marques vickers

TWISTED TOUR GUIDE:
WASHINGTON D.C.
SHOCKING HISTORY, SCANDALS AND VICE

1

TWISTED TOUR GUIDE:
WASHINGTON D. C.

SHOCKING HISTORY, SCANDALS AND VICE

By Marques Vickers

**MARQUIS PUBLISHING
TACOMA, WASHINGTON**

Version 1.2

Published by Marquis Publishing
Tacoma, Washington
TwistedTourGuides.com

Vickers, Marques, 1957

TWISTED TOUR GUIDE:
WASHINGTON D.C.
Shocking History, Scandals and Vice

Dedication: To my daughters Charline and Caroline. Many thanks to my sister Lisa and brother-in-law Adrian for hosting me and assisting in driving me to photo shootings.

TABLE OF CONTENTS

SOURCES AND ARCHIVES SOURCED

BoundaryStones.weta.org, WashingtonPost.com, Newswise.com, FBI.gov, Chris.org, HistoryToGoUtah.gov, Library.cqpress.com, Wikipedia.org, Google Maps, History.house.gov, ClaraBartonMuseum.org, HistoricSites.DCPreservation.org, IrishTimes.com, WhiteHouseHistory.com, UCPlaces.com, NPS.gov, Forbes.com, Distractify.com, Salon.com, History.com, AmericanHeritage.com, MiamiHerald.com, WTOP.com, YellowPlace.com, SerialKillerCalendar.com, NewYorkTimes.com, NewYorker.com. NPR.org, FreePressJournal.in, Salon.com, Encyclopedia.com, Wamu.org, WeAreTheMighty.com, Battlefields.org, DailyMail.com, CNN.com, Senate.gov, MartinsTavern.com, AtlasObscura.com, HMDB.org, Time.com, TheMayflowerHotel.com, NBCWashingotn.com, Thoughtco.com, LawAndCrime.com, RollingStone.com, ABCNews.go.com, DC.UrbanTurf.com, GhostsOfDC.org, WTOP.com, WashingtonChronicles.com, WashingtonTimes.com, Chrs.org, JewishFoodExperience.com, Washingtonian.com, MentalFloss.com, OffbeatNova.com, TheDailyBeast.com, SmithsonianMag.com, MillerCenter.org, Vault.FBI.gov, Unresolved.me, Bizjournals.com, VRE.org, BostonHerald.com, GQ.com, Hillrag.com, Popville.com, AlphaHistory.com, ArlNow.com, InmateAid.com, NOLA.com, DCTourGuideOnline.com, TheGuardian.com, GGWash.org, StreetsofWashington.com, DCTravelMag.com, HistoricHotels.org, PostalMuseum.si.edu, Nerdable.com, Living-In-WashingtonDC.com, Dcist.com and WhiteHouse.org.

Photography shot during 2022. Some of the locations may have altered with time and ownership changes. Many of the locations are still privately inhabited. Please don't disturb the residents.

TWISTED TOUR GUIDE TO WASHINGTON D. C.

Avoid The Tourist Herds.

What could be more uninspiring than seeing the identical attractions that everyone else has for decades?

This Twisted Tour Guide escorts you to the places locals don't want to talk about anymore...the same places people once couldn't stop talking about. Long after the screaming headlines and sensationalism has subsided, these bizarre, infamous and obscure historical sites remain hidden awaiting rediscovery.

Each visitation site in this guide is accompanied by a story. Many of the narratives defy believability, yet they are true. The profiled cast of characters feature saints and sinners (with emphasis towards the latter).

Notorious crimes, murders, accidental deaths, suicides, kidnappings, vice and scandal are captivating human interest tales. Paranormal activity in the aftermath is common.

The photography from each profile showcases the precise location where each event occurred. The scenes can seem ordinary, weird and sometimes very revealing towards clarifying the background behind events.

If you're seeking an alternative to conventional tourism, this Twisted Tourist Guide is ideal. Each directory accommodates the restless traveler and even resident looking for something unique and different. You will never imagine or scrutinize the Washington D. C. Metropolitan area through rose tinted glasses again.

An Assortment of Spirits With D.C.'s Oldest Residence
Old Stone House: 3051 M Street NW, Washington D.C.

Georgetown's Old Stone House is reputed to be the oldest structure within Washington D.C. dating back to 1766. The documented history of the property has ranged from serving as a brothel to a car dealership. Three separate individuals owned the property before the federal government acquired it in 1953.

Today it is operated as a tourist site and the interior is staged to represent an evolution of Americana. There has been speculation that the attention initially lavished upon the modest dwelling was undertaken because the structure was erroneously mistaken for George Washington's headquarters.

With such an extended pedigree, there is little wonder that sightings of apparitions have become increasingly common. Most of the viewings have involved Colonial era men, women and children in period dress. The most frequent specter has been a misogynist named George accused of shoving and sexually assaulting any woman who dares enter his third-floor bedroom. The majority of pedestrians that pass the longtime institution merely ignore the dwelling surrounded by contemporary boutiques, restaurants and indifferent vehicle traffic.

**Georgetown's Most Reportedly Haunted Mansion
Halcyon House:
3400 Prospect Street NW, Washington D.C.**

The Halcyon House is considered one of Georgetown's most haunted mansions built in 1787 by Benjamin Stoddert. The gardens were designed by Pierre L'Enfant, responsible for the city layout of Washington D.C.

Stoddert served as the first Secretary of the Navy and became President George Washington's confidential agent for defining the parameters of D.C. He was also one of the original 19 proprietors who signed off on the agreement to establish the 10-square mile District.

The Halcyon House became the only hillside-developed lot and served as a party center for local socialites and politicians. This role proved brief. Stoddert's rise to prominence tapered with the death of his wife Rebecca Lowndes in 1800 and subsequent decline in finances. Two years later, he would transfer ownership to his daughter Elizabeth and her husband Thomas Ewell. Their son Richard Ewell would later become a distinguished Confederate general during the Civil War under the command of Stonewall Jackson and Robert E. Lee.

The Ewell's vacated the home in 1818. Over the next eight decades, a succession of owners would inhabit the property.

The Halcyon House was sold to Albert Clemens in 1900, a reputed but never confirmed nephew of writer Mark Twain (real name: Samuel Clemens). Clemens was a confirmed eccentric who believed that his life would only continue provided that he continually build on and redesigned the property. He enlarged the structure and added a succession of smaller rooms, many that he rented out. He purportedly disfigured the north front and side wings with an odd collection of architectural detailing from demolished buildings.

Speculation regarding his means of funding resulted in a *Washington Times-Herald* article that credited his estranged wife Elizabeth White as the source. She was the daughter of Senator White of New Hampshire. Her lone stipulation for the monies was that Clemens stay away from her.

Upon his death, the Halcyon House remained vacant for four years before being purchased by Fredrick Sterling, the former U. S. Ambassador to Sweden in 1942. As Sterling began to normalize the interior design, they discovered dozens of tiny rooms, staircases that led nowhere, doors that opened into blank walls and closets extending into other closets.

Reports of paranormal activity and apparition sightings began shortly following their ownership. Some of the identifiable figures included Benjamin Stoddert, Albert Clemens and a ghostly woman in an upstairs window.

Ownership of the house would change once again in 1952 before Georgetown University purchased the property in 1961 and used it as a dormitory.

Prospect
3400

Scrapped Grandeur, Political Protest and Scandalous Murder
Lafayette Square Park:

Pennsylvania Avenue NW at 16th Street NW, Washington D.C.
St. John's Episcopal Church:
1525 H Street NW, Washington D.C.

Washington D.C.'s seven-acre Lafayette Park is situated due north of the White House. From the outset, the land parcel was included with the planning for a grandiose presidential palace. The final White House construction would become significantly scaled down.

French born architect Pierre Charles L'Enfant's 1791 vision featured a palatial structure fronted by an extensive ceremonial entrance with three approaching avenues. The entrance trio would terminate into a semicircular forecourt.

The ambitious plans were scrapped. L'Enfant would be removed from his position the following year. The planned forecourt entrance land would be auctioned off. Land speculator Samuel Davidson owned the intact land parcel that would one day become Lafayette Square. He became incensed when L'Enfant's original grand entrance design was abandoned. Surrounding his intact parcel were smaller city lots that would be auctioned off and developed.

He attempted to sell the property during the 1790s, but none of the transactions materialized. His continued unhappiness and claims of being misled elevated into disputes with D.C. planning commissioners and President George Washington's administration. His death in 1810 concluded the controversy.

White House construction would begin with the laying of the cornerstone on October 13, 1792. The entire project would require eight years to complete. The initial step involved the excavation of the cellar. Huts were constructed on the future park property to house the slave laborers.

A carpenter's workshop was built later along with twenty wooden structures housing American, English, Scottish and Irish laborers. Future brick barracks followed to house slaves that were contracted out for construction work by their owners.

In the fall of 1793, a kiln operation was installed to create bricks for the structure. The property was entirely cleared of trees. The wood was sold to the government to fuel the fires of the kilns. In 1790, a racetrack was built that extended slightly into the current northwest corner of the park.

John Adams officially moved into the White House on November 1, 1800. Not until the subsequent Thomas Jefferson administration did the construction clean up process begin in earnest. Jefferson drew up plans to install a straight section of wall along the north side of the White House (today's Pennsylvania Avenue) to create privacy. The wall was never built.

The grounds surrounding the White House were pastoral. The public of all races interacted, strolled leisurely on the grounds and conducted their business affairs. Jefferson frequently intermingled with the citizenry.

During the War of 1812, the British Army would burn the White House on the evening of August 24, 1814. Reconstruction began almost immediately completed in 1817. In October, the area that would ultimately become Lafayette Square began a grading process and landscape improvement schedule. The territory was designated as *President's Square.*

The project would be completed in 1834 and honor French

General the Marquis de Lafayette. Lafayette was an important ally during the American Revolution. His death had occurred that same year on May 20. Congress allocated $1,000 to plant trees and install fencing. In 1891, a statue honoring Lafayette was positioned in the southwest corner of the park.

Additional landscape detailing, statuary and ornamentation would be augmented during the subsequent decades. The park evolved beyond a leisure grounds. Its location across from the White House made it a visual center for protest.

The first public demonstrators called *Silent Sentinels* began in 1917. Marchers protested President Woodrow Wilson refusal to support the women's suffrage movement. White House policemen arrested picketers on charges of obstructing traffic.

The suffragette's strategy and pressure from his own Democratic Party shifted Wilson's policy. He advocated passage of the Twentieth Amendment eliminating gender as a constraint to voting. The law became Wilson's final acknowledged victory. The Amendment was ratified on August 26, 1920, but Wilson was unable to join any celebrations. He'd become severely incapacitated by a stroke that he'd suffered in October 1919.

Since 1920, a divergence of groups and causes has peacefully protested on the roadway separating the White House fence and Lafayette Park. Among these have included Anti-War protestors, Civil Rights activists, Anti-Lynching groups, Women's Rights proponents, HIV/AIDS awareness groups and LGBTQ equality organizations. Each has been allowed to actively promote and express their message.

The right of free assembly, however, has been periodically challenged.

On June 1, 2020, concerned citizens protesting George Floyd's murder by a Minneapolis policeman became an unwelcome intrusion into a presidential photo opportunity. Armed riot squad personnel and law enforcement officials aggressively disbursed their protest with teargas and arrests clearing the area. Donald Trump and his entourage were enabled to march briskly through Lafayette Park unimpeded. He posed outside of St. John's Episcopal Church located directly south behind the park. He displayed a bible as a prop and cited the necessity of maintaining law and order.

Political protest is not the exclusive distinction of the park. One of the most scandalous murders transpired in broad daylight during the mid-nineteenth century.

On the morning of February 27, 1859, Lafayette Square was the scene of one of the most sensationalized killings. U. S. attorney Philip Barton Key, 40, the son of *Star Spangled Banner* composer Francis Scott Key was conducting a dangerous liaison with a friend's wife.

The cuckolded husband was Congressman Daniel Sickles, a promising young politician from New York. The Sickles couple was popular hosts within Washington society. Key was a frequent guest to their lavish events. He evolved into an even more accommodating escort for 22-year-old Teresa Sickles, who had originally married her husband at the age of sixteen.

Key had rented a front room in the Cosmos Club across Lafayette Park from the Sickles home. He entertained Teresa Sickles frequently and intimately. They often communicated via a white handkerchief indicating availability as he passed in front of her house.

Their affair became common insider knowledge except to Daniel Sickles. He received an anonymous letter detailing

Key's hideaway location and the unseemly behavior practiced inside. He extracted a confession from Teresa and then witnessed Sickles passing twice in front of his house brazenly signaling to his wife with the telltale white handkerchief.

Sickles invested no time with marriage counseling, divorce negotiations or reflecting on the causes behind their estrangement. He heatedly approached Key in Lafayette Square and shot him fatally. He turned himself in shortly afterwards.

His murder trial became litmus testing for employing a *temporary insanity* defense and *justifiable homicide* based on Key's defiling his marriage bed. Key was vilified throughout testimony for leading Teresa Sickles astray from her sacred marital vows.

The tactic succeeded and Sickles was released. His actions were celebrated and worse duplicated by jealous husbands during the subsequent half-century. Post-trial, the couple reconciled until Teresa Sickles death in 1867 from tuberculosis.

Daniel Sickles regrouped professionally completing his congressional term. When the Civil War broke out, he became initially one of the Union's most prominent political generals. He served with distinction before his career ended at the Battle of Gettysburg. His New York Excelsior Brigade suffered a 40% casualty rate and he was wounded by canon fire that necessitated having his leg amputated.

He was eventually awarded the Medal of Honor for his actions, yet became one of the few senior generals at Gettysburg not memorialized with public statues. Following the war, he was appointed as a commander for military districts in the South during Reconstruction.

Under the presidency of Ulysses S. Grant, he was appointed as the U.S. Minister to Spain. He would be elected back to the Congress in 1856 for a single term. He helped pass legislation to preserve the Gettysburg Battlefield. In 1871, he married Carmina Creagh dying in New York City in May 1914 at the age of 94.

ST. JOHN'S CHURCH
PROTESTANT EPISCOPAL
COMPLETED IN 1816
SUNDAY SERVICES
7:45 9:00 & 11:00 AM
HOLY EUCHARIST
LOVE
THY
NEIGHBOR

Supreme Court Scandals Staining The Guardians of The Constitution
Supreme Court Building:
1 First Street NE, Washington D.C.

Supreme Court appointments are lifelong, but mental health issues and ethical scandals have periodically intervened to shorten the length.

John Rutledge served as a Supreme Court justice in 1795, but the unforeseen death of his wife three years earlier triggered a gradual unraveling of his mind. An impassioned rant that he delivered opposing the Jay Treaty exposed his declining capacity towards reason. The Senate voted him out of office in December 1795. He attempted suicide shortly afterwards. He holds the distinction of being the first and only justice to be officially ousted.

During approximately the same period, Justice John Blair complained of *blinding headaches* and rattling inside his head. His face reportedly would go numb and he would blank out towards his surroundings. He spared the Senate a second vote by resigning in October 1795.

In one of the oddest scandals, a California Supreme Court judge nearly killed a U.S. Supreme Court Judge. California Justice David Terry's wife Sarah lost a divorce and alimony case. The case involved her alleged relationship with silver millionaire William Sharon. He maintained the couple had never wed and she was unable to prove otherwise. Future Supreme Court justice Stephen Field was the presiding judge and ruled against Sarah. David Terry married her afterwards and spotted Field on a train on August 14, 1889. He attacked Field, but was shot to death by the U. S. Marshall assigned to protect Field.

James Clark McReynolds was arguably the least popular

justice in the court's history. McReynolds exhibited consistent bias against Jews, blacks, women and Germans. President Woodrow Wilson nominated him in 1914 after serving two years as the United States Attorney General. He remained on the court until January 1941. Following his death on August 24, 1946, not a single Justice despite his extended tenure attended his funeral.

Supreme Court Justice Hugo Black was a member of the Alabama Ku Klux Klan during the 1920s. When President Franklin Roosevelt appointed him to the court in 1937, there were lingering suspicions regarding his prior background. The Senate confirmed him, but his past became publicly outed a month later. He survived the national outcry and refused to resign. His tenure of 34 years is regarded as a mixed legacy since he was a strong proponent of Roosevelt's New Deal programs and considered one of the most liberal oriented justices in the court's history.

Potter Stewart was author Bob Woodward's primary source for a 1979 novel *The Brethren*. The unflattering portrait and background descriptions of the Warren Burger Supreme Court darkened the integrity of Stewart's colleagues. Stewart naturally remained unscathed by his own commentary, but his resignation in 1981 was popular amongst his peers.

Justice Abe Fortas elevated bribery to the highest court in the land. He was appointed by President Lyndon Johnson in 1965 and accused of improperly promoting Johnson's political career. His acceptance of a legal retainer from friend and client financier Louis Wolfson in 1969 sealed his demise. The agreement paid Fortas $20,000 annually for life in return for *consultation* in Wolfson's pending security fraud trial. His assistance helped little. Wolfson was sent to federal prison. Fortas denied accepting the funds, but opted to resign instead of undergoing closer scrutiny.

Clarence Thomas' 1991 confirmation hearings raised the initial specter of sexual harassment in the workplace. Attorney Anita Hill claimed Thomas had aggressively sexually pursued her during the time she had worked for him at the Department of Education and the EEOC. Thomas vehemently denied the accusations and most Republican backers contended her claims were motivated to prevent a black conservative judge to ascend to the court. Thomas was narrowly confirmed along party lines, but Hill's compelling testimony left a permanent stain on his reputation.

The process of sexual impropriety continued in October 2018 with the confirmation hearings of Brett Kavanaugh. The charges brought by Dr. Christine Blasey Ford contended that Kavanaugh sexually assaulted her while he was intoxicated in 1982 at a fraternity party. As with the charges against Thomas, the credibility of the accuser appeared hard to refute. Kavanaugh's nomination was narrowly confirmed on October 6, 2018.

A Marine Commandant's Residence Spared During The Sacking of the Capitol
Commandant's Residence:
8th and G Streets SE, Washington D.C.

One of the lesser-known anecdotes of American history was the *Battle of York* staged on April 27, 1813. The United States had gained their independence from Great Britain, but harbored ambitions of expanding territory into Canada. During the War of 1812 against Britain, the American invasion strategy concentrated on securing Lake Ontario and the Niagara Frontier as a southern front for further gains.

American soldiers were massed in New York's Sackets Harbor with the intention of crossing over and attacking Kingston, an English naval vessel hub. The plan would be followed by attacks on other British positions including Fort York. Once seized, these footholds would become ideal launching grounds for upper Canadian land attacks.

Aware that Fort York was barely guarded by only 700 troops, American General Henry Dearborn reversed the strategy. He decided to secure an easy victory there first and afterwards attack Kingston. As the late spring ice cleared on Lake Ontario, American forcers stormed the Fort York beachhead.

The awaiting British and Indian troops were overwhelmingly outnumbered and retreated to the east. As they abandoned their positions, they ignited gunpowder kegs to prevent them from falling into American possession.

An entire magazine containing hundreds of barrels of gunpowder detonated. American soldiers who were rounding up prisoners near the fort became the immediate victims of the explosion. Over 200 men were killed or wounded including the commander General Pike. Seeking revenge, American soldiers swarmed upon the capitol city of York (now Toronto). They ransacked the town, burning public buildings and businesses.

The easy military victory later bore minimal value. The American attacks into Canada did not secure dominance of their waterways or enable further land expansion. The invasion of York, however, fueled an act of British revenge.

On August 23, 1814, over 4,000 British troops landed at Chesapeake Bay and headed directly towards Washington D.C. The landing surprised the unprepared American military. The British forces only impediment to attacking the Capitol was 6,500 raggedy militiamen and a battalion of 420 United States Marines and sailors. The disciplined British soldiers routed the militia forces swiftly forcing a hasty retreat.

Navy Captain Joshua Barney did not receive his unit's order to retreat. His small detachment of less than 500 sailors and Marines were left to combat the entire British invasion. They bought precious time with their efforts. They were able to hold back the invaders for two hours before succumbing to their numerical disadvantage. The conflict would later called the *Battle of Bladensburg*. Their futile stand enabled President James Madison and his wife Dolley Madison and members of Congress sufficient time to escape the city. The fleeing presidential party carted off selected national artifacts with them.

Washington D.C. became an open city and British forces flooded inside to exact revenge from the previous years humiliation. It would be the sole time Washington D.C. was occupied by a foreign power. British troops brazenly dined inside the White House before setting it on fire. The majority of the city structures were set ablaze with a notable exception. The Marine Corps Commandant's House and the accompanying barracks were spared.

There are two explanations offered for their restraint. One is that amidst the chaos, the torching was simply overlooked. The British troops had temporarily used the facilities for their headquarters. The other reason has become more palatable and part of Marine Corps lore. The restraint by the British soldiers towards the building was a gesture of respect for the intensity of resistance exhibited by the American soldiers.

The Initial First Lady of Social Prominence
Octagon House:
1799 New York Avenue NW, Washington D.C.
Dolley Madison House:
701 Madison Place NW, Washington D.C.
Benjamin Ogle Tayloe House:
21 Madison Place NW, Washington D.C.

Dolley Madison was the celebrated wife of fourth President James Madison. As first lady, she became a social conduit between political parties by staging functions where both parties could amicably intermingle without fear of violence. Prior heated social gatherings with conflicting political parties frequently resulted in physical altercations and duels.

Madison was born on May 20, 1768 in a modest log cabin in New Garden, North Carolina. Her family would relocate to Virginia where they could practice their Quaker religious beliefs and cultivate a 176-acre farm. At 15, the family relocated to Philadelphia and she was married by arrangement to local attorney John Todd in January 1790. They had two sons together.

In August 1793, a yellow fever epidemic scorched Philadelphia. Madison would lose her husband, one of her sons and her parents-in-law. Two of her older brothers would die two years later. She inherited minimal resources, but her brother-in-law serving as executor withheld the funds. She would have to sue him in court for the proceeds. Dolley, renowned for her beauty, was introduced to numerous potential suiters.

Attorney and politician Aaron Burr assisted her with legal advice He would be named the guardian of Dolley's only surviving son, Payne Todd. Burr introduced her to his friend James Madison, 43, a longtime bachelor seventeen years older than her.

The couple married on September 15, 1794 following a brief courtship. She was expelled from the Quaker community for marrying outside of her faith. Following their marriage, Madison would complete four more years in the House of Representatives. He retired from politics and relocated to Montpelier, the Madison family plantation in Virginia.

His repose was brief. When Thomas Jefferson was elected president in 1800, he asked Madison to serve as his Secretary of State. The couple relocated to Washington D.C. Jefferson, a widower, periodically requested Dolley to serve as hostess for official ceremonial functions. She became an important element of the Washington social circle and the glue that cemented participation and relationships with many foreign ambassadors' wives.

Towards the conclusion of Jefferson's second term, he decided to retire. His party, the Democratic-Republican caucus nominated James Madison to replace him. Madison was elected for two terms from 1809 to 1817. Dolley Madison would achieve the pinnacle of her recognition for an act that she didn't do herself.

In 1813, the United States resumed hostilities with England and attempted to invade Canada the following year. British forces attacked Washington D.C. on the afternoon of August 23, 1814. As they approached the White House, a panicked household retreat became necessary. She instructed her personal slave Paul Jennings to save and carry off the premises a large portrait of George Washington. The detachment process proved slow and laborious. She instructed Jennings to break apart the frame and remove the canvas.

The canvas was successfully detached and transferred to New York for safekeeping. Madison was heralded nationally for her patriotism and composure under duress. Most accounts presumed that she had hauled the painting off single handedly.

The invading British forces would burn the White House. Dolley Madison hurried out of the city with other local families via Georgetown before crossing the Potomac into Virginia. When the couple returned on September 8th, the White House was uninhabitable. They moved into the Octagon House until February 17, 1815. Owner John Tayloe III was compensated $500 for rent during the 6-month Madison residency.

Upon the completion of the presidency, the Madison's returned to their Montpelier plantation for the subsequent twenty years. She never anticipated the misfortunes that would darken her declining years.

Dolley's son Payne Todd had never found a career or earned a livelihood. In 1830, he was interned in a Philadelphia debtors' prison. The Madison sold land in Kentucky and mortgaged half of their Montpelier plantation to pay his debts.

James Madison died in 1836 and Dolley remained for a year at Montpelier organizing her husband's presidential papers and notes from the 1787 convention. The allocated purchase by Congress appeared to maintain her financial stability for the remainder of her life. It didn't.

In the fall of 1837, she returned to Washington D.C. and moved in with her sister Anna and husband, Massachusetts Congressman Richard Cutts on Lafayette Square. The residence had been constructed in 1819. She brought Paul Jennings to accompany her as a butler, forcing him to leave his wife and children in Virginia. She ceded Montpelier to the care of her son.

Predictably, Payne Todd could not handle the responsibility. His alcoholism and related illnesses plunged the property into massive debt. Madison was obliged to sell Montpellier, its furnishings and inventory of slaves. Her money concerns became desperate. Efforts to sell the remainder of her husband's writings were unsuccessful.

She rescinded an earlier promise to Paul Jennings to enable his freedom. In 1846, living destitute and desperate for funds, she sold Jennings to an insurance agent for $200. Six months later, Senator Daniel Webster intervened and purchased him back. Webster compensated the agent and then officially freed Jennings. He kept Jennings employed as a paid servant often sending him to Madison's residence with provisions and petty cash.

Her final two years were salvaged by a purchase from Congress of her husband's remaining writings. She would die inside her home on July 12, 1849 at the age of 81. She was later interred to Montpelier beside her husband.

The renamed *Dolley Madison House* would cultivate a notable history of its own. In 1851, naval officer Charles Wilkes purchased the property. He had commanded the U.S. Exploring Expedition to the Pacific between 1838-1842.

During the Civil War, Major General George B. McClellan resided in the residence. He was named the Commanding General of the Union Army on November 1, 1861. He was notorious for his arrogance. On two occasions, he deliberately kept President Abraham Lincoln and Secretary of War Edwin Stanton waiting in the parlor for extended periods during planned strategy sessions. Lincoln developed a grave distrust over his leadership skills and removed from the position after only four months.

McClellan would never receive another field command. He ran unsuccessfully as the Democratic Party nominee against Lincoln in the 1864 presidential election. In 1886, the Cosmos Club purchased the property for organizational amenities, events and activities.

During the initial term of President William McKinley's administration in 1897, Vice President Garret Hobart rented the adjacent property known as the Benjamin Ogle Tayloe House for two years. The house entertained the politically powerful and social affluent, particularly McKinley and his wife. Hobart's residence became known as McKinley's *Little White House* for its low-key gatherings and prestigious guests. The McKinley's enjoyed this diversion from the strain imposed by formal White House functions.

Hobart's two year abbreviated tenure as Vice President was caused by his ill health and a prickly assignment McKinley had thrust upon him. By late 1898, Hobart was suffering from a serious heart ailment concealed to the public. McKinley had requested that Hobart inform Secretary of War Russell Alger that his resignation was requested. McKinley had provided Alger hints before that he'd opted to ignore.

Hobart invited Alger to his Long Branch retreat for a weekend to deliver the disagreeable news. Alger submitted his resignation afterwards. Hobart's heart condition worsened days later and he became bedridden. His health continued to deteriorate rapidly. The government announced that he would not be returning to public service on November 1, 1889. He died twenty days later.

The office of Vice President remained vacant during the remainder of 1900. McKinley would win re-election with Republican rising star New York Governor Theodore Roosevelt as his running mate. On September 6, 1901, Leon Czolgosz would shoot McKinley in the abdomen during a public reception at the Pan-American Exposition in Buffalo, New York.

Doctors were unable to locate a second bullet and gangrene soon was spread onto the walls of his stomach. X-ray machines were not available and drugs to control infection did not exist. McKinley appeared to improve according to medical reports. These published observations were premature. One week later his condition deteriorated. His drifted in and out of consciousness until he expired at 2:15 a.m. on September 14.

Roosevelt rushed to Buffalo that same day to take the oath of office as president. Czolgosz would be swiftly put on trial nine days following McKinley's death. He was found guilty, sentenced to death on September 26th and executed by electric chair on October 29, 1901.

The Dolley Madison house would subsequently converted into government offices including the operations of NASA. In April 1959, the first seven Mercury astronauts were introduced to the press inside the ballroom.

During the late 1950s until 1960, the residence was debated for potential demolition. First Lady Jacqueline Kennedy made the preservation of Lafayette Square properties a priority. The Dolley Madison house was spared and renovated. It is currently used by the United States Court of Appeals for the Federal Circuit.

DOLLEY MADISON HOUSE

BENJAMIN OGLE TAYLOE HOUSE

**The Original City Hall Featuring A Litany of
Distinguished Trials
District of Columbia Court of Appeals:
451 Indiana Avenue NW, Washington D.C.**

The initial building constructed for local governmental use in Washington D.C. was the City Hall. Construction began in 1820 while the city's distinctive layout was still being formalized. The federal government was chronically underfunded and the structure's composition of brick and stucco reflected the necessitated economies. The majority of federal structures in the neighborhood were fitted with stone.

The center section was completed first in 1822 and housed the mayor and registrar offices. The east wing followed in 1826 and west wing was completed in 1849. Portions were leased out to various tenants including the Recorder of Deed office and the U.S. Circuit Court.

Notable trials began with house painter Richard Lawrence who in January 1835 tried to assassinate President Andrew Jackson. He attempted to shoot Jackson outside of the Capitol building while he was attending the funeral services for Congressman Warren Davis. Lawrence's two pistols misfired attributed to being vulnerable to moisture. The weather that day was gloomy and misting.

His prosecuting attorney Francis Scott Key had a relatively easy task due to Lawrence's wild rants and refusal to recognize the legitimacy of the proceedings. Following five minutes of deliberation, his jury found him *not guilty by reason of insanity*. He was interned subsequently inside several institutions and hospitals. His final residence became St. Elizabeths Hospital where he remained until his death on June 13, 1861.

Francis Scott Key would become better known for his

amateur poetry and creating the lyrics for the American national anthem *The Star-Spangled Banner*. During his legal tenure of four decades, he suppressed abolitionists and sometimes represented the owners of runaway slaves. He publicly criticized slavery and offered free legal representation to certain slaves seeking freedom. He had freed some of his own slaves in the 1830s, but at the time of his death from pleurisy in 1843, he still possessed eight.

Sixteen years later, Key's son, Phillip Barton, would have his murderer tried in the same building. Congressman Daniel Sickles was the defendant in a revenge killing. Key and Sickles were once close friends. Sickles' political clout with President James Buchanan had secured Key's earlier appointment as D.C.'s district attorney.

Key's adulterous affair with Sickles wife prompted a broad daytime shooting on the sidewalk surrounding Lafayette Park. His case introduced the *temporary insanity* plea for the first time. Sickles' acquittal confirmed jealous husbands the right to kill their wife's mistresses for nearly half a century. The reverse scenario for the wife remained homicide.

In 1863, the federal government purchased the City Hall building from the D.C. government for use by the Supreme Court of the District of Columbia. Federal courts would occupy the offices for several decades until being briefly abandoned in 1910.

Before the closure, two additional presidential assassination trials would be staged. The first involved John Surratt, Jr. during the summer of 1867. Surratt was 18 when the Civil War began. He was raised in Maryland and left school to become a Confederate courier. During his service he became acquainted with President Abraham Lincoln's future assassin John Wilkes Booth. He confessed to being a part of a plot to kidnap Lincoln that met in his mother's rooming house a few years previously. He denied any involvement with the assassination.

When Surratt learned of Lincoln's murder, he fled immediately to Montreal where a Catholic priest gave him sanctuary in the small village of St. Liboire. He remained there during the military trials of his mother and other Lincoln assassination conspirators.

Aided by ex-Confederate agents, he disguised himself and booked passage to Liverpool, England under a false name. He lodged in the oratory at the Church of the Holy Cross. Evading his capture by US officials became problematic for any knowledgeably hosting country.

Surratt escaped one detainment and then lived with supporters of Italian revolutionary general Giuseppe Garibaldi within the Kingdom of Italy. He posed as a Canadian citizen named Walters and booked passage to Alexandria, Egypt. He was arrested by U.S. officials on November 23, 1866 and shipped back for trial via the USS Swatara in early 1867.

His two-month trial involved a myriad of prosecution and defense witnesses. American newspapers anxiously followed the daily proceedings. They were disappointed by the result. A hung jury voted Surratt innocent by an 8-4 margin. He would never be retried. The statute of limitations on charges other than murder had run out and he was released on bail.

Surratt briefly became a tobacco farmer and then taught at the Rockville Female Academy. Attempting to capitalize on his notoriety, he attempted a public lecture tour in 1870. Public outrage limited the tour to a single 75-minute speech. He returned to teaching in Maryland, living in Baltimore. He married and had seven children. Later he began working at the Baltimore Steam Packet Company where he eventually became their treasurer. He retired in 1914 and died of pneumonia two years later at the age of 72.

The second presidential assassination trial was conducted in 1882 against Charles Guiteau who'd fatally shot President James Garfield. Guiteau was a writer and lawyer who'd convinced himself that he had played an important role in Garfield's election victory of 1881. A speech that he had delivered only twice on behalf of Garfield was his presumption of importance. He was convinced that he was due a consulship in either Vienna or Paris.

He became enraged by the Garfield administration's rejection of his multiple applications, letters and personal appeals. He became considered a nuisance and gadfly. During March 1881 when Garfield assumed office, he was living nearly destitute and began tracking Garfield's movements. Barely six months into his term, Guiteau would shoot Garfield at the Baltimore and Potomac Railroad Station on July 2, 1881. Garfield would die two months later from medical malpractice and fatal infections.

Upon Garfield's death, Guiteau was placed on trial for murder. He attempted to employ the popular *temporary insanity* plea. He did little to aid his defense with consistently narcissist and bizarre behavior. He frequently cursed and insulted the judge, the prosecution, the majority of witnesses and even his legal defense team. He recited epic poems during his testimony and even dictated an autobiography to the *New York Herald*. He frequently smiled and waved at spectators and reporters throughout the proceedings.

He claimed that he had merely shot Garfield, but that the President's doctors were responsible for his death. He planned a lecture tour upon his imagined acquittal and release crowned by a presidential run in 1884.

Guiteau was found guilty on January 25, 1882 and sentenced to death. He screamed obscenities at the jury. Guards escorted the toothless lion to his prison cell. Guiteau appealed his conviction certain that the Supreme Court would consider it. His appeal was denied. He was hung on June 30, 1882, just two days shy before the first anniversary of the shooting.

As he was led to his execution, he continued his erratic smiling and waving. He even danced en route before shaking hands with his executioner. On the scaffold, he recited a poem that he had composed during his incarceration. His request for an orchestra to accompany him was denied. He signaled that he was ready for death by dropping the paper containing his poem. The gallows trapdoor was sprung and the rope instantly broke his neck with the ensuing fall.

The old City Hall building was renovated between 1916 and 1918. Beginning in 1922 for the subsequent three decades, it was used as a U.S. Courthouse. When the federal courts moved out in 1952, the building became the headquarters of the Selective Service System. It was named a historic landmark in 1960 and returned to the local D.C. government. It currently is the home of the D.C. Court of Appeals.

The Scandalous Innkeeper's Daughter and the Petticoat Scandal
Franklin House Site (Currently Hotel Lombardy):
2019 I Street NW, Washington D.C.
Lockiell House Site (Demolished):
512 Ninth Street NW, Washington D.C.

One of Washington D.C.'s earlier settlers William O'Neale arrived at Mount Vernon in 1794 to establish a stone quarry. His intention was to supply material for the city's newly constructed public buildings. The work proved arduous and too grueling. O'Neale scaled down his commerce to felling trees and selling firewood, building stoves and retailing coal and feed. He saved enough capital from his enterprises to construct both a wood-frame and a brick house for speculative resale.

Neither sold. He converted the brick house into O'Neale's Tavern, offering lodging and a general store. By 1813, the ambitious O'Neale built an extension adding an additional twenty rooms. The larger structure became known as the Franklin House.

O'Neale and his wife Rhoda bore a daughter in 1799 that they named Margaret. She would be known as *Peggy*. The innkeeper's daughter was described as beautiful, flirty and well educated. She spoke French and became renowned for her piano playing. She was a Franklin House celebrity and desirable object for marriageable bachelors. William O'Neale prevented an initial elopement when he caught her trying to secretly sneak out of a window.

He couldn't prevent her at fifteen resisting the allure of 39-year-old U.S. Navy purser John Timberlake. The couple rushed into marriage, but soon after he was commissioned on a four-year voyage with the USS Constitution. The Timberlake's had become good friends with 28-year-old widower John Henry Eaton who'd arrived into D.C. as a newly elected U.S. Senator from Tennessee. Eaton was a close friend of fellow Tennessean Andrew Jackson. Peggy was stranded locally, but soon found companionship with Eaton. The pair promenaded the public streets together prompting rumors of extramarital relations.

Peggy's husband John Timberlake conveniently died of a reported pulmonary disease while away in 1828. Malicious rumors circulated that his death had instead been suicide due to her infidelity. Peggy generated immediate controversy when she abandoned the grieving widow role then necessitated for a year. She married Eaton only months following her husband's death. Andrew Jackson who had recently been elected President encouraged the union.

Peggy Eaton did not conform to any female submissive stereotype. She was the antithesis of most political wives and ostracized as a pariah.

Floride, the wife of Jackson's Vice-President John C. Calhoun was incensed by Peggy's perceived scandal and remorselessness. She orchestrated a social snub of Peggy Eaton within political circles.

Jackson enflamed her resentment by choosing John Eaton as his Secretary of War. The move infuriated other cabinet member's wives. By the spring of 1831, all but one had submitted their resignation. Jackson was elated. He replaced each with his most trusted friends and advisers. The collective became labeled as his *Kitchen Cabinet*. They sometimes convened together informally within the White House kitchen. The movement to ostracize Peggy Eaton and the subsequent cabinet resignations became known as the *Petticoat Scandal*.

The events only heightened John Eaton's political rise. He

would be appointed by Jackson to become the governor of Florida. In 1836, he was selected as the U.S. Minister to the Spanish Court. Peggy soon became an intimate with Queen Christina of Spain. William O'Neale died at his Dupont Circle farm in 1837 at the age of 86. Following his wife's death in 1860, Peggy inherited their substantial real estate holdings. Four years earlier, statesman John Eaton had died. Peggy had finally attained a matronly esteem and respect from the local social elite.

Now wealthy, respected and vibrant at fifty-nine, such acclaim meant little. The merry widow still possessed another lifetime of adventure and a fortune to squander. She had always been the pursued during her captivating years. She would evolve into the tragic pursuer and victim.

She married her granddaughter's 19-year-old Italian dancing instructor, Antonio Gabriele Buchignani. Afterwards, she once again suffered the wrath of societal scorn. Peggy attempted to establish Buchignani locally even try to secure him a job at the Library of Congress. His capabilities were limited and all doors of opportunity shuttered.

He blamed Eaton for his failure. She couldn't do enough for him or provide him with the sufficient resources that he desired. She gave freely and fully while he spent lavishly. He even stole and attempted to resell the family silver. They couple moved to New York City to avert further scandal. He established an import business for Italian wines. Predictably it failed.

In 1866, Buchignani issued one final demand in order to keep the marriage intact. He insisted that Peggy assign the entirety of her assets to him. Her portfolio included nineteen houses and six square blocks of central D.C. She kept only the family home at Twentieth and I Streets in her name. He promptly liquidated the real estate holdings and vanished to

Italy with the proceeds. He traveled there accompanied by Peggy's 17-year-old granddaughter, Emily Randolph.

Buchignani would officially divorce Peggy in 1869 and marry Randolph. The couple lived lavishly until the money ran out. He bounced from one attempted scam or delusional prospect to another. He reportedly lived in Paris, Montreal, Memphis and New York City. Peggy was still living in New York when he arrived and she had him arrested. He was bailed out and escaped to Montreal. He would finally die in New York City in 1891 at the age of 57.

Having lost her wealth and former beauty, Peggy Easton spent her remaining years in poverty. At 80, she was admitted to the Lockiell House, a home for destitute women. She died within the following year subsisting only on her melancholy reminiscences from the past. She would be buried in Oak Hill Cemetery next to John Eaton. Many of her current neighbors are the tormentors who scorned her socially during their lifetime.

The Franklin House would be razed in 1914 and replaced by Penn Gardens featuring two movie theatres and a dance hall. The entertainment venue lasted twelve years before being demolished. An apartment complex and then hotel would replace it. The Lockiell House would also be razed and supplanted by commercial development.

The Historical Madam on the Mall
Former Mary Ann Hall's Brothel Site
National Museum of the American Indian:
349 Maryland Avenue, Washington D.C.
Congressional Cemetery:
1801 E Street SE, Washington D.C.

Mary Ann Hall would earn the distinction during the mid-19th century of being called the *Madam on the Mall*. During her reign surpassing 40 years, she presided over a notorious brothel that spanned 14 presidential terms.

Hall was born in Washington D.C. in 1815, one of nine children. Little is known regarding her formative years, by her early twenties, she had become a prostitute with an entrepreneur's foresight. In her early twenties, she purchased a swampy and unkempt lot along a canal currently known as the National Mall.

Her purchase was in August 1839 and she promptly erected a multi-storied brick house. She employed five white and one black female under the age of twenty. Ten years later as her establishment grew in renowned, she added her younger sister Elizabeth and a 50-year old mulatto woman named Judy Fleet.

Mary Ann Hall attempted to gear her property towards a higher end clientele despite the surround squalid neighborhood. Her business peaked during the Civil War. Her employment base rose to 17 women.

The interior was decorated with enormous oil paintings, parlor furniture, expensive carpets and fashionable silver plate items. She insisted upon the best cuisine for her meals that often included exotic foreign dishes. The French champagne flowed habitually.

Due to her clientele connections, she avoided legal entanglements until January 18, 1964. Police raided her establishment and she was arrested. She was charged with keeping a bawdy house and disorderly conduct. At her trial, she hired the best legal protection, but was found guilty and ordered to pay a significant fine.

One of the interest revelations from the case was an elaborate screening device she employed with her front door. The entrance had a ball and chain attached so that the portal could only be opened approximately six inches. Hall would determine who was eligible for admittance. The year ended badly for Hall when more bad press was published regarding her establishment.

A fight broke out between two women inside her parlor. After a harsh verbal exchange, one of the women battered the other with three crisp blows to the left eye.

Following the war, Mary Ann Hall's brothel continued to flourish, but as he approached her late 50s, she lost interest in the management responsibilities. She entrusted the operation to her sister and spent her leisure time on her farm in nearby Alexandria County.

The neighborhood began a transformation around her property. Working class families began populating the sector and more diminutive alley houses proliferated. In June 1883, Hall shuttered her brothel and rented out a portion of her property for a women's health clinic. The medical center was operated by two female doctors and funded by donations.

On Friday, January 29, 1886, Hall died form a cerebral hemorrhage. She was buried in the Congressional Cemetery with duo monuments towering over her neighbors. Her fortune was disputed by family members who ultimately agreed to distribute it equally.

President H. W. Bush would raise the legacy of Mary Ann Hall to the surface with the signed creation of a new museum in 1996. Part of the selected site was located on Mary Ann Hall's former brothel location. Before construction could commence, an unorthodox archaeological excavation was undertaken.

Female adornments, hundred of champagne corks and broken bottles, expensive porcelain and remnants of decadence past were unearthed. The treasured trash became exhibited artifacts stored at the Historical Society of Washington D.C. Private viewings are available by appointment.

During the excavation process, Mary Ann Hall was christened with her moniker *Madam on the Mall*. In 2004, the finally completed National Museum of American Indian Act was opened. The site's previous exploitation has become historically ironic.

NATIONAL MUSEUM OF THE AMERICAN INDIAN

**The Rarest Stamp Collection Gems
National Postal Museum:
2 Massachusetts Avenue NE, Washington D.C.**

The Smithsonian's National Postal Museum is a complimentary visitor attraction dedicated to the study, preservation and presentation of postal history and stamp collecting. The museum incorporates exhibitions, displays and historical research to educate Americans on mail delivery that may be in the throes of its final breath.

Email and texting have supplanted traditional letter delivery services. Private commercial delivery companies have carved out a significant niche from the lucrative package and parcel business.

Stamp collecting remains attractive to an aging and dwindling population. The most valuable specimens will not be found within the museum walls. Rather their ownership has shifted into the open trading market and/or auction houses. These valuable collectables are products of scarcity and sometimes printing errors.

Three of the rarest stamps portray statesman Benjamin Franklin. Two 1¢ stamps were printed in 1851 and 1868. Both examples feature him in a left facing profile pose. Slight imperfections in the printing process for these commonly issued stamp have distinguished the two versions. In both cases, only two samples remain in mint condition. Their value has ranged from $375,000 to $850,000 based on the last published auction in October 2007. The third Franklin scarcity printed in 1908-1909 features his profile facing right. The highly valued item is actually a vertical pair employing double lined paper and a watermark from the U.S. Postal Service. One unused pair last sold for $310,000 in 2015.

The oldest rare stamp was printed in 1847, the first year that the public could purchase stamps from the government. George Washington adorned the 3¢ cent issue that earned its excessive value due to scarcity and a B grade grill design. There were a reported 1,000 stamps of this stamp issued, but only four are known to exist today. In 2008, one of these stamps sold for $900,000.

The distinction elevating the most valuable American postal stamp was an erroneous printing of a 1918 airmail stamp with a face value of 24¢. The famed *Inverted Jenny* stamp features an airplane upside down. Reportedly the clerk who initially sold over 100 of these stamps had never seen an airplane and sold them without noticing the error. The latest auction sale for one in 2016 was a reported $1.35 million.

**Political, Funding and Construction Dilemmas Honoring
George Washington
Washington Monument:
2 Fifteenth Street NW, Washington D.C.**

Honoring George Washington would have seemed a priority
for the nation upon his death in 1799. He had served as the
commander-in-chief of the Continental Army (1775-1784)
and as the first President (1789-1797). The U.S. Congress had
authorized a suitable memorial to be included with the
ongoing Washington D.C. construction that had been in
process since 1791. The presidential election of 1800
changed everything.

The Democratic-Republican Party led by Thomas Jefferson
prevailed in the voting and took control of Congress.
Washington had symbolized their political rival, the
Federalist Party. Many of Jefferson's contemporaries felt
hostile towards the concept of honoring powerful men,
particularly Washington. The new Congress reversed their
predecessor's decision to commemorate him. They prevented
his image from being used on coins or currency and even
banned the celebration of his birthday.

Amongst the previous tributes envisioned included a tomb
erected within the Capitol building accompanied by his crypt
below the rotunda of the dome. Two obstacles thwarted this
proposal. The first was a lack of funding and the second was
the Washington family's reluctance to relocate his body from
Mount Vernon.

Over thirty years would pass before a citizenry group formed
an organization called the Washington National Monument
Society. They raised significant donations and announced a
competition for the memorial design. They stated lofty
expectations for the construction. The design competition
began in 1836. Architect Robert Mills was selected with the

winning entry in 1845. He was reputed to be the first native-born American to be professionally trained as an architect.

In 1814, he had designed a monument of Washington for the city of Baltimore. His proposed creation was an elaborately decorated Greek column with balconies featuring Washington at the summit. The design would later be simplified to a plain column shaft with a toga-clad Washington. It was completed in 1829, but moved from the courthouse due to its height over to the rural hills to the north. The city population would eventually expand to encompass it.

Mills' Washington D.C. proposal featured a massive circular colonnade structure 250 feet in diameter and 100 feet high. This circular base would support an obelisk in the center. The four-sided obelisk was intended to rise 500 feet high above the colonnade with a slightly peaked roof. The height of 600 feet total would substantially exceed any known building of that era.

Both the obelisk and pillar would be hollow inside with an upwardly spiraling railway. On top of the base of the building, a sculptural work of Washington would be standing in a chariot holding the reins of six horses. The interior of the colonnade would feature 30 Revolutionary War sculptured heroes along with the 56 signers of the Declaration of Independence.

This grandiose overkill version was not budgeted economically. Mills' estimated the cost at an unprecedented $1 million prompting the selection committee to hesitate. Three years later, the committee determined that the price tag was too excessive. They decided to scale back the majority of the elaborate embellishments and maintain a streamlined 600-foot high obelisk.

Mills' design was considered audacious, ambitious and

unprecedented. The first phase was begun in 1848 privately funded. The cornerstone was laid on July 4th with an estimated 20,000 people in attendance. Builders first began work on the blue gneiss foundation, an 80-foot square step pyramid. Upon the completion of the substructure, the aboveground marble structure rose 55 feet. The structure inched forward until 1854 when the monument reached 156 feet above ground.

Two impediments then stalled construction. The Washington National Monument Society went bankrupt in 1854. Robert Mills died the following year, never seeing his most renowned project to fruition.

For over the next two decades, monument construction stagnated. The response invoked ridicule and became a national embarrassment. Congress attempted to intervene but failed due to conflicting issues. Their priorities drifted away from the partially completed obelisk towards clamors advocating regional secessionism and then Civil War.

Following the completion of the war and the turbulent era of Reconstruction, Congress resumed their efforts to finish the Washington Monument. In 1876, Congress passed a funding bill. The U.S. Army Corps of Engineers headed by Lt. Colonel Thomas Lincoln Casey were assigned to complete the construction. Casey's first task was to strengthen the support at the base of the foundation that he determined was inadequate. The fortification required four years.

A second problem arose when the original Baltimore quarry stone was no longer available. Casey was obliged to use two additional quarries to try and color match. The stone was tinted slightly differently. Three different stone shades from three separate quarries are noticeable today.

Casey modified Mills' intentioned height of 600 feet. He decided to re-calculate the height ratio of the structure as ten times the width of the base. This limited an optimal height to 555-feet. Excessively planned ornamentation was scrapped creating a minimalist appearance. His design modification reduced labor expenses and sped up construction. Starting at the 150-160 foot level, Casey reduced the thickness of the walls from thirteen to nine feet.

At the 470-foot level, the contractors began angling buttresses inward to support a 300-ton marble pyramidion at the top. On a windy December 6, 1884, the capstone was lifted through one of the windows and hoisted to the top of the monument. A 9-inch aluminum tip was then placed atop the capstone to act as a lightening rod. The aluminum cap featured inscriptions of notable names and dates involved with the project. Inscribed facing the sun, the Latin words *Laus Deo* were etched translating into *Praise be to God*.

The completed Washington Monument reigned for five years as the world's tallest building. Measuring slightly over 555 feet, the obelisk surpassed the Cologne Cathedral in Germany. The completion of the Eiffel Tower in Paris during 1889 replaced the designation.

The solitary pointed aluminum apex lasted merely six months before lightning damaged the marble blocks of the pyramidion. A net of gold-plated copper rods supporting 200 spaced 3-inch points was installed over the entire pyramidion. In 2014, the originals tip system was removed and replaced by two thick solid aluminum lightning rods.

PACIFIC

ATLANTIC

**A Resonating Voice From A Disenfranchised Population
Frederick Douglass House:
316-318 A Street NE, Washington D.C.**

For most individuals caged by the tyranny of slavery, their thoughts and voices were echoed by the speeches and writings of Frederick Douglass during the mid to late nineteenth century.

Frederick Bailey Douglass was born into slavery in 1818 in Talbot County, Maryland. His father was of white European descent and his mother an enslaved black woman. He was separated from her as an infant. He lived with his grandmother for a few years before being relocated at six to work on the Wye House plantation in Maryland owned by Thomas Auld.

He was later shuffled to his brother Hugh's property in Baltimore. Hugh's wife Sophia bestowed upon Frederick a life-changing gift by teaching him the alphabet. He taught himself to read and write which ultimately empowered him with his natural gift for eloquence. He was encouraged to teach other slaves how to read using the Bible.

Thomas and Hugh Auld got into a nasty dispute. Douglass and the other enslaved workers returned to Thomas' estate. He resumed work as a field hand.

His teenage years were brutal. Thomas Auld proved a cruel and impatient overseer. Frederick was leased out to other slave owners intent on deflating his independent spirit. He was whipped regularly. He attempted to escape on several occasions before successfully boarding a train that arrived into free-state New York. He was lodged at a safe house owned by abolitionist David Ruggles.

Briefly settled in New York, he sent for Anna Murray from Baltimore, a free black woman he'd met while in captivity. She joined him and they were married in September 1838. They would have five children together.

The couple moved to New Bedford, Massachusetts. Another couple that they had befriended encouraged Frederick to take the surname *Douglass*, a character in Sir Walter Scott's poem *The Lady of the Lake*.

Douglass began attending meetings of the anti-slavery abolitionist movement. He was exposed to the public speeches and perspective of journalist and abolitionist William Lloyd Garrison.

Garrison encouraged Douglass to share his narrative regarding his enslavement and escape after hearing him speak. He was impressed by Douglass' oratory and potential leadership skills.

In 1843, Douglass would participate in a six-month speaking tour of the United States. Many of his audiences were unreceptive towards his message. He was physically assaulted numerous times during the tour. A fractured hand from one assault would never fully heal during the remainder of his lifetime.

In 1860, he published the first of his autobiographies entitled *Narrative of the Life of Frederick Douglass, An American Slave*. Over the next thirty-five years, he would articulate passionately the cruelty and darkness associated with this foulest of institutions. He vilified the cruelty imposed upon him by Thomas Auld. He advocated that *slavery was the enemy of both the slave and the slaveholder*.

Douglass developed a broader perspective behind the evils of slavery. His travels to Ireland and Great Britain transformed his global understanding. Prejudice based on race, cultural and gender differences was an international disease dividing individuals from understanding and acceptance of each other.

He frequently concentrated scorn on American religious institutions and patriots that accepted slavery as an essential institution. He denounced their hypocrisy in boasting of their adoration of justice and purity. *Such ideals didn't exist for millions of enslaved individuals deprived of essential freedoms and dignity.*

He tirelessly advocated that the end of slavery should be accompanied by granting voting rights. He extended his activism into women's rights issues, often a lonely voice advocating on their behalf.

Douglass quarreled with President Abraham Lincoln following the Emancipation Proclamation of 1863 that ended the institution of slavery. He was disappointed that the formally enslaved people were not given the immediate right to vote. The pair reportedly reconciled before Lincoln's assassination.

The passage of the 13th, 14th and 15th amendments to the U.S. Constitution cemented Douglass' objectives. He spoke at the dedication of the Emancipation Memorial in D.C.'s Lincoln Park in 1876. Lincoln's widow, Mary Todd Lincoln reportedly presented the late president's favorite walking stick to him following the speech.

During the Reconstruction era, Douglas remained relevant serving in numerous governmental positions. He was appointed as the ambassador to the Dominican Republic, becoming the first black man to hold recognizable national high office.

In 1877, Douglass met with his former slave owner Thomas Auld. The unimaginable reunion was emotional for both men as Auld was nearing the conclusion of his life. The formerly cruel and vindictive master had become a pitiful remnant. Both men found commonality with the individuals that had been part of their lives. They spoke on the subject of death. The men parted with a deeper respect and understanding towards each other. Their shared tears had bridged reconciliation. Douglass published the account of their reunion in newspapers then and in a later memoir.

Douglass' struggle against inequality could never be entirely satisfied or extinguished. He realized that hating slavery was different than despising its practitioners. His reconciliation with Auld proved that both men shared a similar bond of humanity that skin color could not eradicate. Their meeting proved a reminder that forgiveness and even progress was still possible in healing the racial divide that continued to incapacitate America.

Douglass' wife Anna died in 1882. Six years later, he married white activist Helen Pitts. He continued his public speaking despite his pace and health slowing. He died in 1895 after suffering a heart attack on his way home from a meeting of the National Council of Women, a women's rights organization based in D.C.

His steady voice and example of racial and gender empowerment had been stilled. His published words and expression remain pertinent today.

**The Wild Rose and Her Civil War Espionage Exploits
Rose O'Neal Greenhow Residential Site:
Corner 16th Street and K Streets NW (Currently the Hay-
Adams Hotel), Washington D.C.**

Only 108 miles separated the capitals of the Union and
Confederate States during the Civil War. Today Washington
D.C. and Richmond, Virginia can be driven from each
extremity in less than two hours via Interstate 95. During the
early stages of the conflict, loyalties were frequently
interspersed within the two cities.

Rose O'Neal and her sister Ellen were orphaned as children.
In 1830, they began living with their aunt in a stylish
boarding house at the former temporary Capitol Building
(later a prison during the Civil War). Through her aunt's
acquaintance, she met many renowned figures within
Washington D.C. society. Her olive skin earned her the
nickname *Wild Rose*. She would meet and marry prominent
doctor, lawyer and linguist Robert Greenhow five years later.
He worked inside the U.S. Department of State.

Her Capitol connections would form an important network in
her future. She became considered a renowned socialite
fixture. Her husband's work relocated their growing family to
Mexico City in 1850 and later San Francisco.

In 1853, she returned to D.C. with her three daughters, a
voyage requiring several months. Upon arrival, she gave birth
to the couple's final daughter. The following year, her
husband died from an accident in San Francisco. Her
widowhood did not affect her social standing. In 1856, her
niece married widower Stephen A. Douglas, the senator from
Illinois renowned as Abraham Lincoln's famous debating
adversary.

As the divided nation headed towards armed conflict, Rose O'Neal Greenhow remained attached to the Confederate cause. She was strongly influenced by her friendship with South Carolina Senator John C. Calhoun and other prominent southern personalities. She advocated secession and preservation of a Southern culture corrupted by slavery. Her known political views and social access made her an ideal candidate for espionage on behalf of the Confederate Army.

During April 1861, she was expediently recruited into a Pro-Southern cause spy network within D.C. By the summer months, she forwarded regular dispatches in ciphered code via couriers. Presumably her messages were distributed to the formulating Confederate Secret Service and government leaders in Richmond.

There is serious question how valuable her observations impacted the war. She claimed that she obtained and passed along valuable intelligence regarding Union military intentions. She had befriended and entertained Union officers and Republican politicians along with former President Buchanan and Secretary of State William Seward. Her most valuable contact was rumored to be already married suitor Massachusetts Senator Henry Wilson, Chairman of the Committee on Military Affairs.

Her most noteworthy messages were credited with exposing Union military movements to Confederate General Beauregard for the impending First Battle of Bull Run. Confederate President Jefferson Davis would also credit her with supplying invaluable information aiding the victorious battle of Manassas. Some historians have questioned whether her messages were merely stale society gossip of marginal value.

By August 23, 1861, intelligence correspondence had been tracked to her D.C. residence, the present site of the Hay-

Adams Hotel. Allan Pinkerton, head of the newly formed Union Secret Service, placed her under house arrest. A search of her house uncovered significant compromising printed materials including fortifications and detailed notes on military movements. Reportedly discovered love letters from Senator Henry Wilson became questionable when their handwriting and signature did not match his.

Greenhow would evade trial for her spying activities. She reportedly continued to distribute messages even during her confinement. On May 31, 1862, she was escorted to Fortress Monroe at Hampton Roads, Virginia and released. The sole condition imposed was that she remain within Confederate boundaries. She traveled to Richmond and was honored upon arrival as a Southern heroine.

She had no intention of remaining an idle socialite. The Confederate government employed her as a courier overseas to promote their cause within French and British aristocratic circles. She authored a successful memoir entitled *My Imprisonment and the First Year of Abolition Rule in Washington*. The work sold well in Britain, but would ultimately prompt her premature death.

On August 19, 1864, Greenhow departed England with important dispatches on the *Condor*, a British blockade running ship. The Union gunboat *USS Niphon* began fervent pursuit on October 1st as the ship neared Wilmington, North Carolina waters. The Condor ran aground at the mouth of the Cape Fear River. Fearing capture and imprisonment, Greenhow attempted to flee by rowboat.

Her vessel was capsized by a wave. She drowned weighted down by $2,000 worth of gold sewn into her undergarments and hung around her neck. The gold was sourced from the royalties of her memoirs. She was given a military funeral at the St. Thomas Catholic Church in Wilmington.

Rose O'Neal Greenhow has been subsequently portrayed in film, television and theatre. Her exploits have become legendary and some of the stories may even be accurate.

Floating Trade Outside The Traditional Box
Example of Remaining Potomac Ark:
McIlhenny Seaport Center
0 Thompsons Alley, Alexandria, VA

One of the most innovative forms of brothels and gambling parlors began floating along the Potomac River during the mid 19th century. Nicknamed the *Potomac Arks*, drifting houseboats, generally twenty-four feet in length moored near the water's edge.

The arks concentrated near Alexandria, Virginia because the state had no jurisdiction over the river while Maryland and D.C. law enforcement generally ignored them. Although the houseboats were generally slow and cumbersome, periodic police raids were generally easy to evade. Madames would simply pull up the anchor and in thirty seconds float out of the pursuing vice squads jurisdiction.

The diminutive floating houses of prostitution were color-coded. The elite boats were typically painted white with blue roofs and shutters. Some were two-story. Individual entrepreneurs painted their *houses* red. Many clustered around gambling casino boats with convenient transfer shuttle service available.

At the outset of the Civil War in 1861, there were approximately 450 brothels recorded in Washington D.C. One year later, there were 5,000 sex workers in D.C. and over 2,500 in Georgetown and Alexandria. Practitioners followed the influx of soldiers and shifted to the waters edge following the conclusion of the conflict.

Few stories regarding the brothel fleet were reported in the press. There was a sharp decline in the number of arks nearing 1927. During the Great Depression and World War II, scrutiny was lessened significantly. By the 1960s, their presence had evaporated. Most of the arks had been abandoned or burned by the harbor police.

In 1993, Alexandria city workers uncovered a wooden barge sunken in the dirt while demolishing a section of the waterfront. The ark was recovered, restored and donated to the Alexandria Seaport Foundation. The boat currently serves as the headquarters for the foundation oriented as a safe haven for troubled teenagers.

A Hooker's Influence on the Union Army and Washington D.C.

Hooker's Division Boundaries:

Pennsylvania Avenue (North), Ohio Avenue (South), 15th Street (West) and 10th Street (East), Washington D.C.

The term *Hooker* evolved into a derogative term for prostitutes and sex workers. Many sources attribute the origins to the women for hire who worked the shipyards and ferry terminals of the Corlear's Hook area of Manhattan, New York in the mid 19th Century.

Twenty years later, Union General Joseph Hooker provided a face to the term. There was a legend that Hooker's military brigades lacked discipline and were accused of excessive intoxication and debauchery. Bands of prostitutes reputedly followed his division and were referred to sarcastically as *Hooker's Brigade*.

As a soldier, Hooker developed a steady upward climb following his graduation from the United States Military Academy in 1837. His first assignment was in Florida fighting in the second Seminole War. He continued with staff positions in the Mexican-American War until 1848.

His military reputation became damaged when he testified against his former commander General Winfield Scott in the court-martial trial of Major General Gideon Johnson Pillow. He was sidelined to Sonoma, California where he held a commission as a colonel in the California militia. During the next thirteen tedious years, he became a farmer and land developer, running unsuccessfully for the California legislature.

When the Civil War erupted, he requested a commission with

the Union army. General Winfield Scott's lingering resentment towards him thwarted his request. Scott was the initial general-in-chief of the Army. Hooker borrowed money to make a train trip east and appeal directly to President Abraham Lincoln.

He witnessed the disastrous Union Army defeat at the First Battle of Bull Run. He wrote a critique to Lincoln of the military mismanagement he observed and promoted his own unique credentials. On August 1861, he was appointed as a brigadier general of volunteers.

His rise within the Union Army was swift. He distinguished himself in the Peninsula Campaign in 1862, followed by battles in Williamsburg, Seven Pines and the Second Battle of Bull Run. He fought to a standstill in bloody skirmishes against Lt. General Stonewall Jackson of the Confederate at South Mountain and Antieam.

He made few friends amongst his officer peers, criticizing their extreme caution in the battlefield, particularly commanding General George McClellan. Following the December 1862 Union disaster at the Battle of Fredericksburg, Hooker had similar condemnation for McClellan's successor Ambrose Burnside bordering on subordination. Burnside's most notable life distinction was as the model for the facial term *sideburns*. He intended to demote Hooker, but instead Lincoln removed Burnside.

Lincoln was impressed by Hooker's reputation for aggressive fighting, sorely lacking within the Union Army. He appointed Hooker to command the Army of the Potomac on January 26, 1863.

During the spring of 1863, Hooker concentrated on restoring the morale of his soldiers and shoring up the administration of the army. He created the Bureau of Military Information, the first intelligence service. He made critical changes in military command and established better training preparedness for his troops.

His major criticism during this period was that he established a very poor example for the conduct of his generals and their staffs. His headquarters were described as being a *combination of a bar-room and brothel.*

Hooker was popularly known as *Fighting Joe Hooker* originating from a newspaper dispatch during the 1862 Peninsula campaign. His reputation as a hard-drinking ladies man trailed him throughout the remainder of his life. He was parodied in the press and even lampooned as Mr. F. J. Hooker by Confederate Army General Robert E. Lee.

Lincoln overlooked his character flaws desiring decisive leadership and an aggressive launch into Confederate lines. Hooker boasted an ambitious strategy, but selected the wrong commander, Brigadier General George Stoneman to lead the attack. Robert E. Lee would outmaneuver and soundly defeat Hooker extinguishing Lincoln's confidence in his leadership. Hooker's tenure only lasted five months. He was replaced on June 28, 1863 only three days before the Battle of Gettysburg.

History would credit this decisive Union victory to Major General George Meade. Hooker was reassigned to other posts, but never given the credit he thought that he'd earned. He led the funeral procession for Abraham Lincoln on May 4, 1865 in Springfield, Illinois. His influence had long ago waned and he served in various command posts in the Department of the East and Lakes post war. His libertine lifestyle finally felled him with poor health and partial paralysis from a stroke. He retired from the Army in October 1868 and died in 1879 while visiting Garden City, New York.

Hooker's influence within Washington D. C. became most pronounced during the Civil War. The Federal Triangle was a large parcel of the city located east, but within sight of the White House. The parameters included Pennsylvania Avenue to the north and Ohio Avenue to the south. The western periphery was 15th Street extending to the east at 10th street.

The territory would be snidely labeled *Hooker's Division* and contain over 50 saloons and 100 houses of prostitution. It was considered the city's concentration of vice, gambling, and red light district. Reformers labeled the neighborhood an embarrassing scourge. Hooker became the infamous namesake in 1862 while guarding the city against a Confederate military incursion. A tract of land designated *Murder Bay* became so dangerous, even the police were reluctant to patrol or respond to the crime and violence. Bodies would reportedly be discovered floating in the canal or buried in ash dumps. Following the Civil War, the neighborhood became more gentrified and residential properties began displacing brothels. By the conclusion of the First World War, *Hooker's Division* became a distant memory even if the honoree's name would persist even out of context.

The National Mall
Smithsonian Museums
Freedom Plaza
Ronald Reagan Building
White House Visitor Center
National Archives
Federal Triangle

WORLD TRADE CENTER

**The Origins of Lobbying and Presidential Exposure
The Willard Intercontinental Hotel:
1401 Pennsylvania Avenue NW, Washington D.C.**

President Ulysses S. Grant had an extended affiliation with the Willard Hotel during his lifetime. He reportedly lodged there on four occasions while he was the commander of the Union Army during the Civil War.

The Willard Hotel began as a series of row houses on Pennsylvania Avenue in 1816. The property was known by several names and owners until Henry Willard leased the entirety and combined them into a single structure.

Like several of his presidential predecessors dating back to Franklin Pierce, the Willard became a quiet oasis following a stressful workday in the Oval Office.

Grant used to stroll from the White House to the nearby property's lobby during his tenure. He reposed over a brandy and cigar. Heads of industry, politicians and other favor seekers anxious to informally pitch their respective proposals knew Grant's habit.

Grant labeled many of these petitioners *lobbyists*. This account became known as the popular origin of the name. Several newspapers repeated the account securing it into briefly legendary status. Sticklers for factual history, however, have been passionate to denounce this media reinforced myth.

The term *lobbyist* supposedly originated as far removed as 1640 within the lobbies of the English House of Commons. These lobbies enabled the general public to speak directly to members of the House. Another American account placed the origins to the 1820s inside the New York State Capitol building lobby in Albany. Like the British version, the general public was able to interact with legislators.

Lobbyists since the late nineteen-century have multiplied as pestilence swarms. Presidents no longer may linger during leisure hours inside a publicly accessible hotel lobby. It is ironic and tragic that a former head of the American military and future president felt unthreatened enough to cultivate this accessible exposure and habit. That level of informality and security will never return.

A Curse Of Infamy Upon A Playhouse Of Tragedy
Ford's Theatre
511 Tenth Street NW, Washington D.C.

Ford's Theatre secured its residence in infamy with the April 14, 1865 assassination of President Abraham Lincoln. The President and his wife were attending a performance of *Our American Cousin*. Major Henry Rathbone and his fiancée Clara Harris were seated with the Lincoln's.

The popular and renowned 26-year-old actor John Wilkes Booth had previously performed the production at Ford's Theatre. He was intimately aware of the layout and presidential box when he entered from the rear. He also was intimately familiar with the dialogue. Following one of the actor's delivered line that always provoked audience laughter, he shot Lincoln in the back of the head. Lincoln's male seating companion, Major Henry Rathbone was stabbed attempting to prevent Booth's escape

Booth leapt down to the stage before escaping through a rear door. He would remain a fugitive twelve days before his own death.

Following the assassination, the government appropriated the theatre and paid the owner John T. Ford compensation. Congress issued an order prohibiting the theatre from ever being used as a location for public amusement. The U.S. military would convert the building into a succession of offices.

The building would share a disproportionate history of ill fortune. It was originally constructed in 1833 as the second meeting house of the First Baptist Church. Pastor Obadiah Bruen Brown sold the building to John T. Ford in 1861 once his congregation moved to a newly completed third structure.

Ford converted the former church into a theatre and called it Ford's Athenaeum. The first of multiple curses followed the year afterwards when it was destroyed by fire. The building would be reconstructed.

The next calamity following Lincoln's killing occurred on June 9, 1893. The front section of the three interior columns collapsed. A supporting pillar was undermined during a cellar excavation. Twenty-two clerks were killed and another 68 injured. Rumors of a terminal curse upon the building began.

In 1928, the building was turned over to the Office of Public Buildings and five years later to the National Park Service. Over nearly the subsequent four decades, lobbying efforts were directed towards restoring the building to contemporary standards. On January 30, 1968, the theatre reopened with a gala performance.

Since the reopening, Ford's Theatre has produced plays and musicals celebrating Abraham Lincoln's legacy and various American themes. A collection of Lincoln memorabilia is housed for display. During performances, the presidential box is never occupied.

A Nearby House To Die Softly In The Early Morning
William A. Petersen House:
516 Tenth Street NW, Washington D.C.

In 1849, William A. Petersen, a German tailor constructed a Federal style row house across the street from the First Baptist Church. The church would sell their property to John T. Ford in 1861. Fire destroyed the structure the following year, but the reconstruction became known as Ford's Theatre.

In 1852, Petersen would rent the property to John C. Breckinridge who was serving as Kentucky's 8th district Congressman. Breckinridge would become President James Buchanan's Vice President between 1857-1861. He would be elected to the U.S. Senate following in March 1861. He was expelled nine months later upon being commissioned a brigadier general for the Confederate Army. Towards the end of the Civil War, he would serve as the Confederate States Secretary of War urging President Jefferson Davis to surrender.

Harry Safford was Petersen's lodger during the fateful evening of April 14, 1865. The Civil War had only concluded four days earlier when President Abraham Lincoln and his wife Mary Todd attended a performance of *Our American Cousin* that evening. John Wilkes Booth entered the presidential box from the rear and shot Lincoln in the back of the head. One of the Lincoln's seating companions Major Henry Rathbone suffered serious stab wounds attempting to prevent Booth's escape. Booth leapt upon the stage and exited via a back door.

Doctors Charles Leale and Charles Sabin Taft examined Lincoln in the seating box before having him carried across the street to the Petersen house. Lincoln's initial prognosis for survival was poor.

His doctors noted that Lincoln's extremities were already frigid and blood clots had formed over the wound. They attempted to drain excess brain fluid and matter from where the bullet had entered Lincoln's head to relieve pressure on the brain. There were no reports that Lincoln regained consciousness as the external and internal hemorrhaging continued until the early morning.

Guards patrolled outside the house to prevent curious spectators from entering. Cabinet members, generals, Congressmen and son Robert Todd Lincoln were allowed to view the President as his condition deteriorated. He died the next morning at 7:22 a.m. at the age of 56. His death site would be preserved as a historical museum recreating the scene at the time when Lincoln expired.

**The Lincoln Conspiracy and Aftermath
Mary Surratt Boarding House
604 H Street NW, Washington D. C.**

Actor John Wilkes Booth evaded immediate capture following his assassination of President Abraham Lincoln. In an attempted coup d'etat undertaken on April 14, 1865, Booth and his intimate band of conspirators planned to simultaneously murder Lincoln, Vice-President Andrew Johnson and Secretary of State William Seward.

The Civil War had officially ended four days previously. Only Lincoln would be successfully murdered. Seward was severely wounded by five stabbings in the face and neck. His attacker Lewis Powell was convinced that he'd left Seward for dead.

Powell would be captured the following day at Mary Surratt's boarding house. Seward's wife Mary never recovered from the shock of the brazen attack on her husband. She died two months later in June. William Seward would live an additional seven years.

Booth had a getaway horse waiting for him following his exit from Ford's Theatre. Edman Spangler who likely had no idea of his plans tended the horse. Booth fractured his leg while either leaping onto the stage from Lincoln's box or while galloping away when his spooked horse reportedly fell on him. He traveled 25 miles southward before stopping at the home of Dr. Samuel Mudd in St. Catherine, Maryland. The doctor treated his injury, although he later claimed that he didn't realize who Booth was.

Booth and his companion David Herold followed a planned escape route through swamp and forestland in southern Maryland. They rested in a few Confederate sympathizer residences and in concealed woods. Booth was shocked and dismayed by the public's reaction towards Lincoln's murder and himself.

Had the killing been completed during the war several months before, the act might have been considered a strategic military strike. Instead of being considered a Southern hero, Booth was shunned as a *madman, monster* and *wretched fiend*. Only hardcore confederate supporters found his deed admirable.

Ironically some of the prior fiercest anti-Lincoln newspapers condemned Booth's actions. Confederate General Joseph E. Johnston called Booth's action *a disgrace to the age*. Robert E. Lee expressed regret for Booth's deed. The war's ending had altered the perspective of his act.

Abraham Lincoln was mourned internationally and with great reverence. His death elevated his virtues, patience and objective towards reconciliation that had previously been mocked and criticized. It is arguable, but probably accurate to credit Lincoln as being the sole individual capable of preserving the United States intact during the darkest period in our history.

Booth would be tracked down by federal troops after twelve days to the Garrett farm in rural Northern Virginia. He was aware that his co-conspirators had been captured and strategy to kill Andrew Johnson and William Seward had failed. On April 26th at dawn he awoke surrounded by soldiers inside a tobacco barn at Garrett's farm.

Fugitives Booth and Herold were requested to surrender. Herold did but Booth refused. The pursuing soldiers set the barn on fire. While Booth was shifting his position inside, he was shot against orders in the neck. The wound pierced three vertebrae and partially severed his spinal cord leaving him paralyzed. He was dragged to the porch of Garrett's farmhouse where he expired three hours later.

A dramatist to the end, he reportedly whispered near death: *Tell my mother I died for my country*. His final words were *Useless, useless*. He died clouded by infamy and a disgrace that he had never envisioned.

Throughout the two weeks encompassing Booth's pursuit, hundreds of individuals were detained. Several were questioned and imprisoned as federal agents attempted to determine who was responsible for Lincoln's assassination. Investigators identified ten individuals including Booth as prime suspects. Each was charged with conspiracy to murder the President and labeled *The Lincoln Conspirators*.

Eight would be brought before a military tribunal. Testimony from 366 witnesses required seven weeks. Four of the accused were sentenced to hang, three imprisoned for life at hard labor and one for six years. Defendant John Surratt, Jr. had already fled to Canada remaining absent during the trial. He would be arrested two years later and undergo a juried public trial. His case resulted in a hung jury and he was eventually released.

The most sympathetic of the condemned was Mary Elizabeth Surratt who owned the boarding house where the conspirators reportedly met. Her role if any was minimal regarding any planning. She was convicted to death primarily on hearsay and for transferring a package to Booth. She would become the first woman to be executed by the federal government. Five of the judges asked her to be granted clemency by new President Andrew Johnson due to her age and sex. He declined and she was hung with three others on July 7, 1865.

Three men joined her on the scaffold. George Atzerodt lost his nerve to slay then Vice-President Andrew Johnson on the night Lincoln was shot. He wandered the D. C. streets the entire evening. He was arrested on April 20th in Germantown, Maryland. Lewis Powell was responsible for stabbing Secretary of State William Seward. David Herold guided Powell to Seward's residence. He later accompanied Booth during his fugitive run.

Three other men were sentenced to life in prison with hard labor. Dr. Samuel Mudd treated Booth's injury. The two others Michael O'Laughlen and Samuel Arnold had backed out of an earlier plan in 1864 to kidnap Lincoln. Edman Spangler would be sentenced to six years for tending Booth's horse the night of the assassination behind Ford's Theatre.

O'Laughlen died of yellow fever while incarcerated in 1867. President Andrew Johnson pardoned Mudd, Arnold and Spangler in 1869.

The Surratt house remains today in Chinatown where the conspiracy to kidnap and then murder Lincoln was originally planned. Jonathan T. Walker built the structure in 1843 in the Early Republic or Federal design style. John Surratt purchased the house in 1853 and operated it afterwards as a boarding house. Upon his death in 1862, his wife Mary would move into the property permanently. Her decision ultimately resulted in her own demise and infamy three years later.

WOK and ROLL RESTAURANT
WOK AND ROLL Restaurant
OPEN
Chinese Food Sushi Karaoke

Nurse, Activist and American Red Cross Founder
Clara Barton Residence and The Missing Soldiers Office:
437 Seventh Street NW, Washington D.C.

Clara Barton is best known for her founding of the American Red Cross. Her lifetime of service was heightened by humanitarian exploits and civil right advocacy. Her era was dominated by silenced women's voices. She led by initiative and example.

Her formative years provided scant evidence towards her future dynamic personality. She born on Christmas Day 1821 and named after the title character from writer Samuel Richardson's novel *Clarissa*.

Her father was captain Stephen Barton, a member of the local militia and a politician who inspired his daughter towards patriotism and a broader vision of humanity. Unfortunately, his perspective did not extend to the Native American tribes he fought against under the command of General Anthony Wayne.

When Clara was ten, her brother David fell from the roof of a barn and suffered a severe head injury. Doctors have given up on his recovery. She nursed him back to health. She learned how to distribute prescribed medication and properly employ leeches on his body for bleeding purposes. The practice of medicine then was rudimentary.

Clara suffered from extreme timidity. Efforts to enroll her at a local high school only made her withdrawal worse, accentuating her depression and an eating disorder. Her only remedy came from active service helping others.

At seventeen, she became a schoolteacher, thriving within that environment. She embraced several progressive educational projects that bolstered her confidence into demanding equal pay for teaching. She continued instructing for twelve years in schools based in Canada and West Georgia. Upon her mother's death in 1851, she decided to further her own education and advancement in New York at the Clinton Liberal Institute. Her perspective of the world continued to expand and she was recognized at the institute for her unique communicative skills and work ethic.

In 1852, she was contracted to open a *free school* in Bordentown, New Jersey. Her enthusiasm and successful management enabled her to hire another woman to teach over 600 students. Her accomplishment prompted the town to raise nearly $4,000 to construct a new school building.

She would experience her first bitter taste of discrimination shortly afterwards. Upon the building's completion, the school board elected a male as principal and demoted Barton to *female assistant*. Their rationale was that the position was *unfitting for a woman*. The injustice prompted a nervous breakdown and other health ailments. She resigned her position.

In 1855, she relocated to Washington D.C. and began employment as a clerk in the US Patent Office. She became one of the first women to receive such a substantial position within the federal government and comparable male salary. For three years, she endured torment and verbal abuse from her peer male clerks.

Political opposition towards women working in government offices reduced her title to *copyist*. Her political views and opposition to slavery prompted her firing in 1858. She would live with relatives in Massachusetts for the next three years before returning to D.C. and a temporary copyist position with the patent office.

The trajectory of her seemingly dead-ended career was

altered by the Civil War. On Friday, April 19, 1861, the *Baltimore Riot* ignited. The skirmish was a civil conflict between antiwar Democrats and other Confederate sympathizers and members of the Union 6th Massachusetts Militia.

Casualties were transported from the battle site to the D.C. railroad station. They were then housed inside the unfinished Capitol Building. She voluntarily arrived at the train station and took charge of nursing 40 men. She carried supplies to the wounded, offered emotional support, read to them and wrote letters on their behalf to their families.

Her patients pricked an intimate nerve. She knew many of them as acquaintances or had taught them previously. She discovered her niche for existence. She launched a personal campaign to assist in tending the wounded. She used her own living quarters as a storeroom for distributing provisions and medical supplies. She ran newspaper advertisements requesting supplies and was inundated by the response.

Her *Ladies Aid Society* sent bandages, food and clothing to the front lines beginning in early 1862. The War Department and many field surgeons opposed these efforts. Senator Henry Wilson of Massachusetts became an important political patron recognizing the selflessness behind her contributions.

She was granted her wish to serve on the front lines. She labored to distribute goods, clean field hospitals, apply dressings and serve food to wounded soldiers in close proximity to several major battle sites. Supplies were not always readily available. There are accounts of her employing cornhusks in place of bandages. She treated both Union and Confederate soldiers.

In 1864, she was appointed by Union General Benjamin

Butler as the *lady in charge* of the hospitals at the front of the *Army of the James*. She was frequently compared with Florence Nightingale and many parent later christened their newborn daughters with her first name. Her most traumatic battlefield experience came when a bullet ripped through the sleeve of her dress and struck a soldier that she was tending. He died from the wound.

She continued her duties uncompensated financially until the closure of the war. Her legacy was only midway complete.

Following the peace settlement, thousands of letters were arriving to the War Department and left unanswered. Most concerned the fate of family members or relatives who had never returned home following the conflict. She wrote a letter to President Lincoln asking permission to be allowed to respond officially to these inquiries.

She was granted permission and established the Office of Missing Soldiers. She operated inside her third floor apartment at her own expense. The organization's official purpose was to find or identify soldiers that had been killed or were missing in action. Many were presumed buried in unmarked battlefield graves. She and her assistants wrote nearly 42,000 replies and helped locate more than 22,000 missing soldiers.

Many of the identified dead would be properly buried in marked graves. The project would continue until 1868 with Congress eventually appropriating $15,000 towards the financing.

Clara Barton began to receive widespread recognition by delivering lectures throughout the United States between 1865-1868. She related her war experiences. This exposure brought her into direct contact with woman's suffragette Susan B. Anthony and civil rights activist Frederick

Douglass. She subsequently championed both of their causes.

Her frenzied workload had left her physically and mentally spent. Following her speaking tour, she closed the Missing Soldiers Office and traveled to Europe under doctor's orders the following year.

Clara was incapable of lounging through a relaxing vacation without purpose. In 1869, while visiting Geneva, Switzerland, she was introduced to Dr. Louis Appia, a specialist in the area of military medicine. He was a founding member of the International Red Cross that provided relief efforts voluntarily on a neutral basis.

Appia determined that Clara was the ideal representative for an American branch. Her confidence and documented exploits had elevated her into a capacity to locate necessary financial backers for the organization. She consented.

During her European stay, she became indispensable. At the beginning of the Franco-Prussian War in 1870, she assisted the Grand Duchess of Baden in the preparation of military hospitals. She represented the Red Cross in various aid activities. She concentrated her energies primarily in Strasbourg and Paris maintaining her personal neutrality. She was honored by the victorious Prussian nation at the conclusion of the war.

When Clara returned back to the United States in 1873, she initiated a movement to gain governmental recognition of the International Red Cross. She met with President Rutherford B. Hayes, who responded indifferently to her proposal. His attitude represented the popular opinion that the United States would never be plagued again by an internal military conflict.

Clara modified her approach and eventually persuaded President Chester Arthur that an American Red Cross could respond to crises other than simply war. Natural disasters were added to their responsibilities. She became the President of the American branch of the society holding their first official meeting at her I Street NW apartment. The first local society would be chartered in Dansville, New York where she maintained a country home.

The American organization became invaluable during the late 19th century. They responded to disastrous flooding, famine, yellow fever outbreaks, tornados and hurricanes. Beyond American shores, the organization offered relief during the 1894-96 Armenian (Hamidian) massacres within the Ottoman Empire and 1898 Spanish-American War.

Dissension towards Clara Barton's role, personality and autocratic management style created inevitable clashes. Questions arose over her co-mingling professional and personal resources. Her idealistic humanitarian approach did not adapt well with evolving contemporary fundraising and charities. By the beginning of the 20th century, she had become estranged with the organization she had been responsible for founding.

At the age of 83, she was unceremoniously forced to resign as president in 1904. A new generation of male scientific experts promoted a self-professed era of realistic efficiency. Wounded by her rejection, Clara founded the National First Aid Society oriented towards promoting local first aid programs. The American Red Cross later absorbed the organization.

Clara continued to reside in her Glen Echo, Maryland residence. It was used as the Red Cross Headquarters upon her initial arrival in 1897. She published her autobiography in 1908 and four years later died of pneumonia. Her life of achievement became the inspiration for numerous theatrical, television and film portrayals posthumously. The majority of her personal residences remain standing and have been designated as historical monuments and/or museums.

**A Structural Discard Becomes Urban Chic
Alleyway Housing:
1-8 Terrace Court NE, Washington D. C.
512 F Street Terrace SE, Washington D.C.**

Historical alley dwellings are an important component
framing the residential layout of Capitol Hill. The majority
emerged following the Civil War. Many of the planned alleys
were meant to provide access to the rear of large lots where
there might exist kitchens, animals or stables. Post-Civil War,
the majority of the city's alley dwellers were unskilled
laborers and 81% African Americans.

The biggest problem sustaining alley housing was their
construction without building permits. Materials were often
lower grade, workmanship inferior and room dimensions
constricted. Their employment for low-income housing often
created overcrowding and slum conditions creating a public
eyesore.

The institution of city building permits in 1877 forced the
disclosure of slumlord identities. By 1894, citizen groups
became more vocal and proactive regarding the elimination
of alley dwellings. A 1912 alley survey listed over 15 alleys
in the Capitol Hill neighborhood. The inward facing
structures often conveyed a sense of isolation for residents.
Yet neighborhood bonds remained tightly supportive as an
extended family.

Numerous progressive movements and urban renewal
programs sought to eliminate alley dwellings. Inexpensive
automobiles, roadways and suburban development
redistributed population concentrations away from the city
core. In 1934, Congress created The Alley Dwelling
Authority whose commission was the discontinuation of alley
constructed buildings. Their mandate became clear: no alley
houses were to be inhabited after July 1, 1944.

Despite their commitment to eliminate these structures, World War II and the subsequent housing shortage postponed enforcement. The deadline was set back another decade and then permanently repealed in 1954. By 1950, nearly all of the alley dwellings included electricity and indoor plumbing. As working class homeowners began making structural and interior upgrades, the properties developed a following. By 1970, at least 20 inhabited alleys remained accommodating an estimated 192 heads of households. Forty-two structures were listed then as vacant.

Today, brick constructed alleyway homes remain diminutive, but no longer bargains. Some properties in desirable neighborhoods have leapt up into million dollar valuations. Their popularity has inflated financially due to their location on Capitol Hill and distinctive *American* style. Such a transformation would have seemed incredulous during the mid-twentieth century and before.

Historic D.C. Institutions Weathering Property Development Trends
Ebenezer United Methodist Church:

4th and D Streets SE, Washington D.C.
Thaddeus Stevens Elementary School:

1050 21st Street NW, Washington D.C.

As historic property continues to feel the financial temptation from real estate appreciation and gentrification, two edifices remain committed towards survival.

The original *old* Ebenezer Church site was located on 4th Street SE hosting the parent Ebenezer United Methodist Church. The building dated back to 1811 and is currently a condominium complex. It's replacement, *Little Ebenezer* was constructed in 1838. Interracial congregations were common then although black members were generally relegated to sitting in the upper galleries.

Schisms and splintering off developed within the membership over this seating practice. Many white ministers refused to take African American babies in their arms. Ultimately by the early 1860s, *Little Ebenezer* began to sponsor its own African American preachers. The church's original wood frame building would be employed as a temporary school for the neighborhood. The student population expanded to over 100 pupils. A year later, a larger permanent school was opened a few blocks away.

By 1870, work began on replacing the church's original frame building with a larger red brick structure. The moniker *Little Ebenezer* was dropped. Three years later the renovation would be completed. On September 1896, a tornado destroyed the structure. Another replacement church was built on the same site the following year and remains today.

Thaddeus Stevens was a Congressman from Pennsylvania and the leader of a *radical* faction of the Republican Party during the 1860s. He was an uncompromising opponent of slavery and discrimination against black Americans. He led the movement to secure their rights during Reconstruction leading to explosive conflict with President Andrew Johnson's marginal reforms.

Stevens had been the Chairman of the House Ways and Means Committee during Abraham Lincoln's tenure. He was a political outsider with a pronounced limp due to a clubfoot from birth. He avoided the social circuit and never married. He was rumored to have a twenty-year relationship with his widowed housekeeper and companion, Lydia Hamilton Smith, a light skinned African American.

Nearing death while suffering through a variety of painful ailments, he confessed that his life had been a failure. Post-Civil War violence in the southern states initiated by the Ku Klux Klan, the failure of his political party to accelerate reforms and his hatred towards President Johnson aggravated his suffering. History would ultimately disagree with Steven's personal condemnation.

The House of Representatives initiated a movement to impeach Johnson in February1868. The process would require three months before their final favorable vote on May 26. The U.S. Senate would acquit Johnson afterwards enabling him to complete his term. Johnson would become the first presidential impeachment, but not the last. Stevens endured a summer of endless physical agony pain before expiring in mid August.

His civil rights legacy made him an ideal namesake for the first D.C. elementary school constructed for African-American children. The school opened on the year of his death and remained segregated for the initial 86 years of its existence. In 1977, Amy Carter, the daughter of President Jimmy Carter enrolled there. She became the first President's child to attend public school since the beginning of the 20th century.

In 2001, the district government planned to convert the Stevens building into residential use due to low enrollment. Public opposition prevented the sale. In 2017, the school district announced the building would re-open as a child development center for infants and toddlers. It would also be employed as additional classroom space for the nearby Francis-Stevens Educational Campus.

TWISTED TOUR GUIDES.com

Shameful Compensation For Exemplary Courage Under Fire
Anna Etheridge Hooks Residence:
115 6th Street SE, Washington D.C.
U.S. Treasury Building:
1500 Pennsylvania Avenue NW, Washington D.C.

Anna Etheridge Hooks exhibited courage under fire that few Civil War infantrymen could emulate. She initially entered the Union army as a laundress when her husband enlisted in the 2nd Michigan Infantry Regiment. He soon deserted. She remained with the Fifth Michigan Infantry. When the regiment went on campaign, the other laundresses went home. She chose to accompany them into battle.

Etheridge was described as young, attractive, quiet, modest and fearless. Her regiment adored her and permitted no disrespect towards her. When General Philip Kearny viewed her caring for wounded soldiers during the July 1862 Peninsula military campaign, he secured her services for his III Corp division. She was outfitted with a horse, saddle and commissioned sergeant's pay (never received). She reportedly wore a black riding habit with sergeant's chevrons.

Her official title was *cook* for the officer's mess, but her role evolved far more significantly and inspirationally. She was renowned for riding to the front lines to aid wounded soldiers exposing her to extreme danger. Her saddlebags were completely filled with medical supplies. Her skirt was frequently ripped by bullet strikes. She endured the identical hardships as infantry soldiers that included sleeping on the bare campgrounds.

Etheridge reportedly never flinched from death. Her steadfast encouragement and example boasted morale. She once fortified an artillery battery near retreat to continue fighting despite their heavy losses. Her greatest acknowledgement occurred when General Grant ordered all women out of military camps and the front lines in 1864. Numerous officers signed a petition requesting that Etheridge be allowed to remain in service on the field.

She would be transferred to aid in the transportation of wounded men from the ports of Alexandria, Virginia to Philadelphia, New York City and D.C. She would be awarded the Kearny Cross for service and bravery. Her military tenure ended on July 1, 1865. She was never financially compensated for her military service. Her health would be compromised with her front line exposure for the balance of her life.

In 1870, she married Charles Hooks, a war veteran from Connecticut. Three years later, they purchased a D. C. residence. She worked at the Treasury Department for eight years before being discharged in favor of someone else. Her former soldiers gathered hundreds of signatures protesting her treatment and petitioned her reinstatement. Their request was ignored.

In 1886, she wrote a deposition requesting a $50 monthly pension for her wartime service. The following year, Congress allocated a $25 monthly pension. She died on January 23, 1913 at the Georgetown University Hospital and was buried with full veteran's honors at Arlington National Cemetery.

**The Science of Metrology and Accurate Predictions
Cleveland Abbe-James Monroe House:
2017 I Street NW, Washington D.C.**

Cleveland Abbe is the individual to credit or blame for our cultural dependence on weather forecasting. During his lifetime, he was referred to as *Old Probability* based on the reliability of his forecasts. He was born and raised in New York City distinguishing himself in mathematic and chemistry and earned his Bachelors degree at City College. He taught engineering at the University of Michigan while studying astronomy before returning to City College to earn his Masters degree.

When the Civil War erupted, he enlisted with the Union Army, however he failed the vision test due to his myopia. He spent the war years attending Harvard and invested significant time with leading scientists and intellectuals of the era. He studied abroad in Russia at the Observatory of Pulkovo. Upon his return, he was offered the director position at the Cincinnati Observatory, which he held for five years before being let go due to funding issues.

While in Cincinnati, he first began predicting the weather based on presumptions that forecasts could be generated based on astronomical conditions.

By 1871, he had become responsible for elevating the science of meteorology with a coordinated team of volunteer observers. He was appointed the official Meteorologist for the United States Signal Corps and the United States Weather Bureau. He is credited as the founder of the National Weather Service. His published works and forecasts became an integral part of military and commercial operations and forecasting. North American railroad companies accepted his published works advocating the implementation of time zones in 1880s.

He continued to accumulate honors, professorships and credibility until his death in 1916 after more than 45 years of achievement. His townhouse residence near Foggy Bottom features an equally storied history. Built in 1805 in the Federalist architectural style, it was the residence of President James Monroe and later historian Henry Adams. Monroe has a park named after him across the street. The property is currently the headquarters for the Arts Club of Washington.

Abbe doubtlessly would have found amusement and possibly contempt in the current state of weather forecasting. The reports are still drawn from scientific research, but few of the televised presenters have the slightest metrology background. Instead they've become fashion templates or comic entertainment reciting forecasts flashed on teleprompters. Few if any are labeled *Old Probability* based on the accuracy of their predictions.

A Scandal That Nearly Toppled A Civil War Hero's Legacy
Ulysses S. Grant Sculpture:
U.S. Capitol Building Facing The Reflecting Pool
Former D.C. Residence:
3238 R Street NW, Washington D.C.

Ulysses S. Grant's genius as a military commander was nearly eclipsed by the 1872 Credit Mobilier scandal. The financial swindle darkened his presidential re-election campaign and had the potential to ruin his enduring legacy. The scandal's origins dated back to the close of the Civil War in 1864 when Congress chartered the Union Pacific Railroad. An associated affiliate called the Credit Mobilier of America was established at the same time.

Congress authorized funding with the Pacific Railroad Act of 1864-68 for the completion of a transcontinental rail line west from the Missouri River to the Pacific Coast. Treacherous desert and mountain terrain, hostile native inhabitants and virtually no consumer demand at that period plagued working conditions and elevated construction costs.

The Credit Mobilier operation was a complicated financial scheme masking as a railroad construction entity. Credit Mobilier organizers invoiced Congress $94.6 million for construction while incurring operating expenses of only $50 million. The organizers pocketed the difference, a gluttonous windfall. They used portions from this graft to bribe influential federal politicians to create laws, funding sources and regulatory rulings favorable to the Union Pacific Railroad.

President Grant was unaware of the unlawful proceedings, but many among his closest political circle were deeply involved.

On September 4, 1872, preceding his upcoming presidential election, the *New York Sun* revealed some of the financial improprieties behind the construction overbilling. The newspaper had been historically harsh towards the Grant administration and Republican Party. Compromising letters were revealed implicating members of the Credit Mobilier management team and certain Republican members of Congress.

The public disclosure left the Union Pacific and other investors nearly bankrupt. Eight members of Congress and Grant's sitting Vice President Schuyler Colfax were investigated. Grant's running mate in the 1872 campaign Henry Wilson was also included. Five additional congressmen would be investigated later. Wilson emphatically denied any involvement initially, but later altered his account. He admitted accepting stock but confessed to reversing the transaction based on his personal doubts regarding the ethics of his acceptance.

Despite the tarnish, Grant and Wilson easily prevailed in the election.

A follow-up Department of Justice investigation revealed that over 30 politicians from both parties had received stock. James A. Garfield, elected president in 1880 was part of that contingent but denied involvement. No charges were ever filed against any of the participants. Grant's two-term presidency has been appraised with mixed reviews. Two additional scandals would tarnish his administration along with the *Panic of 1873* economic depression.

His stewardship of post-Civil War finances was generally lauded and his foreign policy remained peaceful avoiding war. He is credited with advancing the civil rights movement and civil service public hiring practices.

One of his unsuccessful projects was the annexation of the Dominican Republic. The Senate rejected flatly his proposal.

The financial uncertainty caused by the *Panic of 1873* enabled the Democratic Party to regain the White House with Rutherford B. Hayes along with a majority in the House of Representatives. Despite varied Hayes administration problems and his general unpopularity, Grant was unsuccessful in securing the Republican nomination for a third term in the 1880 election. James Garfield would sweep the nomination and general election, but hold office only briefly. When a reporter advised Grant of Garfield's assassination on July 2, 1881, he wept openly for his peer and friend.

During his retirement, Grant toured the world dining with England's Queen Victoria and numerous prominent world leaders. Following his worldwide jettison, his fortunes plummeted. He was an inexperienced financier and chased poor advice. A Wall Street brokerage firm involving his son Buck resulted in his worst setback. He was diagnosed during October 1884 with terminal throat cancer prompted by an adulthood of cigar smoking.

Recognizing the precarious financial position his family could face following his death, he wrote his two volume biographical memoirs. The work detailed comprehensively the Civil War and became a critical and financial success posthumously. He completed the manuscript only a few days before his death on July 23, 1885 at the age of 63. Subsequent generations of readers, literary critics and military historians consider the work a literary masterpiece for its clarity, insightfulness and blunt honesty.

Grant's death had been expected. The magnitude of public response rivaled Abraham Lincoln's. Over 1.5 million people attended his New York City funeral. Numerous ceremonies were held nationally. President Grover Cleveland ordered a 30-day nationwide period of mourning. He was initially buried in Riverside Park in New York inside a temporary tomb. Twelve years later he would be relocated to the newly completed *General Grant National Memorial*, the largest mausoleum in North America.

Within Washington D.C., a Grant memorial sculpture was commissioned and dedicated in 1922 at the foot of Capitol Hill. The memorial overlooks the Capitol Reflecting Pool. The historic house that he resided in post-Civil War remains occupied in the Georgetown district.

Grant has been historically eulogized as a skillful leader, strategic planner and symbol of national unity. The Credit Mobilier affair briefly dimmed his reputation. An acknowledgement over his life accomplishments and his own broader vision towards humanity fortunately prevailed.

A Lincoln Statue Accused of Promoting Inaccurate Racial Stereotypes
Lincoln Park:

11th and East Capitol Street NE, Washington D.C.

Lincoln Park was the first designated memorial to honor President Abraham Lincoln by Congress two years following his 1865 assassination. It is the largest of the Capitol Hill Parks and features a monument honoring its namesake along with educator and civil rights leader Mary McLeod Bethune. The space was originally included as part of Pierre L'Enfant's original 1791 plan for the city.

During the Civil War, the location was used as a hospital for wounded troops, visited periodically by poet Walt Whitman. Intended to honor Lincoln and the freeing of slaves, a bronze casted statue designed by Thomas Bell depicts Lincoln holding the Emancipation Proclamation before a kneeling black man. The slave's arm is extended to show that his shackles have been broken.

The slave model was Archer Alexander, the last person captured under the Fugitive Slave Act. Charlotte Scott, a former enslaved woman living in Virginia initiated the fundraising program to finance the statue. The majority of the monies accepted were exclusively from formerly enslaved individuals.

The Lincoln statue was dedicated inside the park on April 14, 1876 with over 25,000 people in attendance. Frederick Douglass delivered the keynote address before President Ulysses S. Grant, his cabinet and members of Congress.

Douglass had mixed emotions regarding the monument. He felt the imagery *perpetuated negative stereotypes regarding African Americans*. Additional critics and protests have since joined his voice of dissent over the ensuing decades.

In 1974, the memorial was shifted from originally facing the U.S. Capitol to face the Bethune Memorial. In 2020, a petition was initiated to remove the monument and relocate it to a museum with an explanation of its origin. As perspectives continue to shift regarding racially themed memorials, it is foreseeable to imagine that Lincoln may sooner than later occupy another space besides his namesake public park.

A Shooting in the Back of a Recently Elected President
President James Garfield Assassination Site:
National Gallery of Art West Building Rotunda
6th and Constitution Avenue NW, Washington D.C.
Garfield Monument:
U.S. Capitol Building Facing The Reflecting Pool,
Washington D.C.

In 1941, the National Gallery of Art West building was completed in the neoclassical style of architecture. That museum section replaced plans to construct a George Washington Memorial Building that never materialized. The structure established an important public venue to exhibit an extensive collection of paintings, drawings and sculptures by European masters from the medieval period through the late 19th century. The display also includes pre-20th century works by American artists.

The West Building's immediate predecessor was an infamous site of American history. Opened on July 2, 1872, the Baltimore and Potomac Railroad Station operated there until its closure in 1907. President Theodore Roosevelt ordered its demolition in late 1908 without authority or notice to the public. The train station lobby was the site where President James A. Garfield was fatally shot.

Little is remembered regarding Garfield's tenure as President. He was a Union army general and Ohio congressman prior to becoming American's 20th chief executive following Rutherford B. Hayes. By his fourth month in office, the prestige of the title had already begun to rust. He clashed frequently with Republican power brokers over patronage appointments. His wife had nearly succumbed to a case of malaria.

He was anxious to escape the oppressive heat of D.C. for a

summer trip to New England. On July 2' 1881, he was scheduled to give a speech at his alma mater, William College. He departed in the morning from the White House via carriage with his two teenage sons and Secretary of State James G. Blaine.

They left unaccompanied by bodyguards or security personnel. The carriage pulled up outside the entrance of the Baltimore and Potomac rail station.

Awaiting his arrival was a restless and spurned political applicant named Charles Guiteau. He was already pacing the waiting room. Guiteau, 39, was known by White House insiders for his persistent complaints of being discarded as a worthy candidate for an appointed position in the new administration. Garfield once even granted him a personal meeting. Blaine had become infuriated by his presence. The deluded Guiteau persisted in his conviction that two speeches he had delivered promoting Garfield's candidacy had elevated him to the presidency.

Family members and acquaintances considered Guiteau an eccentric and mentally imbalanced. Some considered him dangerously insane. He barely escaped commitment to a mental institution. Those who knew him underestimated his resolve.

During May and June 1881, he had roamed around Washington D.C. lodging in rooming houses and then sneaking away without paying for his lodging and meals. He passed days loitering in hotel lobbies, writing letters of application and reading old newspapers. He circulated often inside State Department offices and the White House waiting room pestering officials while wearing the same shabby clothes.

He had stalked Garfield's movements throughout June and had meticulously prepared for his presumed historical destiny. He had acquired a .44 caliber pistol with an ivory handle. He chose ivory because he felt that it would display better in a museum. He toured the District jail assuming that it might become his temporary home following his perceived *heroic* act. Most brazenly, he carried a letter in his coat pocket addressed to the White House. He cited his impending murder as a justified and unifying action for the Republican Party.

At 9:30 a.m., Guiteau strode up to Garfield from behind. He drew his pistol and fired steadily into Garfield. The first shot only grazed his right arm. Garfield responded with: *My God! What is this?*

The second shot lodged in his lower back and knocked him to the floor. The bullet passed the first lumbar but missed his spinal chord. Amidst the accompanying screams, Guiteau calmly placed his pistol back into his pocket and headed towards the exit to escape via an awaiting cab.

He inadvertently bumped into policeman Patrick Kearney who was entering the station upon hearing the gunfire. A ticket agent and other police officers then apprehended Guiteau. An enraged crowd surrounded him and urged his immediate lynching. Police transferred him to the anticipated D.C. jailhouse a few blocks away for his own safety.

Garfield remained on the train station floor bleeding profusely. He was carried to a room on an upstairs floor of the station. Ten different doctors arrived to examine him and attempt unsuccessfully to locate the missing second bullet inside him. The shot had missed his vital organs and arteries, but lodged behind his pancreas.

These physicians worsened the damage by using their

unsterilized fingers and instrument to probe the injury. Germs were doubtlessly introduced with infection resulting. One doctor accidentally punctured his liver. Following an hour of medical probing and excruciating agony, Garfield was transferred to a bedroom of the White House. He was fully conscious and alert. Doctors presumed that he would die that evening. The following morning, his vital signs were sound and there was fresh hope that he might survive.

Garfield should have survived the wound. The problem persisted that his doctors could not locate the bullet. They even experimented with a metal detector to locate the projectile. The lead doctor employed the machine exclusively on the wrong side of Garfield's body. The evasive bullet ultimately resulted in fatal consequences.

Garfield spent a miserable summer weathering the oppressive D.C. heat. Infection ravaged his body and he struggled to keep down and digest solid foods. He subsisted primarily on liquids and dropped nearly half of his body weight. He was tormented by fever, abscesses over his body and a weakened heart rate.

He did meet once with his Cabinet, but his prognosis for recovery continued to decline. No official business or major decisions were conducted during his decline. On September 6th, he was relocated by train to Elberon on the New Jersey Shoreline. Any hoped-for tranquility and/or seaside air could not effectively combat the infection that had overwhelmed his system.

He died two weeks later on September 19th, two months before his 50th birthday. An autopsy would reveal his doctors' miscalculation in tracking the path of the fatal bullet. His body would lie in state in the Capitol Rotunda and House of Representatives chamber. His body was transferred to Cleveland, Ohio where his funeral services were conducted on September 26th.

Vice President Chester Arthur would immediately succeed Garfield. Their combined legacies have been generally downplayed in chronologies of American history. Arthur would lose in the 1884 Republican primary to James Blaine. Democrat Grover Cleveland would defeat Blaine in a close general election.

Garfield spent nearly as many days incapacitated as he did navigating the treacherous currents of the presidency. His 40-year old assassin would be hung nearly one year following the day of the shooting. The prized pistol Guiteau employed was recovered and displayed in the Smithsonian Institute during the early 20th century. An elaborate plaque adorned a wall on the inside of the train station stating the details of the treacherous act. A gold star embedded on the floor designated the location of the shooting. All three items have reportedly since vanished.

In 2018, the National Park Service installed replacement signage to designate the assassination site. A few blocks nearby, the James A. Garfield Monument is located on the southwest corner of the U.S. Capitol grounds near the Reflecting Pool.

Garfield's assassination did not conclude fatal violence against American presidents. Twenty years later, President William McKinley would be killed by a shot at close range during a public reception. Following McKinley's death, Congress assigned the United States Secret Service to assume the responsibility of ensuring the president's personal safety. With the exception of President John Kennedy, none have been killed since.

A Woman Constrained Seeks Her Own Exit
Hay-Adams Hotel:

800 16th Street NW, Washington DC

Marian *Clover* Adams had an admittedly happy marriage and was considered an accomplished photographer. It wasn't enough to sustain her happiness or longevity.

Born in 1843 and raised in Boston, during the American Civil War, she volunteered for the Sanitary Commission. She insisted on watching the reviews of Union General Sherman and Grant's armies in 1865, considered unconventional for a woman.

In 1866, she traveled to Europe where she met writer Henry Adams in London. She would marry Adams and while he taught at Harvard, they established a gathering place for intellectuals. In 1877, they moved to Washington D.C. where their home on Lafayette Square became a popular social center.

The Adams mansion was adjacent to the residence of influential statesman and official John Hay. He had begun his career as a private secretary to Abraham Lincoln crowning his political achievements as U.S. Secretary of State under Presidents William McKinley and Theodore Roosevelt.

Clover Adams wrote extensively and was suggested to be the true author of *Democracy: An American Novel* in 1980. The work was credited to her husband 43 years following publication. She has been cited as the inspiration for two of Henry James's writings *Daisy Miller* and *The Portrait of a Lady*.

Her passion towards photography and subject themes documented the role of women in the 19th century. She did all of her own developing. Although her work was widely admired, Henry Adams would not allow her to earn a livelihood. He discouraged any publication of her photographs.

Clover Adams suffered from severe depression following her father's death in April 1885. The disruption caused by the construction process of their residence deepened the darkness and control surrounding her.

The Adams had relocated temporarily to a nearby rented house on H Street. Alone in her bedroom in early December 1885, she swallowed potassium cyanide one of her photo developing chemicals. She was 42. Henry Adams would find her prostate on the rug before her bedroom fire.

He became devastated by the loss and destroyed all of the letters she had ever written to him. Those letters reportedly documented a generally content family life and love towards her husband. Consumed by grief, Henry Adams commissioned the famed *Adams Memorial* designed by architect Stanford White with a bronze sculpture designed by Augustus Saint-Gaudens. The haunting memorial marks her grave in Rock Creek Cemetery.

Henry Adams would never remarry. In 1912, he suffered a stroke speculated to be prompted by news of the *Titanic* sinking. He had tickets for the return voyage to Europe. His scholarly works diminished afterwards and he died at the age of 80 in 1918. He would be interred beside his wife Clover.

In 1927, developer Harry Wardman purchased the Adams and Hay mansion properties. He razed both residences and built a 138-room residential hotel in the Italian Renaissance style. In 1928, the Hay-Adams House opened.

Wardman's fortunes sunk during the Great Depression and real estate his empire collapsed. The Hay-Adams House was one of his last properties that he defaulted on. In 1932 another hotel magnate Julius Manger purchased the property at auction and renamed it the Hay-Adams Hotel. Prior to moving into the White House in 2008, President-elect Barack Obama moved his family and security entourage into an entire wing of the hotel.

Ownership has changed several times subsequently, but one guest has never vacated. The spirit of Clover Adams reported roams the floors trailed by a distinct scent of almond. Potassium cyanide, her death-provoking chemical smells like almonds.

Mapping Segregation Within A Gated Community
LeDroit Park Gate Entrance
286 V Street NW, Washington D.C.

The LeDroit Park development was Washington D.C.'s first gated community. The boundary outline, which resembled a tracing of the state of Nevada, encompassed Elm Street NW (North), Florida Avenue NW (South), 5th Avenue NW (West) and 2nd Street NW (East). The housing neighborhood was founded in 1873 by Amzi Barber, a businessman who served on the board of trustees of neighboring Howard University. He named the terrain after his father-in-law.

Exclusivity became one of the prime marketing features touted with the development. The neighborhood was promoted as a *romantic* district provided residents were white. The landscaping featured narrow tree-lined streets with emphasis on planted flowerbeds and trees to attract upwardly scaled professionals. Guards patrolled the gate and fencing to insure security.

Between 1886 and 1891, a *fence war* erupted between LeDroit Park residents and perceived *intruders* seeking a corridor from Howard University to downtown. The protestors inevitably won the skirmish. Over the subsequent decades, the development became fully integrated and considered a desirable elite residence.

Griffith Stadium, the former home of the Washington Redskins and Senators professional sports teams was located on the Northwest corner of the property until 1965. Upon demolition, the Howard University Hospital was constructed on the site.

A Toxic Relationship Ends In Bloodshed on the Capitol Steps
Death Site of Former Congressman William Taulbee: East Staircase of the House of Representatives Wing of the U. S. Capitol

In 1887, *Louisville Times* correspondent Charles Kincaid wrote a story implicating Kentucky Congressman William Taulbee with conducting an extramarital affair. Taulbee was the father of five sons. The dalliance was conducted with a young government employee.

Kincaid also wrote a series of articles accusing Taulbee of financially profiting from his congressional service. The writings severely damaged Taulbee's reputation within his home state. He chose not to run for a third term.

Taulbee did not leave Washington D.C. permanently. Instead he was hired as a lobbyist. He frequently encountered Kincaid who continued his reporting on Congress. Taulbee never forgave Kincaid for the stain attached to his character. They frequently traded verbal insults that often nearly resulted in physical altercations.

Physically, Kincaid was overmatched due to his slight build. On February 28, 1890, the two men scuffled on the second floor of the Capitol outside the House of Representatives. Taulbee grabbed Kincaid by the shirt collar and tossed him backwards.

Taulbee continued on with his daily routine. Kincaid ran home to retrieve his pistol for what he claimed was self-protection.

Later that day, Kincaid was descending the Capitol staircase and viewed Taulbee approaching from below. He sensed more confrontation was forthcoming. At close range, he shot

Taulbee in the face. Taulbee fell onto the steps bleeding profusely. The stains reportedly are still visible today. Kincaid admitted that he'd fired the shot and surrendered voluntarily. Taulbee would linger eleven days before dying at the age of 38 on March 11, 1890.

The murder trial of Charles Kincaid began one year after Taulbee's death due to various delays. The story gripped national readership. U.S. attorney Charles Cole led the prosecution team having only been appointed to the position three weeks previously. Indiana Senator Daniel Voorhees headed Kincaid's defense team. Kincaid pleaded self-defense and a jury found him not guilty.

Kincaid would return to Kentucky with is sister and nephew. He would serve on the Kentucky Railroad Commission and as an American diplomat. He later resumed a career in the newspaper industry as a reporter with the *Cincinnati Enquirer*. His own poor health finally deserted him in 1906 when he died at the age of 52.

A Fall Into Terror Film Infamy
Exorcist Stairs:

Prospect Street and 36th Street NW, Washington D.C.

The concrete steps that descend as a continuance of Georgetown's 36th Street NW are an important part of film history. Located just behind Prospect Street, they were originally constructed in 1895 adjacent to the Capital Traction Company Barn. This facility housed cable cars and is now part of Georgetown University. The staircase served as a public right of way. For decades, the steep descending stairs were known as the *Hitchcock Steps* in honor of the famous suspense and mystery film director Alfred Hitchcock.

The staircase was christened with a more enduring designation when it became attached to the 1973 film *The Exorcist*. The movie cemented a reputation in terror and apocalyptic genres. The steps were a component of a scene depicting a memorable fall by key character Father Damian Karras. An adjacent townhouse constructed in 1950 became the infamous *Exorcist* house.

A Glamorized Portrait Of The Frontier West Fabricated Buffalo Bill's Residence:
28 Ninth Street NE, Washington D.C.

William Frederick Cody compressed several lifetimes within one. He immortalized a fictitious narrative of the American West while experiencing firsthand its gradual disappearance and transformation. Through melodrama and re-creation, Cody, better known as *Buffalo Bill* created a faux impression of the frontier that has subsequently been criticized for its exploitation of Native Americans and endangered animal species. His history is far more complicated than the caricature he successfully marketed with his signature *Wild West Show*.

Cody was born in February 1846 on farm near LeClaire, Iowa on the Mississippi River. His family moved to Kansas where his father Isaac operated a trading post near the Kickapoo Indian Reservation. Isaac was an abolitionist who delivered frequently unpopular anti-slavery speeches. He was stabbed during one and ultimately died from the wound three years later in 1857.

To support his fatherless family, Cody began working at nine as a horseman for the Russell, Majors and Waddell freight company. During his employ that year, he worked on a cattle drive. He would encounter a young peer *Wild Bill* Hickok who intervened on his behalf during a fight Cody was engaged in with an older man. During this same drive, he became reputed as the *youngest Indian fighter* when be killed a Native American who attacked the cattle party.

Cody's exploits and adventures would be frequently embellished through his writings and later shows. At 14, he reportedly began riding for the Pony Express. During the Civil War, he served as a Union scout in campaigns against the Kiowa and Comanche tribes. By 1863, he enlisted with the Seventh Kansas Cavalry that engaged in battles in Missouri and Tennessee.

He continued his scout and dispatch services for the U.S. Army following the war. During this period, he often undertook dangerous assignments that others refused. On April 26, 1872, he was awarded the Medal of Honor by President Ulysses S. Grant. During this period, his reputation expanded and evolved into mythology throughout the frontier. He would be christened the moniker *Buffalo Bill*. The very exploits that propelled his fame would later serve as the condemnation of his life.

Between 1867-68, he hunted buffalo to feed construction crews on the Union Pacific Railroad. He reportedly slaughtered 4,280 head of buffalo himself making him the undisputed slayer of the Great Plains. This killing proficiency of a defenseless animal by hunters nearly decimated the entire population. By the late 1880s, fewer than 100 remained in the wild.

Buffalo hunting on the plains was macabre. The animals were hunted for their skins and tongues. The rest of the animal was left behind to decay. Once they had rotted, their bones were then collected and shipped to the East Coast in large quantities. The practice became later acknowledged as an American disgrace.

Cody became an integral guide for the U.S. Fifth Cavalry between 1868-1876. The Calvary became the American government's systematic vehicle for massacring Native American resistance to land settlement west of the Mississippi River. Cody's acknowledged skills included accurate marksmanship, total terrain recall and intimate knowledge of Native American traits, courage and tactical practices.

He reputedly participated in 16 battle engagements climaxed by his scalping of the Cheyenne warrior *Yellow Hair* in Sioux county, Nebraska. He rationalized the act as a response to the massacre of General George Custer's regiment at the Battle of Little Bighorn earlier in 1878.

Cody discovered early the value of self-promotion. He offered choice material to newspaper reporters and a proliferation of hack novelists. They elevated *Buffalo Bill Cody* into a Western folk hero. As early as 1872, he began stage acting with a performance in the drama *The Scouts of the Prairie*. For many years afterwards, he continued scouting for the army and escorting hunting parties to the West.

His self-promoted mythology morphed in 1883 into his own touring *Wild West Show*. The spectacle featured outdoor entertainment with a cast of hundreds. Dressed in flamboyant leather theatrical clothing, Cody successfully showcased fancy shooting, daring horse riding and glamorized recreations of history that astonished audiences who'd rarely ventured further than their hometowns.

The show played at Queen Victoria's Golden Jubilee in 1887 and was staged throughout Europe. By 1893, over three million spectators had viewed the farce. With his prominent goatee and cascading hair, *Buffalo Bill Cody* became one of the most recognized personalities in the world by the conclusion of the 19th century.

The clichés that defined for generations the Cowboy and Indian culture of the Old West can arguably be attributed to Cody's exaggeration. His *Wild West* show continued until 1916 with his active participation. His speculation into an unproductive gold mine cost him his fortune. His last public appearance was in late 1916. He died at the age of 71 on January 10, 1917 in Denver, Colorado.

Historical Maintenance of the Congressional and Lincoln Memorial Reflecting Pools
Capitol Mall, Washington D.C.

Situated between the Botanic Garden and the Capitol Building, the Capitol Reflecting Pool was envisioned by Pierre L'Enfant in his original city design plans. The original intention was to redirect the waters of Tiber Creek into a canal that would tumble into a cascade and pool at the foot of Capitol Hill.

When the Washington Canal was constructed in 1815, the plans did not incorporate any of L'Enfant's basins or canals. It streamed water down 3rd Street, crossing over the Botanical Garden. It evolved into a disgusting sewer and was eventually channeled into D.C.'s sewer line during the early 1870s.

At the beginning of the twentieth century, the National Mall fronting the Capitol Building was a disgrace. A train station, shops and random buildings obscured the monumental vision L'Enfant had envisioned. The McMillan Commission was established to correct this aesthetic blemish. Their modifications incorporated eight fountains situated off the center axis in Union Square and a large pool along the Mall's center panel from 3rd to 4th Streets.

The effect creates a spectacular image mirroring the Capital Building. The pool is part of a larger plaza including the Grant and Garfield monuments and features sunken walkways along the north, west and south sides of the pool. The Capitol Reflecting Pool has no filtration system and is frequently littered by accumulating dirt and trash. Sections of the retaining wall have settled affecting the seals so that the pool leaks water.

The Lincoln Memorial Reflecting Pool on the other extremity contains 4 million gallons of water when full. The water is drained each winter and flows into both the Tidal Basin and city water system. The full release requires approximately 3-4 days to drain. The discharge is moderated so that it does not overwhelm the city's processing capacity.

A month is allocated for cleaning, repairs and essential maintenance. Refilling the basin requires three to four days and is sourced from the city's filtered water system. This cycle has become absolute necessary to keep the waters circulating, sanitary and bacteria under control during the traditional scorching heat of summer.

Playing With Extramarital Fire and Becoming Scorched
Raleigh Hotel Murder Site: (Demolished)
1111 Pennsylvania Avenue NW, Washington D.C.

Arthur Brown tiptoed through a precarious labyrinth of marriage and adultery that ultimately severed his life. Brown was born in March 1843 on a Michigan farm moving with his family at thirteen to Yellow Springs, Ohio. He attended Antioch College before earning a law degree from the University of Michigan in 1864.

He would establish a successful law practice in Kalamazoo, Michigan, marry and father one child, Alice. His straying eye descended upon Isabel Cameron, the daughter of a Michigan state senator. Their affair destroyed his marriage once it became publicly disclosed. He would relocate to Salt Lake City and reconstruct his life and law practice.

Isabel Cameron would follow him. They married following his divorce and had a son named Max. Brown decided to pursue a political career and steadily rose to prominence within the Republican Party. The state legislature elected him to become one of Utah's first two U.S. senators in 1896 following their admission to American statehood. His brief term concluded on March 4, 1897.

The paths of Brown and Anne Bradley would cross during his Utah political stint. She was actively involved with the Salt Lake City Women's Club, First Unitarian Church and Republican Party. She was married to railroad executive Clarence Bradley and had children. She became estranged from her husband by 1898. Brown seized the opportunity to seduce her. She was thirty years younger.

Their relationship followed a familiar pattern of many extra marital affairs. He promised her that he was divorcing his wife, but property settlement issues had become an obstacle.

He gave her an engagement ring to signify his fidelity. They traveled together to Washington D.C. with his daughter Alice. Bradley posed as Brown's wife.

His actual wife, Isabel Cameron-Brown was well aware of his pattern of deceit. He indicated to her that he was filing for divorce. Adultery was illegal during that era. She hired a private detective to follow Brown and Bradley. On September 28, 1902, both were arrested on charges of adultery.

Isabel was against the divorce proceedings primarily because she wished to be presented at court in England the following year. Divorced women were prohibited from admission. She offered to drop the charges against Brown and his newest mistress if he would cancel the divorce filing.

Arthur Brown delayed upon a resolution. Three months later, he and Bradley were arrested again on adultery charges.

Anne Bradley rejected a marginal financial settlement offered to her by Arthur and Isabel Brown. The two women fought viciously over their unworthy prize. The conflict escalated into a fateful evening of confrontation between the two at a Pocatello, Idaho hotel. Insults and accusations of indiscretions were hurled heatedly between them as errant dishware thrown against a wall.

The evening concluded with an apparent agreement. Arthur Brown promised to create a financial settlement for his wife, pursue a divorce and marry Anne Bradley. He provided her with a revolver for future protection against his wife. He would regret his gift.

Her confidence in Brown's promises was premature. When Bradley returned to Salt Lake City three months pregnant with Brown's child, she discovered that he had reconciled with his wife. The reasons may have revolved around her health. Isabel Brown would die of cancer on August 22, 1905.

For Bradley, a solution now became elemental. She divorced her husband and was now legally available to marry Arthur Brown.

He cooled towards the idea of matrimony. He continually made promises but delayed execution of them. He evaded all attempts to finalize arrangements regarding marriage or even setting her up in a business arrangement he'd vowed.

Like her predecessors, Bradley had wizened to Brown's pattern of duplicity. In December 1906, she trailed him to Washington D.C. uncovering letters addressed to him from actress Annie Adams Kiskadden. She would become the mother of future famed actress Maude Adams.

Bradley became enraged by the discovery. She perceived that Brown intended to marry Kiskadden and confronted him inside his Raleigh Hotel room. On the evening of December 8th, she shot him with the pistol that he had gifted her. Four days later, he would die from his wounds.

At her highly publicized trial, she used a convenient plea employed by cuckolded husbands of *temporary insanity*. The trial revealed that Brown had modified his will. He had renounced Bradley and two sons that she claimed were his. The jury was empathetic towards her plight and convinced of her sincerity. They acquitted her.

She returned to Utah and ultimately operated an antique store in Salt Lake City until her death at 77 on November 11, 1950.

**The Transformation of Swampoodle Into Union Station
Washington Union Station:
50 Massachusetts Avenue NE, Washington D.C.**

At the beginning of the twentieth century, *Swampoodle* was located on the periphery of Washington D.C. development. The area consisted of several blocks around the intersection of North Capitol and K Street. Primarily Irish immigrants settled the neighborhood in the early 1800s with a large influx during the mid-century due to the Great Famine in Ireland.

The name *Swampoodle* was reputed to be derived from newspaper slang covering the 1857 ground breaking of St. Aloysius Church. The land was flush with swamps and puddles that occurred when the Tiber Creek overflowed its banks. Local male gang members were called *poodles*. A reporter simply bridged the two terms to form *Swampoodle*... the name stuck. Crime, illicit vice and gang violence were commonplace.

The district was criticized for overcrowding and frequent outbreaks of malaria, typhoid and dysentery. Tiber Creek was a tributary of the Potomac River and flowed through the center of the district creating an unhygienic open-air sewer system.

Within the district, the Washington Statesmen baseball club played on the Swampoodle Grounds between 1886 to 1889. The team became the forerunners for the Washington Senators. The Grounds could seat 6,000 spectators and featured an outfield tower approximately 20 feet high.

The neighborhood was in close proximity of the U. S. Capital building and considered an eyesore. Residents kept goats, cows and livestock in between their houses. Most of these structures were flimsy shanties constructed from wood scraps.

The terrain became prime new development land for city planners seeking to construct a central railway station and memorial to honor Abraham Lincoln. The Lincoln Memorial would be constructed elsewhere, but Union Station found a permanent home.

Over 100 houses, the baseball field and other commercial structures were razed. Many of the hired construction workers tore down their own houses. The remainder of Tiber Creek was enclosed and became part of the massive D.C. tunnel system. Low lying areas were leveled with landfill.

Union Station would be completed in 1907 and become the largest train station in the world at that time. Commercial office complexes were built nearby. Certain streets would be buried under the railroad tracks. Some were renamed.

ELEVATOR

Walgr
Lowe
Lower L
Amtrak
Gate
B

A New American Meridian Designation
Meridian Hill Park

16th Street NW and W Street NW, Washington D.C.

Meridian Hill Park began its storied legacy as a mansion site in 1819 by John Porter. That mansion would later become the home for departing President John Quincy Adams. After being converted to a public park, Union troops encamped on the grounds during the Civil War. In 1910, the U.S. government purchased the grounds and hired landscape architects George Burnap and Horace Peaslee to design a lush Italian style garden. The highlight of their collaboration features the country's longest cascading fountain.

The park's name is derived from a failed visionary project of President Thomas Jefferson. He believed that capital surveyors should establish a fresh American Meridian, a north-south line running through both poles and the American continent.

Jefferson wanted to reinforce America's independence from England and specifically the Prime Meridian established to service Britain's Royal Navy global navigation. The internationally recognized Prime Meridian then as now passes through Greenwich, England.

The American Meridian is acknowledged by the finials on the Euclid Street fence post entrance of Meridian Hill Park. Jefferson's desire to re-orient global positioning failed to achieve international recognition and acceptance.

Meridian Hill Park evolved into a performance center for established acts and an informal Sunday afternoon drum circle dating back to the 1960s. Many have subsequently renamed the property Malcolm X Park, although the title has never officially been altered.

Restoring A Elevated Panoramic View
The Historic Kalorama Spanish Steps Staircase:

22nd Street NW, Just South of S Street NW, Washington D.C.

Decatur Terrace is more commonly known as the *Spanish Steps* in the Kalorama neighborhood of D.C. The terrace was constructed in 1911 because the Municipal Office of Public Works determined the steepness of the grade made continuation of lower 22nd Street NW impractical.

Such a construction was feared then to potentially compromise several adjacent building sites. A steep ramp was considered too arduous for carriages, automobiles and *uncomfortable* for pedestrians.

The four-level stone steps and originally accompanying fountain were designed employing Beaux-Arts architectural elements. Severe erosion and a subsequent car collision destroyed the original upright support and fountain. A 1999 restoration project restored the damaged steps, fountain and enhanced the surrounding landscaping.

**Separating Genius From An Incomprehensible
Philosophy
Charles August Lindbergh Residence:
115 Fourth Street SE, Washington D.C.**

It is not surprising that aviator Charles Lindbergh would find a hostile public reception towards his remarks and admiration of the leadership of Nazi Germany. His father Charles August Lindbergh endured his own public wrath for supporting Germany at an improper time. Father and son would stir permanent resentment towards their controversial and incomprehensible political stands.

Charles August Lindberg represented Minnesota's 6th congressional district from 1907 to 1917 as a Republican. In 1913, he published *Banking, Currency and the Money Trust*, which attacked the establishment of the Federal Reserve. He cautioned in his writings that the creation of a centralized American bank would create an environment where *the invisible government by the Monetary Power will be legalized*. He foresaw a day of reckoning only a few years removed. The Great Depression beginning in 1929 verified his prophecy according to his limited band of supporters.

Charles August Lindbergh vehemently opposed American involvement in World War I when it initially broke out in 1914. Lindbergh would be one of only fourteen congressmen to vote against the arming of United States merchant ships in 1917. Later that year, he voted against the American entry into the war. His son Charles was 16 and on the periphery of being conscripted.

Charles August would be vilified in the press for his principled but flawed position and greeted by hostile crowds at public events pelting him with eggs and rocks. He ran unsuccessfully for governor of Minnesota in 1918. He decided to run once more in 1924 under the Minnesota

Farmer-Labor Party. His campaign was cut short by his death from brain cancer.

During his years in Congress, the family resided in Washington D.C. during legislative sessions. Charles attended Capitol Hill schools including Eastern High School (since demolished). The Lindbergh marriage was on perpetual shaky status.

Charles August Lindbergh had married Mary LaFond in 1887 and had two daughters together. She died in 1898. He remarried Evangeline Land three years later and they had Charles. She chafed under the responsibility of also raising two stepdaughters and frequently threatened divorce. Charles August would placate her demands fearing a divorce would end his career in Congress. The pair lived separate lives and often in different residences beginning in 1909. They officially separated the year he left Congress.

Son Charles would earn international acclaim on May 21, 1927 with his solo non-stop transatlantic flight between New York City and Paris. He was feted internationally and would return to his former second home Washington D.C. on June 11th aboard the U.S. Navy cruiser *USS Memphis*. A fleet of warships and multiple military aircraft escorted him along the Potomac River to the Washington Navy Yard. President Calvin Coolidge awarded him the Distinguished Flying Cross.

Charles Lindbergh would be showered with adulation and attention over the next decade. He would experience tragedy when on March 1, 1932, his twenty-month infant son, Charles Jr. was kidnapped for ransom. The child's remains would be found two months later in the woods not far from Lindbergh's residence. Intensely private, Lindbergh found the unrelenting public attention towards him stifling. He began investing his time and research into additional projects including an aviator watch, rocket science and heart surgery pumps.

He was requested by the United States Military to travel on several occasions to Germany to evaluate the state of German aviation. He undertook a similar visit to the Soviet Union in 1938. His visits and feedback became invaluable to American military intelligence.

His initial public controversy began in October 1938 when he was honored by the Nazi government with a *Commander Cross of the Order of the German Eagle*. Despite growing European concerns and hostile movements towards war, Lindbergh refused to return the metal.

His public speeches urged the United States towards isolationism, consistent with his father's beliefs. Many of his statements regarding eugenics were interpreted to stress beliefs in the superiority of the white race.

He was publicly criticized for his presumed pro-Nazi sympathies and labeled anti-Semitic for his refusal to condemn Nazi atrocities as they became increasingly documented. Lindbergh passionately believed the war would ultimately be waged between the Soviet Union and Germany. He viewed the United State's greatest threat posed by aggression from East Asia.

Lindbergh eventually fell out of favor with the Nazi's regime for not subscribing wholly to their theories of racial purity. The tarnish to his reputation within the United States had already been done.

Lindbergh had made a crucial enemy in President Franklin Roosevelt who was convinced of his Nazi beliefs. The 1941 surprise attack on Pearl Harbor and resulting damage to the national naval and air fleet shocked Lindbergh and prompted him to action. He sought to be re-commissioned into the

United States Army Air Force. The White House denied his request.

During six months in 1944 amidst the Pacific aerial campaign, he accompanied over 50 fighter bombing raids on Japanese positions as a civilian. He provided valuable consulting advice during this period. Following the war, he toured Nazi concentration camps and wrote about his reaction of *disgust* and *anger*.

The stigma from his previous pre-war public statements and writings would haunt his legacy. Lindbergh was never a personality to simplify or easily comprehend. His remaining years became a mix of adventurous travels, accumulating honors and published writings stressing the needs for conservation and environmentalism. His darker side would ultimately deceive his wife and family with the exposure of three lengthy extramarital relationships resulting in multiple children.

At the time of his death on August 26, 1974 in Kipahulu, Hawaii, his questionable past had already discredited his accomplishments.

Separating the varied achievements of Charles Lindbergh from his presumed philosophy became unfashionable. Any recent movement to acknowledge his unconventional genius and contributions has remained glacial.

The Evolution of Grocery Store Shopping
First Piggly Wiggly Grocery Store:
1403 Independence Avenue SE, Washington D. C.
Former Giant Food Shopping Center Site:
Park Road and Georgia Avenue NW, Washington D. C.

Piggly Wiggly became the first of the modern self-service grocery stores. Founded in Memphis during 1916, the company became originators of checkout stands, individual item price marketing and shopping carts. Prior to the company's creation, grocery stores did not allow customers to select, pay and then leave with their items. Customer would give shopping their list to a clerk, who would gather the inventory from the store. Waiting on customers individually obligated grocers to deliver goods and establish customer credit tabs.

The innovation of self-service shopping substantially reduced labor costs with resulting lowered prices.

In 1919, Piggly Wiggly opened their initial D. C. one-story grocery store designed by architect Frank Hollingshead. The 1,750 square foot building only stocked approximately 1,000 items and was limited to four aisles. The following year, they would open 26 stores in the Washington D. C. Metro region and even more in 1921. Piggly Wiggly's founder Clarence Saunders gambled on the concept that customers would find the shopping experience preferable if they could select their own items, pay immediately and take their purchases home themselves.

Piggly Wiggly's innovation proved popular with customers and more profitable for their independently owned and operated stores. Today, the chain boasts more than 600 outlets in 17 states throughout the Midwest and South.

The original Piggly Wiggly outlet lasted in their building until the end of the 1920s before closing. Between 1929 and 1933, the Crusty Pie Company replaced it. During the 1940s and 50s, a radio and appliance store operated there being replaced in the 1980s by a printing company. Thankful Baptist Church is currently the building owner.

Local grocery store innovation continued in February 1936, when *Giant* opened their first supermarket. Their high-volume business model combined the self-service concept with discounted prices. During their initial year, food prices were lowered an estimated 35%. The original store was eventually razed, but by the 1950s, *Giant* had grown into a regional chain with more than 50 stores. The company remained family owned until 1998. Today it has over 170 stores in the Mid-Atlantic States.

The Debilitating and Crushing Demise of President Woodrow Wilson
Woodrow Wilson Post-Presidency Residence:
2340 S Street NW, Washington D.C.

In November 1918, Germany signed the Armistice ending World War I. American President Woodrow Wilson championed a movement intentioned to end all future global warfare. He had delayed American military entrance into World War I until April 1917. His successful re-election in 1916 had been predicated on keeping American soldiers out of the conflict. Post-war, Europeans were looking for an answer that might eliminate future catastrophe. Woodrow Wilson became their hope and advocate.

There are few instances where a political leader has ascended to meteoric heights and dramatically plummeted into such profound depths as the legacy of Woodrow Wilson. Over the trajectory of two years, Wilson would rise from a potential international savior to a bedridden invalid, discarded by his own political party.

Wilson's delay and discernment regarding American's war entry was regarded by most as prudent and well timed. American forces tipped the balance of power towards victory for the allied nation cause. His clouded judgment ignored the dissipating level of commitment his own country wished to invest into a lasting solution.

On December 13, 1918, Wilson would arrive into Paris to participate in the World War I peace negotiations. He was enthusiastic to promote his vision for a League of Nations, an international organization capable of resolving conflicts between countries. Wilson had ascended his personal summit upon arriving in Paris. He was arguably viewed as the most popular personality in the world. Crowds wildly celebrated his arrival and showered him perpetually with adoration. His idealistic objective of ending war was met with nearly universal acclaim until nationalistic interests, bickering and unresolved resentments derailed the momentum of the process.

The result of his Paris appearance produced the flawed Versailles Treaty containing the covenant for the League of Nations. He became the first sitting American president to travel to Europe. Wilson remained in Europe until June 18, 1919. Following Paris, he traveled to Italy for a week including a Vatican visit. He then returned to Paris for six months of extensive negotiations ironing out the language and specifics of the Versailles Treaty. At no time, did he encourage visitation, input or contributions from the opposition Republican Party. In 1919, he would be awarded the Nobel Peace Prize.

Wilson presumed that his popularity, the accelerated momentum of the process and the objective of securing international stability would be sufficient to earn the necessary two-thirds approval by the U.S. Senate.

He was gravely mistaken.

While remaining in France absorbing the intoxication of acclaim, the political landscape in the United States had altered. During the 1918 mid-term election, the Republican Party had secured majority control of the Senate. Wilson had become increasingly estranged from his own constituency and base of support due to his absence. His refusal to permit any cooperation, dialogue or modifications offered by Republican members of Congress backfired.

Americans had been reticent to enter the war when it initially began in 1914. As the carnage worsened and battle offensives stalled on both sides, remaining neutral appeared the best tactical policy. The United States' ultimate entry had resulted in over 116,000 soldiers deaths. Public enthusiasm towards intervention into future European disputes rapidly shifted towards isolationism following the surrender of Germany.

A consensus regarding the Versailles Treaty was viewed by many observers as excessively punitive towards Germany. Their necessitated repercussion payments spiraled their economy into catastrophe. The terms imposed would result in impossible repayment terms, unprecedented inflation and social disintegration. The subsequent emergence of national leader Adolph Hitler and World War II became a direct consequence.

The League of Nations proposal was perceived by many within the Republican Party as fatally idealistic. Worse, it was product of a president they despised and the opposition Democratic Party.

The Senate failed to vote the required two-thirds majority for acceptance of the Versailles Treaty including the League of Nations. The count was seven votes shy.

Much of the blame was attributed to Wilson's absolute refusal to compromise on any element of the bill or text. He felt betrayed and devastated by the result. He opted to initiate a national speaking tour to stimulate public sentiment for approval of the treaty. He envisioned a third term to insure its passage.

Wilson targeted the Western States from the outset of his tour. Exhaustion and health issues compelled him to return to Washington D.C. in late September 1919. His stamina was fading. On October 7th, he suffered a stroke. He was left paralyzed on his left side and retained only partial vision in his right eye. He was confined to his bed for weeks. His second wife Edith screened all visitors and incoming correspondence to minimal levels. The public was not made aware of his condition until February 1920.

His inner circle constructed a barrier insuring disclosure as to the severity of his condition. He remained physically feeble although his mind was still regarded as clear. The effects of the stroke severely affected his emotional and impulse control resulting in defective judgment. He was an invalid throughout the entire final year of his term.

The timing of his collapse coincided with a challenging domestic agenda. The rise of the Bolsheviks in Russia created a *Red Scare* within the United States. A proliferation of labor unrest, strikes and protests were coupled by racial riots. Postwar unemployment rose to 12% and in 1920, the economy suffered a severe retraction.

Throughout each of these crises, Wilson was absent. The executive branch operated within a vacuum and few major decisions resulted.

Despite his infirmity, Wilson still wanted to run for re-election during 1920. Democratic Party leaders continued to strongly endorse his policies, but not Wilson. They nominated Governor James Cox for President and Assistant Navy Secretary Franklin Roosevelt for Vice-President. Their ticket lost decisively to Ohio Senator Warren Harding.

Wilson's term limped towards an anticlimactic conclusion on March 3, 1921. He shared tea with his successor Warren Harding, but would be physically unable to attend his inauguration. Wilson and his wife relocated to a town house purchased in the Kalorama section of Washington D.C.

He initiated his retirement with ambitious plans. He opened a law practice with former Secretary of State Bainbridge Colby. Wilson showed up on the initial day and never returned. The practice closed within a year.

A formerly prolific writer, he laboriously authored a few short essays. They lacked vitality and direction. He opted not to write his memoirs, but cooperated with writer Ray Standard Baker who compiled his three-volume biography published in 1922. The new majority Republican Congress reversed and eroded many of his political policies. Enthusiasm towards joining the League of Nations was extinguished.

Wilson's life and achievements formed a consistent pattern of irony. He would outlive his presidential successor. He was physically capable of attending Warren Harding's funeral in August 1923. His final national speaking engagement would be a brief radio address on Armistice Day, 1923. He died on February 3, 1924 at the age of 67 and was interred in Washington National Cathedral. Wilson is the only president buried within Washington D.C.

Evaluating Wilson's presidential tenure and historical influence remains under contemporary revision and reassessment.

His harshest criticism has become raised towards his perceived racist attitudes and behavior. He was born and raised in Virginia to a minister who fervently supported slavery and the Confederacy. There is an extended and documented history of Wilson's prejudice and personal bias that has surfaced on critical issues.

Wilson became the first Democratic Party candidate to a receive majority support by black voters. Many would ultimately feel disillusioned and misled by his public policies and indifference towards improving civil liberties.

He maintained segregation within the military, southern states and even D.C. He was criticized repeatedly for overlooking qualified black candidates for public sector employment.

Wilson was wrongly criticized for the implementation of the Volstead Act that introduced the social experiment of Prohibition as the 18th Amendment. Wilson vetoed the original legislation, but Congress overrode his action.

The Wilson presidency features several notable accomplishments besides his handling of American military intervention in World War I. He successfully rallied passage of the 19th Amendment enabling women's voting rights. His support was motivated more by political party gain than personal preference. In 1911, he had publicly expressed his opposition to the women's suffrage movement.

His administration is credited with the Revenue Act of 1914 that lowered trade tariffs and introduced the modern income tax. During his tenure, the Federal Reserve Act was passed resulting in the creation of Federal Reserve System. The Federal Trade Commission and Clayton Anti-Trust Acts were also established.

His vision of international cooperation and diplomacy resulted in the failed League of Nations. Following World War II on October 24, 1945, a similar institution, the United Nations would be established with the full cooperation of participating nations.

The United Nations has neither eliminated nor prevented war. Dialogue has been introduced and certain conflicting issues have been resolved due to cooperating intervention. Five countries called the United Nations Security Council have the capacity to veto any substantive resolution.

Those five include Russia, China, Britain, France and the United States. Unfortunately, the majority of international military conflicts involve at least one of those nations and/or their allies. Consensus between the five counties is rare.

Woodrow Wilson understood that war might perpetually remain a casualty of nationalism and self-interest. He nearly became the architect of a mechanism to peacefully resolve conflict before the escalation of armaments. We are still searching for that possibility.

TWISTED TOUR GUIDES.com

The Curse of the Knickerbocker Theatre and Adams Morgan Plaza
Adams Morgan Plaza:

18th and Columbia Road NW, Washington D.C.

The Knickerbocker Theatre was a premium venue located in the Adams Morgan neighborhood featuring silent movies, concerts, lectures and ballroom dancing. Constructed in 1917, architect Reginald Geare designed the structure to accommodate a seating capacity of 1,700.

On January 28, 1922, the Knickerbocker was showing the comedy *Get-Rich-Quick Wallingford* to an estimated audience of between 300 and 1,000 people. Two days prior, the city had suffered through its worst blizzard since 1899.

The accumulating snow and ice on the theatre's flat roof put a significant strain on the structure. The film was a welcomed distraction to a city paralyzed by the storm. Slightly after 9:00 p.m., the roof of the Knickerbocker abruptly collapsed onto the concrete balcony without creaking or warning indications.

Assistance was immediate by nearby pedestrians. Army Major George S. Patten coordinated a rescue operation involving more than 600 soldiers and Marines. The weather conditions and accumulated snow slowed relief and ambulance response. As a result of the collapse, 98 people died and 133 were injured. The theatre's architect was among the initial responders helping to pull bodies through the wreckage. Neighboring houses were set up as medical treatment facilities and a nearby Christian Science church was employed as a morgue.

An extensive investigation concluded that the collapse was most likely caused by poor design and a defect in the support beams. Theatre employees had discussed removing the snow before the show from the roof, but determined it unnecessary. The following year, a new Ambassador Theatre would be constructed on the site. It would remain until the 1960s when it was razed for an urban renewal project that later became a bank.

The design of the 1960s brick replacement building was meant to evoke the Knickerbocker Theatre structure facilitated with a slanted roof. The building is currently boarded up and the adjacent Adams Morgan Plaza became a homeless encampment.

The theatre disaster became a curse to both the original owner Harry Crandall and architect Reginald Geare. His career effectively ended by the associated notoriety. Geare committed suicide in 1927. Ten years later Crandall would end his life leaving a note for reporters requesting they *not be too hard on him.*

A curse on the Adams Morgan Plaza surfaced with a morbid centennial death during another stretch of inclement winter weather. On March 21, 2022, the homeless encampment was fully cleared of tents, sleeping bags and blankets to enable the assemblage of protective fencing. Long time plaza squatter Miguel Gonzales would die from hypothermia eight days later. His framed portrait hangs upon the fencing, a reminder of the tragic vulnerability and hazards of life without shelter.

A Classic Memorial Eventually Eluding Political Pettiness
Lincoln Memorial:
2 Lincoln Memorial Circle NW, Washington D.C.

Daniel Chester French, Sculptor of Lincoln's 4th Floor
Studio Loft
506 East Capitol Street NE, Washington D.C.

The Lincoln Memorial is arguably Washington D.C.'s most imposing and impressive monument. It is located on the western end of the National Mall, across from the Washington Monument. The Memorial features a Greek Doric temple containing the sculpture of a seated Abraham Lincoln and inscriptions from two of his best-known speeches.

The Memorial showcases numerous symbolic elements. Its 36 columns represent the number of states in America at the time of Lincoln's death. There are 48 stone festoons above the columns representing the number of states in 1922 at the time of the unveiling. The 87 steps ascending from the Reflecting Pool to Lincoln's statue is the equivalent of *four score and 7* extracted from his Gettysburg Address. The Memorial is pictured on the reverse of the U.S. five-dollar bill and penny coin.

The Memorial evolved into an important symbol with the Civil Rights Movement. The grounds became the setting for Martin Luther King Jr.'s historic *I Have A Dream* speech delivered to an estimated 250,000 attendees on August 28, 1963. King's speech delivered on the eighteenth step from the top landing crowned the *March on Washington for Jobs and Freedom*.

The creation of the Memorial became controversial from the outset. Efforts to properly commemorate Lincoln had begun since his death in 1865. Political squabbles, special interest conflicts and choosing an appropriate location delayed completion. Strong public sentiment towards establishing a fitting and distinctive tribute ultimately prevailed. The wait would require 55 years.

A site was eventually narrowed down to two options, the Potomac Flats and nearby the Union Railway Station.

Potomac Flats initially seemed less desirable for many reasons. Its most compelling attraction was it's positioning. The location was aligned between the Washington Monument and the dome of the U.S. Capitol.

The terrain was then isolated marshland previously being a bay expansive enough once to accommodate oceangoing vessels. Erosion from farming upstream had created a significant buildup of soil in the waterway over years. Military engineers leveled the area by dumping millions of cubic yards of mud dredged from the Potomac River. The resulting landfill eradicated former malaria-carrying mosquitoes and the foul stench. The undeveloped land became a haven for vagrants, body dumping, bird hunters and baby turtles in the spring.

Potomac Flats met its fiercest opposition from Illinois Republican Congressman Joe Cannon. As chairman of the House Appropriations Committee and later House Speaker in 1903, he had prestige and clout. He insisted that any public expenditure to honor Lincoln serve the dual purpose of urban renewal. He considered the Potomac Flats merely swampland and better suited for agricultural cultivation.

Cannon would champion a competing proposal to create the Memorial upon a site located in between Union Station and the Capitol. The distance between the two landmarks was approximately six blocks. That stretch of land then had been nicknamed *Swampoodle*. The land parcel had its own marshy conditions, run-down tenement buildings and the existence of numerous fruit vendors.

Cannon felt clearing an unattractive slum and offering convenient access via the train station was both pragmatic and a cost effective public expenditure. Within the artistic community, there existed strong opposition to this site.

Due to his influential position, his site proposal appeared the most likely to pass Congress. He boasted publicly that a bill would be ready for President Roosevelt's signing for the upcoming Lincoln birth centennial on February 12, 1909.

Theodore Roosevelt was neither an artist nor architect, but his instincts leaned towards consulting legitimate experts in the field. He felt steamrolling the process based on an unpopular location might be shortsighted.

Days before the Congressional vote on the train site, Roosevelt invited Glenn Brown, secretary of the American Institute of Architects and three of his colleagues to a meeting at the White House. Each member was vehemently opposed to Cannon's preference. They summed up their arguments against the site by stating it would belittle the dignity of Lincoln by *making his memorial an ornament and part of a railway station.*

They suggested instead that Roosevelt's establish an advisement panel of experts for all new federal buildings. Roosevelt agreed. The Congressional vote was stalled.

In January 1909 nearing the end of his presidential term, Roosevelt created the Council of Fine Arts composed of architects, painters and sculptors. Their initial task was to make a recommendation regarding the Lincoln Memorial site. The group unanimously recommended the Potomac Flats site. Roosevelt signed off on the decision during his final day in office.

His successor, President William Taft favored the Potomac Flats location. He disbanded the Council of Fine Arts in 1909 and created his own advisement group called the Commission of Fine Arts the following year.

During those two years of indecision and political maneuvering, public opinion had shifted away from Cannon's train site. A group of insurgent Republican congressmen revolted against his authority. When Cannon's proposed location came up for a vote in the House, it lost, despite efforts to filibuster.

Lincoln's sculptural design and the Greek Doric encasement would also undergo intense scrutiny and vehement objection from diverse quarters. Belligerent politicians and organizations objected to the Greek Temple, citing a log cabin as more representative of the Lincoln legacy.

Others suggested scrapping the Memorial project entirely and constructing instead a distinctive roadway called the *Lincoln Highway*. Following a collective ten years of debate and political sniping, the Potomac Flats location was selected. The Greek Temple and sculptural positioning of Lincoln by artist Daniel Chester French was also agreed upon intact without modification.

The enormity of the seated Abraham Lincoln radiates power, composure and discernment. His expression is serene and solemn. The 170-ton statue is composed of 28 blocks of white George marble and rises 30 feet from the floor. It includes the 19-foot seated figure of Lincoln complete with armchair and footrest upon an 11-foot high pedestal. Lincoln gazes into the distance and slightly downward. Sculptor French had previously completed a standing memorial of Lincoln for the Nebraska Sate Capitol. Tourists rarely make vacation pilgrimages to visit this Nebraska edition.

The D.C. version features Lincoln seated on a classical chair engraved with fasces, a Roman symbol of authority. The iconic Lincoln signifies kinship with the immortals. His signature modesty, resolve and sense-of-humor might have been overlooked during an uneventful presidency. These character traits saved America.

He successfully prevented the United States from fragmenting irrevocably during one of our darkest historical periods. He remains one our most cherished Presidents by establishing a standard of integrity few successors have come close to rivaling.

French's design and plaster maquette required an entire year to be transferred onto the massive marble blocks. The renowned Italian firm Piccirilli Brothers fabricated the marble carvings. French provided the finishing strokes inside his Bronx studio. He supervised the final installation.

The Memorial has survived periodic defacement and graffiti. The completed work has captivated millions since its formal dedication on May 30, 1922. The vision of renowned artistic professionals ensured the superiority of creation instead of a compromised and mediocre edifice. Politicians, special interest concerns and misguided art critics could not with their limited perspective and experience envision the treasure that ultimately prevailed.

One single design flaw has escaped most public scrutiny. On the north interior wall of the chamber, Lincoln's second inaugural speech has a corrected typo that was initially carved into the limestone. A word *Future* was initially carved *Euture*. Once the mistake was discovered, the bottom base of the *E* was filled in. The mistake is scarcely evident.

IN THIS TEMPLE
AS IN THE HEARTS OF THE PEOPLE
FOR WHOM HE SAVED THE UNION
THE MEMORY OF ABRAHAM LINCOLN
IS ENSHRINED FOREVER

FOR WHOM HE SAVED THE UNION
THE MEMORY OF ABRAHAM LINCOLN
IS ENSHRINED FOREVER

DANIEL CHESTER FRENCH'S D.C. STUDIO

The Rotted Corruption and Demise of the Ohio Gang
The Ohio Gang Meeting House (Razed and Replaced):
1625 K Street NW, Washington D.C.
Department of the Interior: 1849 C Street NW,
Washington D.C.

The *Ohio Gang* became known as a group of unscrupulous politicians appointed by President Warren Harding to high-ranking cabinet positions. The unofficial leader was political operative Harry Daugherty. Other members included Jess Smith, Howard Mannington, Charles Forbes, Will Hays, and Albert Fall.

Howard Mannington was an attorney and manager of the Harding campaign in Ohio. In 1921, he leased a three-story Victorian, 15-room townhouse on K Street as an informal headquarters for the group. The building was constructed of green limestone and featured a healthy magnolia bush in the front yard.

The group regularly met, drank, smoked and played poker. There was reportedly dancing and several members slept overnight with periodic paid companionship. Harding joined the activities occasionally to unwind from the pressures of the presidency. On a more sinister note, the group absent of Harding schemed over plots, taxpayer frauds, scams and scandals. Each booked a unique destiny with infamy.

Wills Hays, appointed Postmaster General, bailed from the group first in 1922. He had been the Chairman of the Republican National Committee and major contributor to Harding's successful 1920 presidential campaign. His reward was the premium postal position. On January 14, 1922, he resigned to become Chairman of the Motion Picture Producers and Distributors of America.

His role was to reform the image of the movie industry

following the alleged rape and murder of actress Virginia Rappe by film star *Fatty* Arbuckle. Hays, a devout Presbyterian deacon imposed a standard of censorship that would continue intact and beyond his tenure. He would ultimately retire in 1945. His Hays Code would define the acceptable moral guidelines for motion picture production. He would only be peripherally attached to the *Ohio Gang* public scandal.

Harry Daugherty had served as Harding's campaign manager during the Republican National Convention. Harding had began the convention as an outsider and emerged as the party's nominee. Daugherty negotiated ethically complicated backroom deals and agreements with party bosses.

He was rewarded the position of Attorney General. His own dealings while in the White House were rumored to include illegal kickbacks, bootlegging and sexual affairs. His associate Jess Smith was appointed an official of the Justice Department. Charles Forbes was named to head the Veteran's Bureau and Albert Fall became the Secretary of the Interior.

As long as Harding remained in power, corruption and inappropriate activities were shielded by presidential protection.

That armor disintegrated in early August 1923. Harding's administration was rumored by the press to be drowning in ethical misdeeds, dishonesty and fraud. His re-election chance for 1924 appeared dire. Harding decided to distance himself from the swirling scandals and launched a two-month arduous *Voyage of Understanding* travel across the continental United States and explore the remote new territory of Alaska. Harding would become the first president to officially visit Canada with Vancouver added as a stop.

Harding, his wife Florence and their entourage departed the

White House on June 20, 1923. The objective was to directly re-connect with the voter base and view firsthand many of America's natural treasures. Shortly before their departure, he dismissed Jess Smith from his position in the Justice Department. Smith reportedly became so distraught that he shot himself to death on May 30th. Some sources suggested that his death was a setup.

Harding's tour was perceived as successful but too exhausting. His health had worsened from the strain of travel by the time he had reached the West Coast. He reportedly summoned his most trusted advisor Herbert Hoover for advice on the scandals nearing exposure within his administration. He wouldn't live to act on Hoover's counsel. On August 2nd, Harding, 57, died from a fatal, but suspicious heart attack.

He was spared the disclosures that would follow forever tarnishing his legacy.

In early 1924, congressional committees began investigating the graft and corruption flagrantly practiced by cabinet members. Charles Forbes was arrested and convicted of fraud and embezzlement of Veteran's Bureau funds. He was sent to Leavenworth Penitentiary in 1926 where he served one year and eight months.

Upon his release, he wrote articles attempting to exonerate any wrongdoing or personal gain by President Harding. He darkened the reputation of additional administration members. In 1927, he wrote about the need of prison reform and the readily available purchase of narcotics inside prison. He suffered ill health in his later years and died at the age of 74 in April 1952 at the Walter Reed Hospital in Washington D.C.

Albert Fall had arrived into Washington D.C. as the consummate outsider from the newly admitted state of New Mexico. He began as a criminal lawyer before being elected U.S. Senator. He became a darling of the Republican right wing for his blunt antagonism of Democratic President Woodrow Wilson. While Fall was permitted to view the ailing Wilson who'd suffered a severe stroke in October 1919, Fall sincerely indicated to Wilson that he'd be praying for him. Wilson responded: *Which way Senator?*

Fall was appointed to the plum financial opportunity of Secretary of the Interior. Harding convinced the Secretary of the Navy that Fall should assume responsibility for the naval Oil Reserves at Elk Hills and Buena Vista, California and more notably Teapot Dome, Wyoming.

Fall maximized his position in 1922 by enabling two of his friends that owned Mammoth Oil and Pan-American Petroleum to be given drilling leases without open bidding. His generosity was rewarded with a significant $385,000 bribe.

The investigation determined that Fall was guilty for the Pan-American Petroleum bribe and sentenced to one year in jail. Fall would lose the entire bribe when Pan-American's President Edward Doheny foreclosed on Fall's New Mexico ranch due to *unpaid loans*. The amount of the loan ending up being the $385,000 bribe. Doheny was exonerated from the scandal. The President of Mammoth Oil was fined and served six months of incarceration for contempt of court.

The year in jail had decimated Fall's financial position and health. He moved to El Paso, Texas where he remained and died in 1944 following an extended illness.

The *Ohio Gang's* unofficial leader and U.S. Attorney General Harry Daugherty initially remained unscathed by the scandal.

Former Vice President and replacement President Calvin Coolidge had been purposely left distant from Harding's inner circle. Initially he resisted demands for Daugherty's removal. The rumors regarding Daugherty's abuse of power intensified. Finally, he concluded that his Attorney General had lost the confidence of the entire county. He demanded and received his resignation on March 28, 1924. Daugherty's replacement was expediently announced as Harlan Fiske Stone, the dean of the Columbia Law School

Daugherty hadn't completely evaded accountability. In 1926, he was indicted on charges that he improperly received funds in the sale of American Metal Company assets seized during World War I. His case went to trial twice with the first ending in a mistrial. A single juror that remained unconvinced of his guilt acquitted him in his second trial.

He returned to practicing law in Ohio until his retirement in 1932. He published a book with the aid of a ghostwriter entitled *The Inside Story of the Harding Tragedy*. He vainly attempted to resuscitate his reputation while spending his final years in Florida and Mackinac, Michigan. He would suffer two heart attacks, survive pneumonia and die bedridden and blind in one eye on October 12, 1941.

The Harding Administration excesses have typically been bundled and combined simply as the *Teapot Dome Scandal*. In truth, the corruption spread far deeper affecting more individuals. The *Ohio Gang* as perpetrators were never able to sanitize their reputations or historical condemnation.

Their K Street limestone headquarters suffered the indignity of being converted into a George Washington University fraternity house for twenty students. The cellar was torn out and used for initiation ceremonies.

The building would be demolished in 1941 and eventually

replaced by a non-descript office building void of historical significance.

Since Albert Fall's conviction, the two most controversial Secretary of the Interior appointments have been James Watt and Ryan Zinke. Watt was appointed by President Ronald Reagan in 1981 and lasted only two and a half years. He was branded as *anti-environmentalist* and his pro-development views sealed his fate as one of Reagan's most disastrous appointments before his resignation.

Ryan Zinke was a congressman from Montana appointed by Donald Trump at the beginning of his administration. He lasted less than two years in the position before his expenditures raised ethical questions and controversy. His deputy replaced him. A 2022 Interior Department inspector general report documented that Zinke had repeatedly violated the department's ethic rules. He officially left his post on January 2, 2019.

A Hotel With An Active Pulse On History and Scandal
Mayflower Renaissance Hotel:
1127 Connecticut Avenue NW, Washington D.C.

The Mayflower Hotel opened on February 18, 1925 to acclaim and offering grandeur and elegance. The standards have never slipped even if some of its famous and notorious guests behavior have.

The first major event staged at the hotel was the inaugural ball of President Calvin Coolidge. The property has entertained every American President since and has been the residence for Vice Presidents, Cabinet members, Supreme Court justices, Senators and Congressman.

The Mayflower has earned a reputation for historic work and play. In room 570, the draft of the Servicemen's Readjustment Act of 1944 was crafted. The result became the GI Bill funding post-military higher education.

Illicit play has captivated more attention. Two presidential mistresses reportedly lodged there amidst their famed trysts. Judith Exner claimed to have an affair with President John Kennedy (take a number) and mafia figures Sam Giancana and John Roselli. During that period, she reportedly kept residence at the hotel.

More recent, an iconic photographed hug between former White House intern Monica Lewinsky and President Bill Clinton was shot at a reception held at the property. The hug transpired more than a year before the media exposed their affair. As the scandal detonated globally, she resided at the hotel.

On March 10, 2008, a *New York Times* article outed New York Governor Eliot Spitzer as *Client 9* in a high-profile prostitution ring. The organization was known as *The*

Emperor's Club. Spitzer shared room 871 with sex worker Ashley Dupre for an exorbitant tariff. Following an embarrassing public admission two days later with his wife beside him, he resigned.

Post-scandal, Spitzer has become a television host and instructor at the City College of New York. He ran unsuccessfully for New York City Controller in 2013. By the end of that year, the Spitzer's marriage had dissolved. Ashley Dupre reportedly terminated her call girl career and concentrated on becoming a singer and sex columnist for the *New York Post*.

Scandal at the Mayflower has spread into politics without sexual spicing. The generally distained and discredited FBI Director J. Edgar Hoover dined in the hotel's Carvery Restaurant nearly every working day for twenty years until his death in 1972. The inflexible Hoover habitually selected the same menu items with each dining experience.

Washington DC Mayor Marion Barry would be found guilty of possessing cocaine during a stay in the fall of 1989. Barry saved his greatest embarrassment for the subsequent year with a crack smoking bust at the Vista International Hotel.

During Donald Trump's administration, an intentional deception created an abbreviated social media uproar. In June 2017, Attorney General Jeff Sessions stated with conviction under oath to a Senate intelligence committee that he had neither communication nor contact with Russian officials during an April 2016 event he attended.

A photo of Sessions next to Russian ambassador Sergey Kislyak contradicted his testimony. There were no repercussions for his deception. In November 2018, Sessions would eventually resign. He was banished back to his home state Alabama where he never regained his prominence. He lost in the 2020 Senate Republican primary attempting to reclaim his former position.

Subsequently, Russian ambassador Kislyak would be linked to other Mayflower Hotel private meetings involving Sessions and Trump's son-in-law Jared Kushner. These accusations would never be fully authenticated or investigated.

**November 1927 Tornado Touchdown Near Lincoln Park
Damaged Rowhouses: 1300 Block of A Street NE,
Washington D.C.
Saint Cyprian Catholic Church Site:
C and 13th Streets SE, Washington D.C.**

Tornados are a relatively scarce phenomenon in America's Mid-Atlantic region. Washington D.C. has recorded at least ten of these damaging storms.

The worst occurred on November 17, 1927 during the mid-afternoon. A tornado initially touched down southwest of Alexandria, Virginia damaging sections of the city. It then crossed the Potomac River and struck the Anacostia Naval Air Station. Several personnel were injured when fierce winds tore off barrack roofs. An airplane hanger was also demolished along with seven airplanes inside.

The tornado's path continued through the Navy Yard and then crossed through the Kingman Park neighborhood where it severely damaged Saint Cyprian Catholic Church, near Lincoln Park. An estimated 372 structures would be damaged including the south side 1300 block of A Street NE. A rare 300-foot tall waterspout would form from the Potomac River.

The speed of the winds were estimated at 125 miles per hour, but lasted less than 25 minutes. Hundreds were reported injured by flying debris. One woman died from a direct lightening strike while crossing a bridge.

Elissa
SILVERMAN
amber
G
VE
anc6a06

An Ascending Staircase to Nowhere
Watergate Steps
620 Ohio Drive SW, Washington D.C.

The Watergate Steps are located between the Potomac River and the Lincoln Memorial. Constructed in 1932, the steps are integrated into the Neoclassical designed Arlington Memorial Bridge complex. Their purposed was never employed as originally intended. The steps were to become connected with a conduit dock where boats could tie up and politicians and dignitaries disembark.

The 40 granite and concrete steps of the majestic staircase are 230 feet wide at river level and 206 feet at the top. On July 14, 1935, a series of concerts commenced in front on a floating barge. The National Symphony Orchestra became the initial act to perform. Extensive crowds up to 12,000 enjoyed the performance sitting on the steps. The *Sunset Symphony* concerts continued until 1965. Noise from airplanes approaching Washington National Airport became oppressive and forced their permanent cancellation. The most common users today are joggers running up the stairs and bicyclists reposing. Their journey to no climatic destination is ideal for a staircase bound for nowhere.

TWISTED TOUR GUIDES.com

The Bonus Act March and Encampment That Became A National Disgrace
Primary Settlement Grounds:
Anacostia Flats, Washington D.C.

Economic prosperity immediately followed the conclusion of World War I for many, but not for every soldier. In the years following, politicians debated offering a bonus payment to veterans that Presidents Warren Harding and Calvin Coolidge both vetoed. In 1926, Congress overrode Coolidge's veto passing the World War Adjustment Compensation Act, commonly known as the *Bonus Act*.

The legislation promised veterans a stipend based on their length of service and whether they served stateside or overseas. The catch was that they were unable to receive the funds until their birthday in 1945, ironically the final year of World War II. The Bonus was nicknamed the *Tombstone Act* since many living veterans would never receive their allocation. If they died before 1945, their estate would be entitled to claim the funds.

By 1932, the Great Depression has escalated unemployment to unprecedented heights. Many World War I veterans became bitter towards the designated waiting period. They desperately needed the cash immediately.

Various veterans groups and unemployed men marched on Washington D.C. during the spring of 1932. An estimated 20,000-40,000 fashioned shantytowns composed of dwellings made from scrap wood and other salvaged materials. They settled primarily on land in the unoccupied Anacostia Flats. Many families joined them. Other homesteads spread out on empty city land and inside vacant buildings within sight of the Capitol dome.

President Herbert Hoover dismissed the movement and

collective march labeling the organizers as communists, hoodlums and ex-convicts. Debate raged fiercely and passionately within the halls of Congress. Tennessee Democratic congressman Edward Eslick suffered a fatal heart attack while addressing the assembly. The House passed a bill authorizing an immediate $2.4 billion payout to the veterans.

The Republican majority Senate voted down the bill on June 17 citing the federal government's own dire shortfall of funds. Had it passed, the bill would have been vetoed by Hoover anyway like his two predecessors.

Once the bill failed in the Senate, a six-week stalemate followed. The veteran's movement advocating immediate bonus act payouts refused to budge. They continued inhabiting their shantytowns and temporary lodgings. Hoover and Attorney General William Mitchell became exasperated and feared further chaos. They ordered the encampments to be disbursed and the men to return home.

The first governmental skirmish against the protestors occurred on July 28th. Police evicted 50 protestors from an empty building along Pennsylvania Avenue. During the ensuing melee, two protestors were shot and killed.

Hoover then ordered the Army to drive the protestors out of the city and back across the Anacostia River to their shantytown. General Douglas MacArthur coordinated the troops along with his aide Major Dwight D. Eisenhower and tank commander Major George S. Patton. These three leaders would become critical components of the American armed forces leadership during World War II.

Their unenviable task became a conflict against soldiers who had fought beside them fifteen years before. Hoover urged caution, but MacArthur ignored his instructions. Once he had driven the protestors beyond the Anacostia River, he followed them across the 11th Street Bridge to their settlement.

His troops advanced expediently with tanks, fixed bayonets and tear gas against the unarmed civilians. The infantry followed igniting the shanties and obliterating the colony. The hospitals were overflowing with wounded. An estimated 259 veterans would die during the onslaught, many consumed by the flames.

MacArthur's conquest was considered a tactical success, but in many eyes, a national disgrace. In November, Franklin Roosevelt would soundly defeat Hoover in the presidential election. The next Republican President wouldn't be elected until twenty years later when Dwight Eisenhower assumed office based on his leadership during World War II.

President Franklin Roosevelt would veto a similar Bonus Act on several occasions before Congress finally overrode his veto in 1936. The initial veterans began cashing checks in June that year averaging $580 per soldier.

A Reminder of Cyclical Historic Events
Holodomor Famine-Genocide Memorial
1 Massachusetts Avenue NW, Washington D.C.

The Holodomor Genocide Memorial is a timely reminder of the forced Ukrainian famine perpetrated by Josef Stalin's Soviet Union regime from 1932 to 1933. Millions of Ukrainians died from starvation due to a poor wheat harvest and the poorly distributed regional collectivization of agriculture. Some historians claim the famine was intentionally planned by Stalin to eliminate a Ukrainian independence movement. Given the recent events of Russia's invasion into the Ukraine, such a scenario appears credible.

The memorial designed by Larysa Kurylas depicts a field of grain. It is one of three D.C. public monuments designed or co-designed by women. The sculptural work, dedicated in November 2015 is a poignant reminder that cultural hatred is rarely extinguished by the passing of a single generation.

**Martin's Tavern: The Site of Political History and
Strategy Sessions
Martin's Tavern:
1264 Wisconsin Avenue NW, Washington D.C.**

William Gloyd Martin was a major leaguer baseball shortstop for the Boston Braves in 1914. He played precisely one professional game before retiring. He had zero hits in three at-bats.

His establishment of Martin's Tavern in the Georgetown district in 1933 quickly overshadowed the brevity of his major league career. Since opening, several of the intimate booths have become aligned with political history. Every U.S. president beginning with Harry S. Truman has reportedly dined on pub food, relaxed and in some instances shaped their legacy and the nation's history.

Plaques above certain booths designate their historical significance. Booth One is considered the *rumble seat* where John Kennedy used to read his Sunday morning newspaper following mass. Booth Two is where Richard Nixon dined on his preferential meatloaf when he was a senator and vice president. President Harry and Bess Truman preferred booth six and Lyndon Johnson and Sam Rayburn met frequently in booth twenty-four during the 1940s to discuss political strategy.

The most renowned booth is number three called *The Proposal Booth*. On Wednesday, June 24, 1953, Senator John Kennedy proposed marriage to Jacqueline Lee Bouvier. She accepted the news and reportedly ran gleefully through the restaurant afterwards.

Martin Tavern's charm extended into the world of baseball where greats Mickey Mantle, Ty Cobb and Yogi Berra dined in The Dugout Room. It is not a particular stretch to assume that Yankee teammate Billy Martin frequently accompanied them.

Baseball's loss ultimately became a political history landmark and comfort food oasis.

The Initial FBI Director Who Drew His Own Legal Boundaries
FBI Headquarters:
935 Pennsylvania Avenue NW, Washington D.C.
J. Edgar Hoover Congressional Cemetery Site:
1801 E Street SE, Washington D.C.

J. Edgar Hoover was born on New Year Day 1895 into a Washington D. C. family whose patriarch was the chief of the printing division for the U.S. Coast and Geodetic Survey. He lived his entire life in D.C. graduating from Central High School and earned his Bachelor of Law degree from George Washington University Law School in 1918.

Hoover evolved into the ultimate political and law enforcement insider. IIe rose quickly initially within the Justice Department assigned to enforce the 1917 Espionage Act. During America's initial communist *Red Scare*, he spearheaded the task of monitoring and disrupting the work of domestic radicals. He was empowered to punish, arrest or deport those who were determined *dangerous*.

By 1921, Hoover rose to become deputy head of the Bureau of Investigation originally created in July 1908. In 1924, the Attorney General designated Hoover as the acting director. President Calvin Coolidge appointed him as the fifth permanent director on May 10, 1924. Hoover was selected for the position based on the fear that his predecessor was involved in the Teapot Dome scandal during President Warren Harding's administration.

When Hoover took over the Bureau, it had 650 employees, including 441 Special Agents. One of his first actions was to fire all female agents and ban the future hiring of them. By 1935, the Bureau of Investigation was renamed the FBI (Federal Bureau of Investigation). Hoover became the initial Director appointed by President Franklin Roosevelt.

In whichever direction the contemporary public perception of the FBI has evolved, most of the reputation can be credited or blamed upon Hoover. He would reign in the director's position for 37 years until his death. He built the agency into a sophisticated crime-fighting agency combating organized crime, foreign espionage, pornography, radical organizations, high profile murders and kidnappings. He instituted numerous modernizations into police technology and forensic development. His national *Most Wanted List* targeted the highest profile fugitives within the United States.

Hoover was an individual with self-interested priorities and personal demons. He became infamous for his secretive abuses of power, disrespect for ethical boundaries, harassing freedom of speech and blackmailing high level politicians and prominently know individuals. He amassed a significant cache of power that he employed to intimidate and threaten with. Even Presidents feared his potentially damaging information against them. None of the governing Chief Executives that he served under dared remove him from office.

Few found him a proponent or protector of the Civil Rights movement. His accustomed non-intervention was blamed for a significant escalation of racial violence.

When he died from a heart attack at his home in 1972, D.C. insiders heaved a collective sigh of relief. His estate was turned over to his personal assistant Clyde Tolson. The pair was rumored to be lovers based on their intimate professional relationship and the inordinate time spent together away from the job. Hoover viciously assailed any accuser that speculated on their relationship publicly. Tolson moved into his Hoover's house upon his death and is buried a few yards away from him and his family within the Congressional Cemetery.

The grip and excesses of his leadership prompted Congress to eventually limit future FBI directors to 10-year terms, subject to extension by the Senate. The current 11-story FBI headquarters was officially completed in September 1975 and named after him. Periodic legislative efforts have been initiated to remove the name. Nothing conclusive has materialized from each proposal.

Hoover's pattern of violating civil liberties in the name of national security has come under increasingly more scrutiny since his passing. His legacy remains a swirling mass of professional acknowledgement, contradiction and disgust. Since Hoover, Robert Mueller III has served the longest tenure as director for 12 years. The majority of candidates have never made it past *Acting Director* status.

TWISTED TOUR GUIDES.com

**A Literary Influence, Fascist and Psychiatric Inmate
St. Elizabeths Hospital:
1100 Alabama Avenue SE, Washington D.C.**

Ezra Pound became an important influence in the early modernist poetry movement. His own early formation stigmatized him as an outsider viewing society distantly. He is credited with his role in developing *Imagism*, a writing movement stressing sparse precision and economy of language.

His influence as foreign editor of several American literary magazines shaped and influenced notable peers including T. S. Eliot, Ernest Hemingway and James Joyce. His own distinguished works would include *Ripostes*, *Hugh Selwyn Mauberley* and *The Cantos* composed during 45 years of his life.

Pound moved to London in 1908 following travels there two years previously. He mixed within literary circles dressing extravagantly in varied color plumage. In March 1910, he visited a friend Walter Rummel in Paris and was introduced to American heiress and pianist Margaret Lanier Cravens. She offered to become his sole patron offering him $1,000 annually. Prior to her death two years later, she provided him with money regularly. He met the novelist Olivia Shakespeare at a social gathering and would later marry her daughter Dorothy in 1914 against her mother's wishes.

The beginning of World War I that same year altered the freedom that writers and poets had formerly enjoyed. Creative works were expected to be patriotic. Pound's own finances dropped precariously. His anti-war themes lessened his popularity. Close literary friends were killed in the conflict that he blamed on *financial capitalist interests*.

He relocated to Paris in 1921 and became part of the impoverished Left Bank art and literary scene. He was older than many of his peers and wasn't a drinker. He became acquainted with the Dada and Surrealist movements.

He moved to Italy in 1928 and throughout the 1930s and 40s promoted Benito Mussolini's fascist philosophy and his own economic theory known as *social credit*. He admired Adolph Hitler during World War II and the Holocaust making hundreds of radio broadcasts on behalf of the Italian government. His contrarian views targeted the United States and Britain, President Roosevelt, international finance, Jews and munitions makers.

When American military forces entered Italy in 1945, he was arrested for treason. He spent months in a U.S. military camp in Pisa including three weeks in an outdoor steel cage.

Pound was shipped back to Washington D.C. where he pled insanity at his trial. Most of the doctors who examined him found him coherent and sane. Dr. Winfred Olverholster who was fascinated by the poet and his works protected him with his compromised testimony portraying him as mentally disturbed. The strategy succeeded.

Pound was admitted into St. Elizabeths Hospital where he would spend the next twelve years in the Chestnut Ward. The facility was plagued by drab surroundings and minimal light. His ward had a wide corridor with few rocking chairs, a television and cubicles for sleeping.

In 1948, Pound controversially won the inaugural Bollingen Prize for his *Pisan Cantos*, written during his imprisonment outside of Pisa. Awarding the highest national poetry award to a convicted traitor led Congress to disassociate the Library of Congress from the award. The Yale University Library would determine future award winners.

Examining psychiatrists did not conclude that Pound ever truly modified his core anti-Semitism or political doctrine. Several of his intimate artist friends including Robert Frost, Ernest Hemingway and T.S. Eliot advocated his release. Frost secured him complimentary legal representation.

At the age of 72, Pound was released in 1958 where he welcomed the awaiting press with a fascist salute. He returned back to Italy to write until his death in 1972.

**A Historical Location Hosting A Modern Worship Facility
New York Avenue Presbyterian Church:
1313 New York Avenue NW, Washington D.C.**

The New York Avenue Presbyterian Church appears deceivingly to resemble one of D.C.'s earliest houses of worship. The original site indeed dates back to 1820 when the Second Presbyterian Church was erected. John Quincy Adams was then the Secretary of State and a member of the board of trustees. He personally lent the church $1,200 to construct a roof on the building.

A replacement church would be completed in 1860 cementing a merger with the Associate Reformed Church who'd previously conducted services on the neighboring site of the current Willard Hotel. President Abraham Lincoln often attended services and became a close friend of the pastor, Reverend Dr. Phineas D. Gurley. Following Lincoln's assassination, Dr. Gurley recited prayers at the funeral and accompanied the casket to Springfield, Illinois for burial.

In 1896, the steeple of the church was blown off onto H Street during a tornado. The family of Lincoln's son Robert Todd donated money for the replacement steeple and chimes. The new steeple would be installed in 1929.

The church remained intact until 1950 when it was determined a larger facility was required. The newest incarnation of the church would be dedicated on December 20, 1951. Wedged amidst contemporary high-rise glass and steel construction, the facility masks well its relative youthful age.

Presidential Assassination Attempt By Two Puerto Rican Nationalists
Blair House:
1651 Pennsylvania Avenue NW, Washington D.C.

During the autumn of 1950, President Harry Truman and his family were living at the Blair House due to a major renovation at the White House for structural issues. On November 1st, two nationalists espousing Puerto Rican independence conducted an attempted assassination. Oscar Collazo engaged Secret Service agents and White House policemen from the east of the building. Grisalio Torresola approached the guard booth on the west corner.

Torresola would fire without warning four shots at duty officer Leslie Coffelt. He was struck three times in the chest and abdomen with a fourth shot passing through his tunic. Torresola continued firing and struck two other officers before needing to reload. Coffelt staggered out of his booth mortally wounded. He fired a single shot hitting Torresola behind the ear from thirty-one feet. The strike killed Torresola instantly. Coffelt staggered back to his booth and collapsed. He would expire four hours later at a nearby hospital.

Coffelt was only 40 at the time of his death. He was considered an expert sharpshooter by acquaintances that knew him during his formative years in Virginia's Shenandoah Valley. He became a Metropolitan Police officer in 1929, but resigned six years later to become a building technician. He would return to the police force in 1941 and the following year was transferred to the White House Police department. During World War II, he served in the Army, but was given a medical discharge after less than two years. He returned to the White House police force following his discharge.

Coffelt would be buried in Arlington National Cemetery. His

widow would receive numerous condolences and expressions of sorrow from Puerto Rican leaders, dignitaries and citizens. She later acknowledged in a speech that the island's people were not responsible for her husband's death.

Co-conspirator Oscar Collazo was convicted and sentenced to death in federal court. Truman commuted the sentence to life imprisonment. In 1979, President Jimmy Carter modified Coffelt's sentence to time served and released him from prison. Collazo returned to Puerto Rico where he died in 1994.

The status of Puerto Rico would be raised via a constitutional vote on the island on March 3, 1952. The vote was intended to reaffirm their American Commonwealth status versus direct United States rule. Neither national independence nor statehood was included options. The vote affirmed the existing preferred status by nearly 82%.

A Beloved University Registrar's Brutal Stabbing
Alma Preinkert Murder Site:
1436 Chapin Street NW, Washington D.C.

Alma Preinkert epitomized all that was honorable about
college education and particularly the University of
Maryland. She was awarded a masters degree in 1923 and
began her first full-time position as a university clerk that
same year. A masters degree was a rarity for a female student
during that era. Preinkert maintained a lifelong fidelity to the
institution.

She became indispensable to university management for over
the thirty years performing a variety of positions before
ascending to the registrar position in 1936. She served on
numerous committees and organizations and even held the
position of President of the Maryland Federation of Women's
Clubs. During a period pre-dating computers, she became the
database and reference source for over 42,000 University of
Maryland students annually worldwide.

The esteemed face of the university would meet a tragic and
vicious fate during the early morning hours of Sunday,
February 28, 1954. She had returned home at approximately
1 a.m. with her sister who shared the dwelling following a
bridge game with friends. She confided to her about a
premonition of something *unsettling*.

An intruder had stolen a stepladder from behind her rooming
house. An hour following her arrival back, he climbed ten
feet up to a window and shattered the glass to unfasten the
lock. The entry awoke Preinkert who caught him ransacking
her second story bedroom. He stabbed both her and her sister
who attempted to intervene. Alma died from her wounds. Her
sister recovered.

Her funeral drew an overflowing attendance. Thirty detectives were assigned to investigate the case and more than 500 individuals were interviewed. The investigation went nowhere despite an offered reward. Her sister never returned again to live in their residence.

Her legacy would be remembered on campus. She was honored with naming rights for a campus women's field house and her painting is included in the archives of the University of Maryland's Hombake Library. Her former residence has since been demolished and replace with a contemporary residential structure.

When The Congressional Assembly Became A Shooting Gallery
Ladies Gallery of the House of Representatives Chamber (South Wing)
United States Capitol
First Street SE, Washington D.C.

On the early afternoon of March 1, 1954, three men and one woman entered the upstairs Female Visitor's Gallery of the U. S. Congress Assembly. The Capitol had few security protocols for visitors during that era. The foursome's presence elicited minimal notice. Hours earlier they had arrived by train from New York City.

Each of the four was a member of the Puerto Rican Nationalist Party and armed with semi-automatic handguns. Members of Congress had gathered on the House floor for a debate on the Mexican economy and upcoming vote on an immigration bill. The four visitors solemnly seated themselves.

At approximately 2:30 p.m., they arose, shouted an epitaph and randomly opened fire towards the congressional members below. Thirty rounds would be discharged. The group unfurled a Puerto Rican flag as a defiant act expressing their cause of island independence. Their actions followed a referendum two years earlier when Puerto Rican voters had reconfirmed Commonwealth status with the United States.

Nationalists were unsatisfied by the 1952 vote, since the option of independence was not offered on the ballot. Puerto Rico had been annexed in 1898 following the Spanish-American War.

Amidst the ensuing chaos, five Congressmen were wounded. Their colleagues, House Pages and police officers detained three of the gunmen outside of the gallery. A fourth escaped, but would be captured later that afternoon. Republican congressman Alvin Morell Bentley from Michigan who had been shot in the chest suffered the most serious injury. All five of the wounded would be treated and ultimately recover.

The four gunmen, Lolita Lebron, Rafael Miranda, Irvin Flores and Andres Cordero would be arrested and jailed. The following morning, a raid was conducted at the Puerto Rican home of Pedro Albizu Campos, president of the Nationalist Party. He would be arrested, brutalized and transported to jail. Despite intense scrutiny by the CIA, FBI and Puerto Rican Insular police, no evidence was discovered linking Campos to the Congressional assault.

Campos would be released from prison, but his pardon later revoked by the governor. He returned to incarceration where he awaited trial for sedition and the attempted overthrow of the U.S. government. He would never face trial. Two years later, he suffered an embolism and stroke while in prison leaving him partially paralyzed and mute. He remained in custody for nine additional years before his release shortly preceding his death in 1965.

The four Capitol gunmen would be tried in federal court during 1954 and convicted of attempted murder charges. Lebron's conviction would be reduced to assault with a deadly weapon. All four defendants were declared guilty of conspiracy. Each received extended sentences that effectively would have amounted to life imprisonment. The four were disbursed into federal penitentiaries in different parts of the United States.

In 1979, President Jimmy Carter commuted the sentences of the four participants. Part of his incentive was President Fidel Castro's release of several American CIA agents being detained in Cuba on espionage charges. American government press representatives denied the connection. An estimated 5,000 people at San Juan International Airport greeted the released prisoners enthusiastically upon their arrival.

A Strange Mirror of Purported Racial Opposites
Uline Arena (Washington Coliseum)
1140 3rd Street NE, Washington D.C.
George Lincoln Rockwell Assassination Site:
Dominion Hills Shopping Center
6011-6035 Wilson Boulevard, Arlington VA

On May 31, 1959, the leader of the Nation of Islam Elijah
Muhammad gave a speech before 10,000 members who had
arrived into Washington D. C. He made his presentation
inside the Uline Arena arriving into town with fanfare. He
was escorted from the airport to the Roosevelt Hotel by a
Metropolitan Police ten-motorcycle motorcade. Part of the
reason for his appearance was motivated by persistently false
rumors circulating that he was a fugitive being pursued by the
FBI.

The motorcade escorted him to the arena. Following his
speech, they accompanied him back to his hotel. His oration
warned against the perils of integration. He also stressed
justice necessitated by *grievous and unprovoked attacks by
the white man*. Back at his hotel, he participated in a
television interview with WNTA of New York. He prophesied
*the pending destruction of the white man will occur before
1970*.

The following year, the Uline Arena would be renamed the
Washington Coliseum by new ownership. In 1961, another
gathering of the Nation of Islam was conducted there with
8,000 in attendance. Elijah Muhammad failed to attend, but
one of his lieutenants, Malcolm X spoke along with two
others. They repeatedly called for *separation, not integration
or segregation*.

Amongst the high-profile attendees in the front rows were
George Lincoln Rockwell and twenty member of his
American Nazi Party in dress uniform. As odd as their

attendance appeared, Rockwell felt perfectly comfortable within that environment. He was a welcomed guest by the Nation of Islam.

He espoused white separatism, a mirrored philosophy of many leaders from the Black separatist movement. He considered the black population *inferior* and urged their return to Africa financed by the U.S. government. Rockwell praised Adolph Hitler, denied the Holocaust and traced the evils of the world to Jewish communists.

He publicly confirmed his concurrence with Elijah Muhammad's views on separatism even if they shared little else in common. Many observers simply dismissed him as a publicity seeker, since no apparent violence had been directly attributed to his group.

His ultra far-right politics, writings and strategies have however continued to influence many white supremacists and hate fueled organizations. His reign as founder and head of the American Nazi Party ended abruptly on August 25, 1967.

He was shot to death from a rooftop at the Dominion Hills Shopping Center in Arlington, Virginia. He was heading towards his car to get bleach in order to wash his clothes at a shopping center laundromat. A former neo-Nazi member named John Patler shot him over ideological differences. Patler would initially serve only eight years in prison for the murder. Following a parole violation, an additional six years was added.

Malcolm X, born Malcolm Little would become disillusioned with the Nation of Islam and Elijah Muhammad shortly following his D.C. address. His relationship with the organization intensified into hatred during 1964. He began receiving dearth threats. On February 21, 1965, he was preparing to give a talk in New York City at the Manhattan

Audubon Ballroom. A disturbance in the rear of the venue camouflaged three men who then approached him. Using a sawed-off shotgun and two semi-automatic handguns, they gunned him down with 21 shotgun wounds.

The Coliseum would host numerous performance events including the first American concert by The Beatles in 1964. It was the home for the NBA and ABA Washington Capitols and the Georgetown and the George Washington University basketball teams. Ice hockey and skating exhibitions, boxing, wrestling and music concerts were popular draws. One of President Eisenhower's inaugural balls was staged inside.

One of the most controversial employments of the Coliseum was as a makeshift detention and processing center. During May 3-5 1971, over a thousand male and female prisoners were arrested during the May Day Protests against the Vietnam War. One hundred and fifty police officers guarded the interned that slept on the floor or on jackets without blankets despite frigid temperatures.

The inmates were all processed with arrest forms, fingerprinting and mug shots. The mood was festive accompanied by singing, chanting and even cheering fresh arrivals. An intimate party of twenty disrobed and began dancing within a large circle. Several sympathetic congressmen and local politicians visited the group. The celebratory mood did little to accelerate the end of the Vietnam conflict, but served as a unifying distraction.

The Coliseum would steadily fall into disrepair and limited use due to competing local venues. The property was leased by a Christian organization during the 1980s that envisioned ambitious plans for its use. The extravagant designs never materialized.

Waste Management purchased the complex in 1994 for use as a trash transfer station. The structure was subsequently targeted for demolition but was spared in November 2006. It was included on the National Register of Historic Places. Its continuing demise created an unruly public appearance with saturation by graffiti scrawls. Its primary use changed into an indoor parking garage.

Salvation and regeneration arrived in 2004 with the opening of the NoMa-Gallaudet U station and an upsurge in neighborhood redevelopment. The property was converted into a mixed-use retail and office development retaining its original *Uline Arena* name. A REI flagship store opened in October 21, 2016 making the space once again relevant and inviting for public patronage.

ULINE ARENA
1140 Third Street

REI
CO·OP

A Mistress' Murder, Innuendo and A Lost Damaging Diary
Mary Pinchot Meyer Murder Site:
Chesapeake and Ohio Canal Towpath, Georgetown, Washington D.C.

Among the numerous purported lovers that President John Kennedy cultivated during his presidency, Mary Pinchot Meyer may have qualified as a *genuine* mistress.

Meyer was raised in New York City, the eldest daughter of Amos Pinchot, a wealthy attorney and key financier for the socialist magazine *The Masses*. Her mother was a journalist published in *The Nation* and *The New Republic*. She was also the niece of Gifford Pinchot, a two-time Governor of Pennsylvania.

She attended the prestigious Brearley School and Vassar College before beginning her own journalist exploits writing for the *United Press* and *Mademoiselle*. Her political orientation was grounded in pacifism and liberalism. While dating future journalist and diplomat William Attwood in 1935, she met Kennedy for the first time.

In 1944, she began dating Marine Corps lieutenant Cord Meyer. Meyer had lost his left eye due to shrapnel injuries suffered in combat during World War II. They married the following year and would quickly have two boys shortly afterwards. In 1950, they had a third son. Despite her pedigree background, experience and education, Mary chose to remain a homemaker and attended art classes at the Art Student League of New York.

Her husband became president of the United World Federalists in May 1947 and worked as an aide to Minnesota Governor Harold Stassen. Four years later, he joined the Central Intelligence Agency (CIA) after being personally recruited by the first civilian director Allen Dulles. Accepting the position meant relocating to Washington D.C. where the couple became highly prominent members of Georgetown society.

By early 1954, Cord Meyer had become disillusioned by his CIA work. The year before, he had been accused by Wisconsin Senator Joseph McCarthy of being a communist. The FBI investigated both he and his wife's political ties and past. During the summer of 1954, newly elected Senator John and Jacqueline Kennedy bought the house next door to the Meyers. Mary cultivated a friendship with Jackie and reportedly they took frequent walks together. At the time, Cord Meyer was often in Europe, operating *Radio Free Europe*, *Radio Liberty* and numerous programs and organizations opposing the Soviet Union.

The couple began drifting apart due to his absences. They weathered the death of their 9-year-old middle son when a car struck him fatally. Her sister would marry Ben Bradlee who would later gain Watergate fame as editor of the *Washington Post*. His own account of her life in his autobiography would confirm the relationship she would share with John Kennedy.

The Meyers were headed in different trajectories and Mary filed for divorce in 1958. Following the divorce, Mary and her two sons moved to Georgetown. She began serious abstract painting inside a converted garage studio at the home of her sister and brother-in-law. Her newfound liberation from marriage freed her from conventional expectations and towards a noteworthy dangerous liaison.

In October 1961, she reportedly visited newly elected President John Kennedy and began an intimate sexual relationship. The affair was not exclusive for Kennedy, but different from others based on their backgrounds, similar ages and intellectual capacities. Their range of conversation doubtlessly transcended social gossip. She maintained cordial relations with Jackie Kennedy. She was an invited guest on the yacht *Sequoia* for a party honoring John Kennedy's 46th birthday celebration. The event was held on May 29, 1963, six months before he would be assassinated in Dallas.

The most conclusive piece of evidence indicating the continuity of their relationship was a letter that surface at auction in June 2016. The note penned by Kennedy implored her to join him for a tryst. The note was handwritten on White House stationary and found in the possession of Kennedy's personal secretary Evelyn Lincoln. It was never mailed.

Her liaison with Kennedy would much later become the subject of intense speculation and revelation. A secret service agent was rumored to chauffeur her two to three times weekly to a discreet White House bedroom. Other accounts indicated that she introduced Kennedy to marijuana. More flattering sources credited her with influencing his thinking on issues including nuclear disarmament and far-left political philosophy. As with most pillow talk between couples, what transpired was never audibly recorded.

Reportedly, she kept a diary that might have proven more revealing and ultimately damaging.

Following Kennedy's death, she continued her painting routine and customary daily walks along the Chesapeake and Ohio Canal towpath in Georgetown. During midday on October 12, 1964, her life ended abruptly.

A car mechanic repairing a vehicle on Canal Road heard a panicked plea for help and two gunshots. He ran to a low wall nearby and witnessed *a black man in a light jacket, dark slacks, and a dark cap standing over the prone body of a white woman.*

The deceased woman was Mary Pinchot Meyer. She had been shot at close range in the left temple and back. An examining FBI forensic expert suggested the killing had the appearance of a professional execution.

A quarter mile away, Ray Crump was soaking wet and walking on the same trail. Police detained him based on his incoherent explanation as to why he was there. He vaguely resembled the mechanic's description but incriminating evidence was absent. The gun was never recovered. During his criminal trial, he was acquitted due to lack of evidence.

Musings towards a more sinister and deliberately planned killing were raised. A suspect or motive never materialized. Former husband Cord Meyer agreed with the police conclusion that *she had been the victim of a sexually motivated assault by a single individual*. Her death resulted in her struggle to escape.

Posthumously, books and articles would be published linking her directly with Kennedy. Her mysterious diary never surfaced publicly. Some accounts maintained that it was ultimately taken by the CIA and later destroyed.

The private indiscretions of public individuals have never ceased to stimulate interest. The early 1960s was an era of selective media disclosure. As all of the affected parties are currently deceased, present and future speculation seems irrelevant. John Kennedy compartmentalized many aspects of his character and varied relationships. Mary Pinchot Meyer was merely a diminutive piece of his clouded personality puzzle.

**The Enduring Fractured Trust Prompted By The
Watergate Scandal**
Watergate Office Building:
2600 Virginia Avenue NW, Suite 610, Washington D.C.
Former Howard Johnson's Motor Lodge Site:
**2610 Virginia Avenue NW, Rooms 419 and 723,
Washington D.C.**
***Deep Throat* Parking Garage:**
1816 N Nash Street, Arlington VA
Former Washington Post Site:
1150 15th Street NW, Washington D.C.

Making sense and perspective of the Watergate Scandal a half-century afterwards requires an understanding of the prevalent expectations most citizens shared towards their Executive branch then. For nearly two and a half centuries, many Americans have harbored a healthy distrust and caution towards political institutions.

This angst and divisiveness was heightened during the early 1970s, particularly following the conclusion of the Vietnam War. Ridicule towards the assumption of political propriety has inflamed dialogue beginning with the presidential tenure of George Washington.

The Watergate scandal distanced itself in severity from precedent improprieties. In the past, national leaders may have misled or misrepresented facts, but never had they been caught and exposed so flagrantly. The scandal pricked an artery of American trust towards an essential presumed truth in public disclosure. This violation of that trust required public accountability and ultimately a change in leadership.

The genesis of President Richard Nixon's administration unraveling began on January 27, 1972 when G. Gordon Liddy, then the Finance Counsel for the Committee for the Re-Election of the President (CRP) presented an intelligence plan to three members of the administration's staff. These three included Attorney General John Mitchell, Presidential Counsel John Dean and acting CRP chairman Jeb Magruder. The project involved extensive illegal activities against the Democratic Party.

The crux of the plan involved burglarizing the Democratic National Committee's headquarters located in the Watergate Complex in Washington D.C. The intent was to photograph campaign documents and wiretap telephones within the office. The break-in occurred on May 28th with two telephones targeted to be wiretapped. The plan seemingly worked flawlessly until it was determined that the listening devices were defective. A second burglary to correct the flaw was planned for three weeks later.

The second break-in attempt would launch the operation into infamy. Shortly after midnight on Saturday, June 17th, a Watergate security guard noticed tape covering the latches on some of the complex's doors leading from the underground parking garage to several offices. He removed the tape and shortly afterwards, noted that upon his return later the locks had been re-taped. He telephoned police.

A series of missteps by the burglars followed. Three plainclothes policemen arrived in an unmarked vehicle. The burglar's spotter watching from across the street at a Howard Johnson's Motel Lodge failed to observe their arrival in front of the Watergate building. The officers advanced to the sixth floor and the Democratic National Committees suite of 29 offices. They would apprehend five men and impound lock picking tools, film, two cameras, three pen-sized tear gas guns and $2,300 in cash.

There was no evidence to suggest that Nixon was cognizant of the operation. His administration team began immediate efforts the following morning to cover-up both the crime and any direct linkage to the CRP.

Nixon's initial error occurred during a conversation with his chief of staff, H. R. Haldeman on June 23rd when he was informed about the break-in. He expressed ignorance regarding the operation to Haldeman, but ordered him to the have the CIA impede the FBI's investigation into the financial sources behind the burglary.

Days afterwards, Ron Ziegler, Nixon's press secretary publicly described the arrests as a *third-rate burglary attempt*. On August 29th, Nixon addressed the issue with a news conference. He indicated that John Dean, his presidential lawyer had fully investigated the incident concluding that no one employed by the White House or administration had any involvement with the operation. The problem with his pronouncement was that Dean hadn't conducted an investigation. Worse, he was amongst the initial three administration members aware of the plan.

On September 15th, a grand jury indicted the five office burglars along with G. Gordon Liddy and former CIA officer E. Howard Hunt on charges of conspiracy, burglary and violation of federal wiretapping laws. Following a juried trial, on January 30, 1973, all seven either pled guilty or were convicted by a jury.

The case might have ended with their sentencing. Nixon was easily re-elected on November 7th in one of the largest landslides in electoral voting history, 520-17. His opponent George McGovern only won the state of Massachusetts and the District of Colombia.

The break-in from the outset was entirely needless. The

revelations to follow the election were only just beginning.

The journey through the labyrinth of darken financing, dirty political tricks and ethically absent perpetrators proved unsettling to the American public palette,

Over the next eighteen months, the scandal would evolve into arguably the worst political scandal in American history. The sustained and accurate accounts by *Washington Post* reporters Bob Woodward and Carl Bernstein revealed that the Watergate break-in was an element of a much larger campaign of political spying and sabotage employed by the Nixon re-election campaign. Their chief anonymous informant was William Mark Felt, Sr., nicknamed *Deep Throat*, deputy director of the FBI. Woodward met clandestinely with Felt at an underground parking garage in Rosslyn, Virginia between June 1972 until January 1973.

As public disclosure regarding the extent of the CRP's activities widened, Nixon's administrative team were ensnared in a web of duplicity. Their efforts to deny guilt or destroy incriminating evidence heightened public distrust of Nixon and his effectiveness as a national leader. Many observers felt that his concealment of the trust was a betrayal that undermined the election process and democracy.

Unable to effectively govern under an enormous weight of suspicion, Nixon resigned as President on August 9. 1974. His desperate action preceded the certainty that he would be impeached by the House of Representatives and removed from office by the Senate. He had increasingly fewer allies defending his actions publicly.

One month later, he was pardoned by his successor, Gerald Ford. Public resentment over the pardon limited Ford's tenure as President to only the conclusion of Nixon's term. Jimmy Carter would defeat him in the 1976 election.

Sixty-nine individuals would be indicted during the follow-up investigation with 48 being convicted. Many of these individuals were the highest-level members of the Nixon administration.

Viewing the scandal in hindsight, the magnitude of actual events involved with the cover-up appear comparatively subdued to subsequent scandals.

Two later Presidents, Bill Clinton and Donald Trump have been impeached. Trump twice. Clinton admitted an extra-marital relationship with a Capitol intern. Trump was impeached first for an inappropriate extortion request with the Ukrainian government and second for inciting an attempted Coup d'Etat on the Capitol steps. Both were narrowly spared conviction by the Senate because their political parties held a narrow majority.

Impeachment remains an aggressive and retaliatory threat towards a sitting President. In the future, such an action will doubtlessly be employed when an opposition party holds a majority in the House of Representatives and US Senate. The ghost of Watergate still haunts the American political legacy. The event merely substantiated a fractured public faith that may never heal within our philosophically divided country.

FORMER HOWARD JOHNSON'S

WATERGATE
INVESTIGATION
DEEP THROAT GARAGE

The Argentine Firecracker and Demise of Congressman Wilbur Mills
Former Silver Slipper Club Site:
815 13th Street NW, Washington D.C.
Tidal Basin:
Located Between the Lincoln and Jefferson Memorials, Washington D.C.

During the early 1970s, Congressman Wilbur Mills represented Arkansas's 2nd district. He'd held the elective office since 1939 and had advanced to becoming the chairman of the House Ways and Means Committee beginning in 1958. Observers considered him one of the most powerful men in Washington. His name was entered in the 1972 presidential primaries in a few states. He performed well in the New Hampshire primary before several decisive losses within several southern states.

In the summer of 1973, Mills was introduced to Annabel Villagra better known as Fanne Foxe at the Silver Slipper club via a mutual friend and fellow performer. Foxe was the club's featured performer stripping under the act the *Argentine Firecracker*.

The 38-year-old Foxe was raised in a town southwest of Buenos Aires. She was a pre-medical student at the University of Buenos Aires before marrying at 20, Eduardo Battistella, a pianist who played in clubs. Their performance act consisted of her dancing to accompany his piano-playing act.

During the early 60s, their act took them to Miami and Baltimore where she began using her stage name and stripping. She officially immigrated in 1963 and became a legal resident two years later. By the late 1960s, she was performing almost exclusively in Washington D.C. The couple's marriage had collapsed, but they continued to live in the Crystal Towers complex in Arlington County, Virginia.

During the sultry summer of 1973, Foxe and Mills grew closer together. They were nightly companions at the Silver Slipper and as their relationship blossomed, she stopped performing at the Silver Slipper.

Wilbur Mills was enveloped in a complicated dilemma. In August 1973, he moved with his wife to the Crystal Towers complex. As boundaries continued to blur, Mills and his wife Polly played bridge with Foxe and her estranged husband.

The arrangement became exceedingly complicated as Mills' drinking worsened. He promised to marry Foxe if he could obtain a divorce from his wife, but didn't seem hurried. He took Foxe on a three week-week vacation to Antigua where she became pregnant. She aborted the child to protect Mills' reputation.

The reprieve became short-lived. Mills infidelity became public knowledge on the evening of October 6, 1974. Mills and Foxe got into an intense argument. They entered the car of a friend. Police observed their driver speeding, swerving and operating without headlights.

When the car was pulled over near the Jefferson Memorial at 2:00 a.m., Foxe panicked and darted out of the car screaming epitaphs in English and Spanish. She attempted to disappear by jumping into the tidal basin, a man-made reservoir located between the Potomac River and Washington Channel.

She was fished out and handcuffed. Her apparent two black eyes prompted police to admit her to St. Elizabeth Hospital for treatment and concern that she might be suicidal. She later would confess that the motive behind her flight was to protect Mill's reputation and her concern an arrest might affect her recent American citizenship.

The incident attracted public scrutiny, but Mills escaped repercussions.

One month later, Mills was narrowly re-elected to his congressional seat. Shortly following his election, he made a fatal error. He attended one of Foxe's burlesque performances at the Pilgrim Theatre in Boston. Intoxicated, he staggered on stage and gave a rambling speech and backstage news conference. His incoherent actions fatally doomed his political career. On December 19, 1974, he resigned from the influential Ways and Mean Chairmanship and soon afterwards checked into a rehabilitation clinic for his worsening alcoholism. He opted not to run for re-election in 1976.

Upon his congressional retirement, he practiced law in Washington D.C. and worked with recovery programs advising other alcoholics in public service. He retired form law in 1991, scaling back his activities in Arkansas. He died in May 1992 at the age of 82. His wife remained with him following the scandal and died nine years later.

Fanne Foxe milked her brief acclaim into additional performance opportunities and appearances. She was arrested and acquitted for indecent exposure for a December 1974 show at the Club Juana in Orlando, Florida.

She divorced Eduardo Battistella when the Mills scandal first broke and married her manager Daniel Montgomery in 1980. They had a daughter together and divorced five years later. She assumed Montgomery's surname and moved to St. Petersburg, Florida where she resumed her college studies. She earned a B.A. and Master's degree and worked as a divemaster for the University of South Florida, participating in underwater filming in Cozumel, Mexico. She died on

February 10, 2021, four days before her 85th birthday.

At the bewitching hour of 3:00 a.m. on June 29, 1981, the fabled Silver Slipper club closed permanently. The city's Alcoholic Beverage Commission had begun a crackdown on burlesque exotic dancing houses. The neighbor had become gritty and infested by crime. The owner had weathered forty years in the DC nightclub business. An attractive buy-out offer made the timing opportune. He confided to a newspaper reporter that he was looking for another location within safer confines. The site was razed and converted into commercial office space.

An Irish Republican Patriot and Peace Negotiations Pub
Robert Emmet Statue:
S Street NW and Massachusetts Avenue NW, Washington D.C.
Phoenix Park Hotel:
North Capitol and F Street NW, Washington D.C

Robert Emmet lived a brief existence of 25 years espousing an Irish Republic and the overthrow of the occupying British Crown. He was a fiery orator and leader of an uprising in Dublin during 1803 that ultimately proved abortive. He would become a standard bearer for future generations proclaiming Irish Nationality.

He would be captured, tried and convicted for high treason on September 19, 1803. He had opted not to mount a defense for his action knowing that his fate was already decided upon. The following day, he was hung and then beheaded on Thomas Street in Dublin in front of St. Catherine's Church. No one would come forward to claim his remains for fear of arrest.

Poet Percy Shelley eulogized him in verse while searching for his grave in Dublin during 1812. A life-size bronze statue of Emmet created by Jerome Connor rises amidst a diminutive land patch along D.C.'s Embassy Row. The setting is partially shrouded in trees and shrubbery, but Emmet's conviction is unmistakable.

The Commodore Hotel was opened in the spring of 1927 diagonally located across from the Union Station. The property became a hotel survivor from an era when travel into D.C. was almost exclusively by rail. As travel shifted towards aviation and airport accommodations, the hotel struggled competitively and resorted to extensive price promotions.

In March 1974, Daniel *Danny* Coleman opened the *Dubliner*

Irish pub in the ground floor restaurant space. In 1980, he purchased the entire building and re-christened the property the Phoenix Park Hotel. He extended the Irish theme throughout and two years later completed a massive renovation.

His investment proved sound and his creation of an Irish oasis has cultivated an impressive roster of political dignitaries and guests. More importantly, its contribution towards Irish stability and history was solemnized by an important peace treaty later known as the *Good Sunday Agreement*. The project was a major initiative headed by Senator George Mitchell brokering a peace deal in Northern Ireland. Irish politicians arriving in D.C. stayed at the Phoenix Park Hotel and negotiated terms and text in the *Dubliner*. The agreement would be ratified in 1998.

TWISTED TOUR GUIDES.com

A Police Shooting Tragedy Compounded Two Decades Later
Former Site of Eastern Liberty Federal Savings:

21st and K Street NW, Washington D.C.
Gail Cobb Murder Site:
20th Street and L Street NW, Washington D.C.

Gail Cobb applied to become a Metropolitan Police office at the age of twenty-three in October 1973. Her decision came as surprise to her friends and family. Her father was a correctional captain for the District of Columbia who had formally applied for the identical position in 1953. His application had been rejected because his height of five foot eight inches was shorter than the mandatory requirement.

Gail Cobb was only five feet tall. By the time she had applied, the minimum height requirement matched hers. This modification would encourage more female applicants. She graduated with her 34-member Police Academy class in April 1974 that included 13 female police cadets. At the time, it was the largest female graduating class of police cadets in the United States. She was given favorable reviews by her instructors and volunteered for training to learn sign language and earn a motorcycle license.

Finding her professional niche had been a challenge after giving birth to a son at twenty. She had dated the boy's father during high school, but he assumed no responsibility for parenting. She raised her son Damon as a single mother. Until her police application was accepted, she had worked as a long-distance operator with aspirations of becoming a fashion designer.

She was assigned uniformed foot patrol as her initial police responsibility. Less than six months following her graduation and still on employment probation, she was working near a pending bank robbery. On Friday, September 20, 1974 at 10:30 a.m., two men, John Curtis Dortch and John William Bryant intended to rob the Eastern Liberty Federal Savings and Loan at the intersection of 21st and L Street NW. They were disguised as construction workers with each carrying a loaded sawed-off shotgun and handgun.

Two plainclothes police officers were tipped off to the robbery in advance. They halted Dortch and Bryant before they entered the bank requesting identification. Both men scattered in different directions before they could be detained.

Cobb was only a block away from the bank issuing a traffic ticket. A bystander informed her that an armed man had run inside a nearby garage. Cobb pursued and confronted John Bryant as he was changing out of his disguise. She ordered him to place his hands on the wall. Instead of handcuffing and disarming him or positioning him on the ground, she radioed for backup assistance.

Her lapse in judgment enabled the still armed Bryant to wheel around and shoot Cobb at close range. The bullet penetrated her wrist, shattering a wristwatch and continued through her police radio. It lodged inside her heart killing her on the scene. Responding officers arrested Bryant. She became the first female MPDC officer and initial black female law enforcement officer nationally to be killed in the line of duty

Her funeral procession was attended by hundreds of police officers from throughout the United States along with numerous government officials including FBI Director Clarence Kelley. She was displayed in an open casket wearing a green pantsuit instead of a traditional police uniform.

Both of the perpetrators were found guilty of second-degree murder and sentenced from fifteen years to life imprisonment. In 1989, John Dortch would be released early on parole for good behavior. He became active with his church and various charitable causes. Dortch was a former U.S. Army officer who'd served in the Vietnam War. He'd also graduated with a degree from Howard University. Following his release, he pursued the prospect of becoming a lawyer. The West Virginia Supreme Court denied his request unanimously.

In 1992, triggerman John Bryant would be released. One year later, he would be arrested for possession of crack cocaine and marijuana. The charges were dismissed in court because the arresting officers did not have probable cause to search him. In July 1997, the D.C. Parole Board revoked his parole for possession of the drugs and for testing positive for marijuana use. Rather than being sent back to prison, he was sentenced to an inpatient program for treatment of alcoholism.

Nineteen years following the murder of Gail Cobb, her son Damon would shoot 21-year-old Gerald Carlton Weaver three times in the back outside of his parents' home. The killing was prompted by Weaver's alleged burglary of a friend's apartment. The action culminated a pattern of Cobb's steady character deterioration. His essential needs had been taken care of by his grandparents and a trust fund set up for his future. His grandparents blamed his mother's death and absence as a major contributing factor to his decline.

He is currently serving a life sentence for first-degree murder at the Western Correctional Institution in Cumberland, Maryland. Ironically, the length of his incarceration has already exceeded that of his mother's killers.

FOR LEASE
papadop.com
HOMESTYLE

2001 L ST   PARKING
PARK

A Mistress Unworthy of A Wedding Invitation
Elizabeth Ray's Office:
Longworth Office Building, Room 1506
15 Independence Avenues SE, Washington D.C.

Congressman Wayne Hays straddled a volatile existence between power and sexual desire. In 1976, he was chairman of the House Administration Committee and served on the International Relations Committee. He was elected to Congress in 1948 and had ascended to become regarded as its second or third most powerful member. He had cultivated a reputation as the meanest man in the House of Representatives.

Hays planned on running as a favorite-son candidate for President in the June 8th Ohio Primary. He was also rumored by close associates to consider a run for governor of Ohio in 1978.

Elizabeth Ray, 27, began working with Hays in April 1974 as a clerk. The annual salary of $11,000 exceeded her previous brief jobs as a flight attendant, waitress, car rental receptionist and clerk on Congressman Kenneth Gray's staff, a Democrat from Illinois. Her prime responsibility appeared to accompany Gray or favorite constituents on dates. She often entertained Gray's male friends aboard his houseboat, docked on the Potomac.

Gray introduced her to Hays who offered her a clerk position in his office. She preferred his position as it required a lighter workload and she had her own desk. Her requirements for appearance in his office were minimal. On average she arrived once or twice a week for a few hours.

Her real position was to serve as Hays' mistress. Once or twice weekly while in Washington D.C., Hays would generally take Ray out for dinner at the Chapparel restaurant at the Key Bridge Marriott at 7:00 p.m. Following a hurried meal, the pair would adjourn to her Arlington apartment. According to Ray, Hays would *never stop in the living room and walked directly to the bedroom*. Keeping a close eye on the clock, he always returned home to his wife by 9:30 p.m.

The arrangement suited Hays, but Ray had other ambitions. She claimed to have known 10-15 other women with similar jobs, but she claimed hers was the cruelest. She confided in a Washington Post article regarding the scandal that *the other congressmen at least treat them like a date*. By the spring of 1975, Ray was tired of her role and quit. She reported traveled top Hollywood to earn her living as a legitimate actress. She claimed that her strongest credential had *been giving Academy Award performances once a week for two years*. The experiment failed and she returned to Hay's office to resume her duties. Her annual salary was upped to $14,000.

By May of 1976, rumor had spread of their relationship to Watergate reporter Bob Woodward of the *Washington Post*. The newspaper began an investigation that would culminate in a May 23rd article exposing the intimate details. A pouting Elizabeth Ray cooperated with their inquiry.

She was hurt because Hays had no intention of allowing their relationship to evolve beyond sex. He had divorced his wife of 36 years during early 1976 and expediently married his longtime Ohio office secretary Patricia Peak. What incensed Ray and triggered her cooperation was that she wasn't invited to their wedding. Ray also became pissed off that Hays demanded she show up for work at least two hours a day for propriety appearances.

Hays consoled Ray before the marriage that their relationship and her job could still continue afterwards...*if she behaved herself.* Ray had no intention of remaining his submissive mistress.

The two *Post* reporters who broke the story, Marion Clark and Rudy Maxa were given access to Rays office, room #1506 in the Longworth Building. Ray was not listed in the directory of House of Representative employees. She enjoyed a *serenely empty* office with a blank entry door. The reporters indicated that the interior contained thick wall-to-wall carpet and a long black leather couch. On her polished wood desk were a book, backgammon set, two red telephones and a color-coordinated red IBM Selectric typewriter with a smoked Plexiglas top.

They noted it was unplugged because Ray confessed she didn't know how to turn it on. Her wall contained a collection of framed and signed photographs from entertainers and other famous individuals.

What Ray provided in access was only superseded by her comic and insightful commentary. She became a memorable quote machine that Hays could not effectively counter.

When asked to define her job, she observed: *Supposedly I'm on the oversight committee. But I call it the Out-of-Sight Committee.* Her most memorable saying became: *I can't type. I can't file. I can't even answer the phone.*

Her ability to adlib candidly overwhelmed Hays' staff's ability to cover up his indiscretion with her. Ray acknowledged her fears towards Hay's retribution, but she had effectively buried him before he could exact revenge against her. Too many witnesses could collaborate her story.

When the scandal detonated, Hays was leaving for London on a Bicentennial congressional trip to bring the Magna Carta back to the United States. His denials of the affair upon his return were useless. He resigned as chairman of the Committee of House Administration on June 18, 1976 and his congressional post on September 1st. He discovered that his cultivated meanness left him with few allies or peer supporters.

He would attempt one last soiree into politics winning a single term in the Ohio House of Representatives in 1978. He was defeated for re-election and retired permanently from politics. He settled into Red Gate Farm, his 300-acre Ohio property where he bred Angus cattle and Tennessee Walking Horses. In February 1989, he suffered a fatal heart attack at his home in Wheeling, West Virginia at the age of 77.

Marion Clark, one of the lead *Washington Post* editors reporting the scandal would meet a gruesome death on September 4, 1997. She reportedly walked into a moving small private airplane propeller at the Iosco County, Michigan airport.

Elizabeth Ray parlayed her notoriety into a book called *The Washington Fringe Benefit*, posing for *Playboy* magazine and work as a stand-up comic. None of these pursuits evolved and she ultimately faded into obscurity and a forgotten historical footnote.

Chilean President Pinochet Bombs An Adversary on American Soil
Car Bombing Site: Sheridan Circle
Massachusetts Avenue NW at 23rd Street NW, Washington D.C.

The ascendance of the military dictatorship of Chilean General Augusto Pinochet was sanctioned and assisted by the CIA in 1973. Pinochet led a successful coup d'etat against reigning President Salvador Allende on September 11, 1973. Allende had escaped an earlier failed coup in June. His three-year experiment with a South American socialist state would not survive a second assault. Civil unrest, strikes, lockouts and economic sanctions plagued his *Unidad Popular* party resulting in factionalism and a minority presence in the Chilean Congress.

The September transition was bloody and brief. The Chilean Air Force bombed the presidential palace. Allende's loyalist forces mounted a fleeting armed resistance, but were soon overwhelmed. Allende committed suicide shortly become Pinochet's troops stormed the palace. Pinochet assumed control of the government immediately. He declared Martial Law aggressively suspending all freedom of speech and conducted military tribunals against his perceived enemies. Throughout the process of regime change, the CIA was intimately involved in supporting his abuses.

Pinochet was ruthless in his pursuit of exiled opposition members to his government. His death squads extended even into Washington D.C.

Orlando Letelier followed a traditional upbringing and at sixteen became a cadet at the Chilean Military Academy. He completed his secondary studies but abandoned a military career. He didn't finish university and worked until 1959 as a research analyst in the copper industry. That year he was fired from the Copper Office for supporting Salvador Allende's unsuccessful presidential campaign. He and his young family relocated to Venezuela where he became a copper consultant to the Finance Ministry.

His extended ties to Allende were rewarded when he was elected to power in 1970. Letelier was appointed as ambassador to the United States in 1971. His mission was to promote the necessity behind the nationalization of the copper industry. This governmental action replaced the previous private ownership business model favored by the United States government. In 1973, he returned to Chile to serve as the Minister of Foreign Affairs, the Interior and Defense.

Following the September 1973 coup, Letelier became the first former high-ranking official to be arrested. He was severely tortured for a year in various prison camps before his release to Venezuela following extensive diplomatic pressure. The sole stipulation was that he immediately leave Chile.

In Venezuela, Letelier might have lived out his life peacefully. He opted to move to Washington D.C. in 1975 where he became a senior fellow at the Institute for Policy Studies. He became the voice of dissent against prominent capitalist economists. He believed that resource dominated economies such as Chile required a socialist government to adequately distribute wealth to the lower and middle class. He soon became a prominent and irritating voice in Chilean resistance preventing several loans from being awarded the new Pinochet government.

Pinochet perceived Letelier as a dangerous threat to his policies. On September 10, 1976 he stripped Letelier of his Chilean nationality. Eleven days later, Pinochet decided to eliminate permanently his nuisance.

Letelier was driving to work on September 21 with an associate Ronni Moffitt and her husband Michael. As the vehicle rounded Sheridan Circle along Embassy Row at 9:35 a.m., a bomb placed underneath the driver side portion of the car detonated. Driver Letelier and front seat passenger Ronni Moffitt would be killed from the explosion. Her husband Michael would crawl out safely from the back seat.

Wires and magnets to the car's underside attached the bomb. It blew a hole two feet in diameter in the driver's seat. The U.S. Department of State expressed *concern* about the death and attributed blame to a series of state-sponsored attempted assassinations against Chilean political exiles.

During the FBI investigation, it was revealed publicly that Letelier had been working in conjunction with Eastern Bloc intelligence agencies for over a decade. Evidence also indicated that he'd been coordinating his activities with the surviving political leadership of the *Unidad Popular* political party exiled in East Berlin.

The FBI determined that Michael Townley, a Chilean secret policeman and American expatriate had organized the assassination on behalf of the Chilean government. Townley and associate Armando Fernandez Larios had been given visas prior to entering the United States.

The messy intrigue resulted in Townley receiving a 10-year prison sentence. He served five years and for the remainder was enrolled in the Witness Protection Program. He forwarded the names of three other participants who pled guilty, but later were acquitted at their second trial. Armando Larios expediently fled Chile with the assistance of the FBI due to fears that Pinochet would liquidate him for his intended American cooperation. Charges against his involvement were later dropped.

Pinochet would die on December 10, 2006 estranged from his American spy contacts and international public opinion. He would never be charged for the deaths of Orlando Letelier and Ronni Moffitt. Over time, it became abundantly clear that he had ordered their murder through his obedient legions of rats.

Approaching Political Figures With Loose Money
Abscam Headquarters:
4407 W Street NW, Washington D.C.

In March 1978, the FBI initiated a sting operation called *Abscam* out of their Long Island, New York office. The intention behind the project was initially targeted towards investigating theft, forgery and stolen art.

The FBI, for reasons unclear, turned to Melvin Weinberg and his girlfriend, Evelyn Knight to organize and conduct the sting. The problem with both Weinberg and Knight was their past. He was a convicted swindler and international con artist and she his accomplice. Both agreed to cooperate and participate in the program because they were each facing three-year prison sentences. Their assistance converted their terms into probation.

The clarity and direction of the operation became blurred and soon drifted into another direction.

The FBI leased a house in Georgetown under the name of L. Robert Johnson, the secretary-treasurer of a bogus company called Olympic Construction. They established and funded a fake company called Abdul Enterprises with FBI agents posing as fictional Arab sheikhs. The name *Abscam* was derived from *Abdul Scam*. The objective behind the program shifted towards political corruption.

The house was wired thoroughly for surveillance. A hidden camera was even located inside a television set. Neighbors found it puzzling that no one stayed in the house overnight and that visitors during the day were generally well-dressed and carrying briefcases.

Prominent political officials ranging from mayors to Senators were approached with cash offers to use their political influence on fictional casino projects intended for Atlantic City. Ethically, the unsolicited inducements shaded into entrapment, but there were plenty of interested takers.

Thirty-one political figures and influential individuals were approached. *Penthouse Magazine* publisher Bob Guccione was included in that list. A majority refused the bribes or requested more detailed background information. Twelve individuals would accept the bait. The FBI recorded and documented each of the money exchanges within their headquarter house before arresting the recipient.

Each of the arrested individuals would be tried separately. A sympathetic judge to the prosecution overruled defense attorney's claims of entrapment. The highest profile conviction was New Jersey U. S. Senator Harrison Williams. Six congressmen, four municipal elected official and one U.S. Immigration inspector were also convicted. They were given prison sentences and their follow-up conviction appeals were denied.

The *Abscam* operation generated a mostly indifferent public reaction. Stricter guidelines for future FBI sting operations would replace *Abscam's* loosely staged parameters. A 2013 feature film entitled *American Hustle* fictionalized the complicated operation. It was nominated for ten Academy Awards, but won none. Criminal coordinator Melvin Weinberg died on May 30, 2018 at the age of 93 in Titusville, Florida.

TWISTED TOUR GUIDES.com

**Historically Innovative Restaurant Torched By
Competitive Fire
Former Bassin's Restaurant Site:
1347 Pennsylvania Avenue NW, Washington D.C.**

The mafia entered the D.C. restaurant landscape during the 1970s for approximately two decades. Front man Salvatore Cottone arrived into the United States in 1947 at the age of twenty from Sicily. Following his arrival, he commenced work humbly in New Jersey as a restaurant dishwasher. He steadily saved and elevated himself into an ownership position. His arrival into the D.C. restaurant trade came via two restaurants named *Pizza Delight*.

Both outlets operated primarily as fronts for various criminal enterprises. Cottone chased his perspective of the *American dream* accompanied by two brothers. Their lucrative crime exploits included the distribution of cocaine, heroin and other illegal substances.

The drug trade proved fierce, but navigating the restaurant industry even more challenging. One of Cottone's more successful competitors was Bassin's Restaurant featuring its own colorful historical background.

Their original structure was completed during the late nineteenth century with a brick Italianate facade featuring ornamental cast-iron window hoods and sills. The neighborhood was then known as *Rum Row* for its distinctive drinking and gambling haunts. The bottom floor operated as a drugstore and upstairs a faro gambling bank. A variety of subsequent commercial interests occupied the premises before Max Bassin opened his restaurant in 1939.

Ten years later, Bassin left the business to concentrate on real estate. He left operations to his sister and Harry Zitelman. Over the following decade, Zitelman promoted the concept of operating a sidewalk café on the premises. His perseverance finally culminated in a 1962 favorable ruling granting his sidewalk café accompanied by serving alcoholic beverages. The following year, twenty additional sidewalk restaurants were in full operation locally.

Zitelman would additionally add the city's first discothèque called the *Top O' the Walk Twist Room* upstairs. He sold the restaurant in 1976 to a wealthy South Vietnamese family interested in operating an *American style* of business.

As a restaurant competitor, Cottone found Bassin's a nuisance. He sought the most expedient way to eliminate his rival. On the early morning of October 17, 1978, he torched the cafe to the ground. The excess amount of gasoline employed blew the restaurant's doors out leaving the structure a smoldering carcass. He likely needn't have bothered. The building was already slated to be torn down to become a massive hotel and office complex.

Cottone evaded both responsibility and arrest for the arson. He continued to expand his restaurant operations in Virginia. His drug enterprise continued to prosper until his younger brother Giuseppe was netted in an FBI sting operation. Salvatore Cottone would spend the subsequent decade dodging and negotiating law enforcement investigations. On March 26, 1990, a federal judge would sentence him to twenty years in federal prison. He would be released in February 2007.

AVENU
BAR

**Garish Admissions and Peculiar Ambition
House of Representatives Corinthian Steps:
First Street SE, Washington D.C.**

Before the Capitol steps became a launching site for coup d'etats, John and Rita Jenrette admittedly established an unusual precedent. If farce is measured on a comparative scale, the former married couple shattered the barometer.

John Jenrette was raised in Loris, South Carolina and earned a degree from Wofford College. He completed his law studies at the University of South Carolina. Afterwards, he worked as a city attorney, then judge before tilting his horizons towards politics. He was elected to the South Carolina House of Representatives as a Democrat in 1964 and retired in 1972 to run for Congress.

He lost during his first 1972 attempt, but was successful the second time two years later. His victory in the normally conservative Republican state was attributed to the voting public's disenchantment with disgraced Richard Nixon and the Watergate scandal. He would win two additional terms before his life briefly tumbled into shambles.

Jenrette's tenure in Congress was unremarkable legislatively and became a mockery personally. He would be identified with two dubious events.

He was charged and convicted in 1980 of accepting a $50,000 bribe in the FBI orchestrated *Abscam* sting operation. He would serve 13 months of a two-year sentence for the offense. His other more anecdotal action upstaged the sexual mile high club on commercial airlines. During an all-night House of Representative session, he and his accommodating wife decided that a sexual liaison during a 3 a.m. break might liven up the banal proceedings.

Illicit sexual activity has probably occurred previously on the darkened periphery of the Capitol building. The allure of the forbidden and the threat of being discovered doubtlessly heighten the stimulation. Most presumably guilty offenders would opt for discretion afterwards. Rita Jenrette included the story in her 1981 *Playboy* photo spread and the accompanying text entitled *The Liberation of a Congressional Wife*.

According to her account, the couple found a shadowy spot on the Capitol portico and *made love on the marble steps that overlooks the monuments and the city below*. Over thirty years later, she would confess to the *New Yorker* that the story was a lie. She added modestly, *why I included it is beyond me*.

Her reason wasn't difficult to understand. Her published admission added sizzle to an ambitious woman's memoirs seeking attention and opportunity. The story, whether true or fictional, contributed towards sales of yet another forgettable political memoir. For a meteorite stretch during 1981, Rita Jenrette became a fashionable *it girl*. No adventure or exaggeration regarding the Jenrette's marriage and subsequent separation seemed improbable.

She divorced John Jenrette, but kept attending D.C. social functions until her novelty dimmed. She posed *tastefully* in *Playboy* and attempted an acting career. The film *The Zombie Island Massacre* in 1984 climaxed her big screen exposure.

She made further headlines by admitting to legal authorities that she'd discovered $25,000 in $100 bills stashed in a brown suede shoe in her husband's closet. He responded that the money he'd *had for years* and had recently brought it to D.C. from his South Carolina law office. One shoe might be reasoned is as secure a hiding location as underneath a mattress.

Gradually the attention and absorption faded towards the couple's carnival sideshow. Both of them drifted into real estate and public obscurity.

In 2003, she met her prince and reinvented herself into a titled princess. Her prince, Nicolo Boncompagni Ludoisi of Piombino, Italy was married at the time to his second wife Ludmilla of St. Petersburg, Russia. They would subsequently divorce. On May 27, 2009, Jenrette became his third wife.

The fairy tale prince was described by one of the his three sons in a *New York Times* profile as *a drunk wastrel who chased women, squandered a fortune and sold off family treasures to pay for the minimum of essential renovations.*

The titled couple lived in a 16th century structure within Rome called the Villa Aurora. One of her immediate priorities became to upgrade the property. Prince Ludovisi died in 2018 halting the ambitious renovation. The villa reportedly features the world's only ceiling mural by Caravaggio along with other classic frescoes, sculptures and paintings.

The property has been labeled *dilapidated* by various sources and a *relic from a nobler era.* The *Times* account noted that the interior remains dimly lit and is seldom heated even during winter.

Jenrette lives within her historic mausoleum in a third-floor apartment with her four dogs. Family relations between her and the Prince's heirs have been contentious from the outset. Harmony and compromise is poisoned by claims and counter charges. An Italian judge ruled that the villa needed to be sold to settle heritage disputes.

In January 2022, an auction house opened the proceedings at

$531 million. The entry level proved excessive. There were
no bidders. On April 20, 2023, Jenrette was evicted.

The Near Assassination of President Ronald Reagan
Washington Hilton Hotel:
1919 Connecticut Avenue NW, Washington D.C.
Park Central Hotel, Room #312: (Demolished)

705 18th Street NW, Washingotn D.C.
John Hinckley Internment: St. Elizabeths Hospital
1100 Alabama Avenue SE, Washington D.C.

John Hinckley Jr. had staked his future on the delusional notion that if he were successful with his assassination of President Ronald Reagan, he would impress actress Jodie Foster. Hinckley had developed an unhealthy obsession towards her. He had stalked her relentlessly, wrote her numerous letters and notes and even telephoned her twice. She absolutely was *not* interested in him.

Hinckley reasoned irrationally that if he became a national figure, her indifference towards him would vanish. He identified strongly with a character in one of her movies *Taxi Driver* named Travis Bickle, portrayed by actor Robert De Niro. Bickle's character attempted to save a child prostitute played by Foster. Towards the end of the film, Bickle attempts to kill a U.S. Senator running for president. Hinckley determined that he should shoot for the top.

Hinckley did a trial run by stalking then President Jimmy Carter. He was able to get close on numerous occasions. He would be arrested in October 1980 at the Nashville International Airport for illegal possession of a firearm. The FBI did not connect this arrest with any plans towards killing the President. They didn't follow through with the Secret Service to identify him.

Hinckley later focused his attention towards Reagan who assumed office on January 20, 1981. Barely two months into his term, Reagan was scheduled to address a luncheon of

AFL-CIO representatives on March 30th at the Washington Hilton Hotel. The venue was considered one of the safest local properties during the 1970s limiting presidential exposure to a small-enclosed passageway called the *President's Walk*.

At 12:15 p.m. on Sunday, March 29th, Hinckley arrived into Washington D. C. from Hollywood via Greyhound Bus service. He'd paid $117 in cash for the ticket. He had been roaming aimlessly around the country for months, riding buses and staying at cheap motels.

He checked into the Park Central Hotel near the White House paying $47 per night. Later that afternoon, he was observed near the fence of the South Lawn of the White House. He made inquiries of several tourists whether the President was staying in town that weekend. He also inquired how an individual might see the President.

On the fateful Monday morning of March 30th, Hinckley had breakfast alone at 8:00 a.m. inside a nearby sandwich shop. He read two Washington newspapers and discovered Reagan's itinerary for the day. He penned a letter to Jody Foster indicating his plans for the afternoon, cognizant that he might not survive them alive. The letter was never mailed.

He reportedly left his hotel room shortly after 1:00 p.m. At 1:50 p.m., he was observed at the Hilton standing amidst a crowd of approximately 285 behind a rope barrier. The barrier was located near a retaining wall only a short distance from the *President's Walk* entrance to the hotel.

Reagan's concluded his speech at the luncheon and then exited the hotel via the VIP entrance at 2:25 p.m. The Secret Service had not mandated him to wear a bulletproof vest that afternoon. As Reagan walked towards his limousine parked fifty feet away, he passed in front of the armed Hinckley.

Walking slightly ahead of Reagan were Secret Service Agent Tim McCarthy, Press Secretary James Brady and Washington D.C. police officer Thomas Delahanty. As Reagan approached the right fender, Hinckley decided this positioning would be his best opportunity. He crouched and rapidly fired six shots from his .22 blue steel revolver.

His second shot had struck Delahanty in the neck. He fell on top of Brady providing Hinckley an instantaneous clear shot at the President. A labor official standing nearby thwarted Hinckley by hitting him on the head and wrestling with him. Other spectators and law enforcement personnel would pile on Hinckley punching him and slamming him against the wall. Their efforts prevented a second round of shooting.

Hinckley's six shots would wound each of the men surrounding Reagan, but miraculously not hit the President directly. The sixth and final bullet ricocheted off the armored side of the limousine passing between the space of the open rear door and vehicle frame. It hit Reagan in the left underarm. The bullet grazed a rib and lodged in his lung causing a partial collapse. It stopped less than an inch from his heart saving certain death.

It would be later determined that the six cartridges Hinckley had fired were intended to explode upon contact. Only a single one that struck James Brady did. He was hit above his left eye causing substantial brain damage.

Delahanty was struck in the back of the neck with a bullet that ricocheted off his spine. Tim McCarthy inserted himself into the direct line of fire. He spread his arms and legs taking a wide stance in front of Reagan to make himself an impediment target. He was struck in the lower abdomen with the bullet traversing his right lung, diaphragm and right lobe of his liver. Only one shot would miss any target.

Initially no one was aware that Reagan had been struck. He had been shoved into the limousine upon the sound of the initial shots. There was debate whether to drive him to the White House or a nearby hospital. He was driven immediately to the George Washington University Hospital emergency department. A superficial search of his body initially revealed no blood. Reagan remained in tremendous pain. His handlers suspected that his rib might have been cracked when he was stuffed into the limo.

Reagan began coughing up blood, but he attributed that to a cut lip. A stretcher was not available when his contingent arrived at the emergency room entrance four minutes later. Reagan exited the limousine and insisted on walking inside. He acted casually and even smiled at onlookers as he strolled inside.

Once inside, serious drama commenced. He complained of having difficulty breathing. His knees buckled and he collapsed to one knee. There was speculation that he was suffering a potential heart attack. His blood pressure had plummeted significantly as he went into shock. The medical team stabilized his condition with intravenous fluids, oxygen, and tetanus toxoid. Over the course of their treatment, the entry location of the gunshot wound was discovered.

After thirty minutes, Reagan left the emergency department for surgery exhibiting normal blood pressure. He entered the operating room conscious and joked with personnel throughout. A 105-minute thoracotomy procedure relieved his persistent bleeding. He had lost over half of his blood volume amidst his emergency room visit and the surgery. His recovery would become complicated by fever that was treated with antibiotics. Most 70-year-old men would not have survived the ordeal.

Reagan survived primarily because he was in excellent physical condition and had been treated expediently and correctly. Had he been driven to the White House first, he likely would have expired.

All of the three other wounded men would survive. Two endured permanent damage. Only Timothy McCarthy recovered fully and became the first man to be released from the hospital. Delahanty suffered permanent nerve damage to his left arm and was forced to retire from the police force. James Brady's head wound incapacitated him with slurred speech and partial paralysis. He would require the permanent use of a wheelchair until his death at 73 in August 2014.

Reagan would not be released from the hospital until the morning of April 11th. His doctors were impressed by his apparent recovery speed. Some of those remarks and showcased appearance were premature. Americans were unaware of how close he'd come to death. The upbeat PR ploy was meant to reassure the nation that he was on an accelerated road to full health. Disclosure of the truth would not be revealed until years afterwards.

During his first week back, he entirely avoided duties in the Oval Office. He gradually spent two hours working daily in his White House residential quarters.

He would not lead a Cabinet meeting until day 26 following his release. He would not leave Washington D.C. until day 49, nor hold an official press conference until day 79. His physician did not consider his recovery complete until October.

In the aftermath, his approval rating rose to a reported 70%. Later controversies, scandals and political confrontations during his two terms prompted divisive dips and rises. The collective issues that he addressed during his tenure became amongst the most varied and turbulent since the Second World War. His administration left office nearly as popular as it had entered eight years previously.

His legacy remained generally popular during his retirement and declining years. In August 1994, Reagan was diagnosed with Alzheimer's disease and his next decade would become a gauzy fog for him. He died of pneumonia inside his Bel Air district home on the afternoon of June 5, 2004. He was 93-years-old.

John Hinckley was a 25-years-old college dropout when he committed his assassination attempt. During his June 1982 trial, he was declared *not guilty by reason of insanity*. The verdict was unpopular when announced.

He was interned full-time into the D.C. mental institution, St. Elizabeths Hospital until 2006. He was gradually permitted to leave the hospital to spend more time at his mother's Williamsburg, Virginia home. On September 10, 2016, he was allowed to permanently leave the facility to live with his mother under court supervision and with mandatory psychiatric treatment.

In 2020, he created a YouTube channel to post his own original songs and guitar playing videos. He reportedly circulates around town, takes walks around his neighborhood nurtures a colony of feral cats. It is an existence few could have imaged following the tragic events of March 30, 1980.

The infamous Park Central Hotel was closed and later demolished. The site became the World Bank-J Building constructed in 1986.

Former Park Central Hotel Site

LICE
PLEASE
PULL
AHEAD

The Abrupt Deaths Of the Halberstam Brothers
Michael Halberstam Residence:
2806 Battery Place NW, Washington D.C.

Brothers Michael and David Halberstam were born in the Bronx, New York to their father Dr. Charles Abraham, a U.S. Army surgeon and Blanche Levy Halberstam, a teacher. Both brothers would professionally adopt their mother's last name and attend Harvard College. Each became a managing editor for the *Harvard Crimson*, the prestigious daily newspaper of the university.

Their career directions would veer upon graduation. Eldest brother Michael would earn an undergraduate history degree before completing his M. D. from the Boston University School of Medicine. David would become a celebrated writer, journalist and historian, best known for his works on American culture, Civil Rights, the Vietnam War and sports journalism.

Michael Halberstam completed his internship and residency in New York City and Burlington, Vermont. In 1962, he became a fellow in cardiology at George Washington University Hospital where he later taught at the medical school. In 1964, he established a private practice. He continued with his writings publishing numerous medical papers in his field. He wrote television reviews on medical shows and a novel called *The Wanting of Levine*.

Halberstam was at the peak of his profession when he was abruptly cut down on December 5, 1980. Returning home that evening, he and his wife surprised Bernard C. Welch Jr., a notorious thief and escaped convict burglarizing their house.

Welch shot Halberstam twice in the chest. Despite his wound, he instructed his wife to drive him to nearby Sibley Hospital. En route, he spotted Welch and swerved the vehicle to strike him. The car hit Welch and then crashed into a tree. Halberstam was immediately transported by ambulance to the emergency ward. He would die on an operating table 90 minutes after he'd been shot.

Welch was arrested and tried for felony murder, second-degree burglary and grand larceny. He was convicted and given a cumulative sentence of 143 years. Halberstam's widow filed a successful wrongful death suit against Welch and his live-in companion. The award of $5.7 million would be a symbolic victory. Welch died incarcerated in 1997.

Halberstam's brother David would perish in a bizarre traffic collision on April 23, 2007 in Menlo Park, California. He was a passenger en route to a research interview when the journalism student driving the car illegally turned into oncoming traffic.

**A Mysterious Killing of a Popular Senate Aide
Raymond Nelson Murder Site: 701 Quincy Street NE,
Washington D.C.**

Raymond *Nels* Nelson crammed sixty years of secrets into his apartment near Catholic University. On June 1, 1981, he was murdered with a large office typewriter inside the dwelling.

Nelson's background was unconventional. Raised in a working class Swedish family, he didn't speak English until the age of six. His twin brother died of spinal meningitis at the age of nine. He enlisted in the Navy and upon his honorable discharge began his professional career with *The Providence Journal* as a typist.

He rose in rank at the *Journal* to bureau chief before managing future Rhode Island Senator Claiborne Pell's campaign during his election in 1960. Pell was the surprise victor for the seat of retiring Senator Theodore Green defeating two former governors in the Democratic primary and the former Rhode Island Republican Party Chairman in the general election. Nelson would join Pell's staff afterwards to serve as his Administrative Assistant.

During his tenure, Nelson was credited with an early drafting of a federally funded college aid program, later known as The Pell Grants. He was proud of establishing Pell's office's *open door* policy and college intern programs, one of the most innovative of the era.

In 1974, Nelson abruptly resigned from Pell's team and joined the staff of the Senate Committee on Rules and Administration. He was in the midst of a turbulent transition in his life. Seemingly happily married, he had three children and a residence in suburban Bethesda, Maryland. In 1976, he announced that he was gay and moved into an apartment in downtown D.C. He remained on good terms with his wife who he never divorced and maintained contact with his children.

His lifestyle upheaval may have ultimately contributed towards his murder. Professionally he was well respected and regarded with affection by his working associates.

On the day of his death, his body was found inside his apartment amidst scattered newspapers and magazines. Prior to sealing off the investigation site, a Senate staff member was allowed entry to remove *sensitive* documents.

Police would never interview family members with him the evening before. Many observers condemned the investigation as *faulty police work*. Credible clues were never revealed.

Only the accustom eulogies and lamentations would follow accompanied by a deafening law enforcement silence. His case remains unsolved.

The Vietnam War Memorial: Enduring Power Via Simplicity
Vietnam War Memorial Site:
5 Henry Bacon Drive NW, Washington D.C.

War Memorials are generally historically imposing, complex and grandiose monuments. They frequently integrate marble, bronze, columns and statues celebrating heroics and sacrifice.

No one disputes the sacrifice the unpopular Vietnam War imposed upon the American population. Over 58,000 soldiers were killed and over 300,000 documented as wounded. There has been little to celebrate within the United States regarding the conflict. The physical and psychological casualties delved far deeper into the societal psyche than simple statistical numbers.

Over 1,400 entrants competed in the Vietnam Memorial design competition conducted by the U.S. Commission of Fine Arts. The entries were judged without accompanying submission names. Maya Lin, a 21-year-old architectural undergraduate at Yale University submitted a design that was a radical conceptual departure.

Integrated into the parkland landscape, she proposed two stark black granite walls that began inside the earth until they met above the surface. The V-shaped design points toward the Lincoln and Washington Memorials and is inscribed with the names of the dead in chronological order.

Her ambition towards contemporary design and symbolism was not greeted favorably universally. Her intention was to create a statement regarding loss and remembrance and remain apolitical.

Boisterous high-profile politicians, veterans, self-appointed critics and media commentators viciously labeled the work as an *affront*, *dishonorable* and *unacceptable*. Some unfairly cited her age and ethnicity (Chinese) as their motivations for attack.

The striking monument would be financed with $8.4 million from private sector funds and individual donations. The location allocated was three acres on the National Mall. The controversy over the design heightened uncomfortably before the 1982 unveiling. To placate the influential critics, the judging commission added a third-place entry from the design competition as a compromise nearby. Maya Lin disagreed strongly with the decision.

The compromise, Frederick Hart's *Three Soldiers* is well crafted and traditional. It receives modest attention. However, Maya Lin's classic simplicity and elegance attracts the majority of viewers. Her design has articulated to many the potential healing power of unconventional remembrance. Her vision is considered by many one of the most beautiful commemoratives of our modern era. The subtle but heart-gripping symbolism touches viewers by its sheer simplicity.

At the 1982 dedication, 57,939 servicemen names were chiseled into the wall. Since then several hundred have been added. A few war survivors would later discover that their names were erroneous etched into the original list.

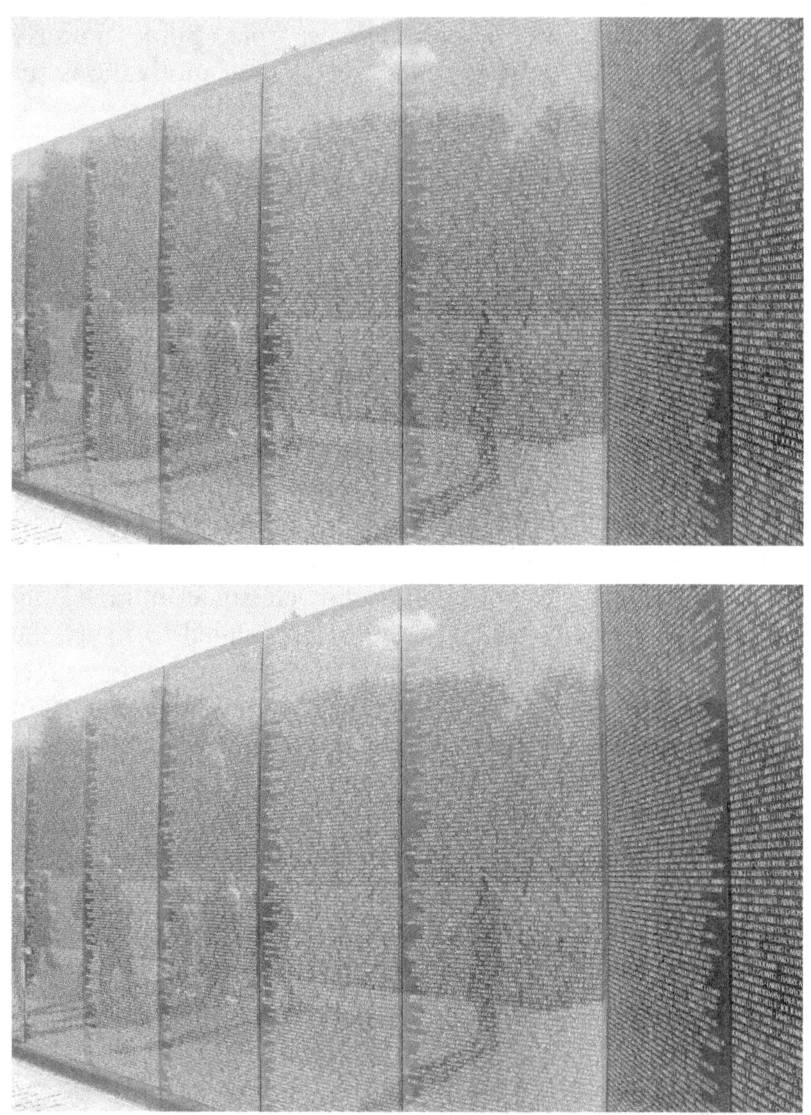

**A Synthetic Designation With Numerous Incarnations
Old Ebbitt Grill:**

675 15th Street NW, Washington D.C.

The original location of the Old Ebbitt Grill began as an unnamed restaurant on the southeastern corner of F and 14th Streets NW. The property distinguished itself as the first local hotel to remain open throughout the summer instead of closing when Congress adjourned. In 1827, the building was demolished and a replacement was constructed at the same site. Ownership would subsequently change multiple times.

In 1856, William E. Ebbitt purchased the property by then called the *Frenchman's Hotel*. He converted the building into a boarding house and bar renaming it the *Ebbitt House*. Ebbitt kept the property only seven years before selling it to his son-in-law. One year later, a fresh owner combined the Ebbitt House with an adjoining property.

The combined structures would serve as offices for the *New York Times*, *Philadelphia Inquirer*, *New York Evening Post*, and other newspapers. For several years prior to the construction of stables, a large house known as the *Bull's Head* was located at the rear of the hotel. That structure was designated as the northeastern corner of the infamous *Murder Bay* district. The *Bull's Head* lodged prostitutes and featured a gambling den.

The Ebbitt House was leveled and rebuilt in 1872 as a six-story structure with a mansard roof and stables behind. The property doubled its size and offered 300 rooms. Massive chandeliers inside led to a dining room called the *Crystal Room*. The property was considered fashionable and its lodging were patronized by politicians and high-ranking military officers.

Future U.S. President William McKinley lodged there during his congressional tenure. The bar and restaurant reportedly served Presidents Ulysses Grant, James Garfield, Andrew Jackson, Grover Cleveland, Theodore Roosevelt and Warren Harding.

By the beginning of the twentieth century, the Ebbitt House had suffered a steep decline in prestige. A fire during August 1913 did extensive damage. Three months later, city officials accused the owner of selling liquor in the bar to underage children. A jury could not reach a verdict during the December 1913 trial. The charges were not dismissed until ten months later.

The property staggered through the next six years with various scenarios debated regarding its future. The building became part of *Rum Row* during Prohibition selling illegal alcohol. The Ebbitt House was finally razed in 1926 to create a site for the National Press Club building.

The newest incarnation opened in 1926 on 1427 F Street NW. Over the next 45 years, the name *Old Ebbitt Grill* replaced the former *Ebbitt House*. Whatever luster the former property once offered steadily tarnished. The operation limped through several successive owners, many of whom found paying sales tax an unnecessary inconvenience. On June 5, 1970, the Internal Revenue Service shuttered the premises. The Grill had not paid sales tax for the previous five years.

In June 1970, co-owners of a Georgetown restaurant successfully purchased the property for the tax bill due of $11,250. Reopened on October 13, 1970, the property slowly cultivated a fresh clientele with an interior refurbishment (including a fern bar upstairs) and an enhanced menu.

Amongst this clientele during 1977 was the genesis of a Soviet Union spy ring. Vladimir Alekseyev, a Soviet reporter from the news agency TASS initiated contact with Ronald Humphrey, an American double agent. Humphrey was a United States Information Agency employee who'd already been outed as a spy for the North Vietnamese government. Facing impending charges by the FBI, Humphrey agreed to meet and cooperate with Alekseyev at the Old Ebbitt Grill in December 1976. Alekseyev was expelled from the United States two months later.

The Grill's F Street location became a redevelopment victim. The structure was razed in early December 1983. Afterwards, the presumably final version of the Old Ebbitt Grill was relocated to its present site. The interior décor was replicated to mimic the prior location.

National scandal soon accompanied the newest version in 1986. A fateful lunch meeting between Assistant Attorney General William Reynolds and Attorney General Edwin Meese revealed damaging evidence regarding the Iran-Contra Affair.

A memo written by Oliver North, a military aide to the National Security Council was brought clandestinely to the lunch by Reynolds. The note was shared with Meese. North's controversial proposal involved diverting funds from the sale of weapons to Iran to an opposition fighting group in Nicaragua called the Contras. The guerillas were attempting to overthrow the ruling socialist regime in their country.

The essential problem with the proposal was twofold. Congress had specifically banned government fundraising for the Contras. The public was likewise unaware that the United States was selling arms to a perceived enemy.

North's memo had previously been submitted to John Poindexter, then the Vice Admiral of the Navy. Poindexter later became the National Security Advisor for the Reagan administration.

The document was considered by many observers to link North's activities directly with the Reagan Administration. Reagan would publicly deny all knowledge of the Contra scheme. He miraculously escaped accountability. North, following his publicly televised testimony would become a folk hero to those who felt defying Congress was sound foreign policy.

The Old Ebbitt Grill markets their current location as D.C.'s *oldest* saloon. Despite their multiple owners, name modification and various re-locations, their claim is superficially if not disjointedly valid.

**Senator Ted Kennedy: Full Frontal Achievements and
Debauchery
La Brasserie Restaurant Site:
239 Massachusetts Avenue NE, Washington D.C.**

Throughout the political career of Senator Edward *Ted*
Kennedy, scandal and impropriety trailed every step. His
legendary bouts of excessive drinking and improper behavior
probably cost him a legitimate chance at the presidency. His
collective abuses tainted the legacy of the youngest of the
four Kennedy brothers.

His most publicized and defining indiscretion occurred on
July 18, 1969 barely a year following his brother Robert's
assassination. He drove his Oldsmobile off a bridge on the
island of Chappaquiddick nearing midnight. His passenger,
28-year-old Mary Jo Kopechne was a former staff secretary
for brother Robert.

Kennedy questionably insisted that he intended to drive
Kopechne to a ferry landing on the island before returning to
his hotel in Edgartown. He claimed that he accidentally made
a wrong turn onto a dirt road leading to a one-lane bridge. His
vehicle skidded off the bridge into Poucha Pond.

Kennedy was able to extricate himself and swim free. He
made claims that he attempted unsuccessfully to rescue
Kopechne. She drowned inside the submerged car. Kennedy's
behavior then veered towards the bizarre. He returned to an
earlier party he'd attended at Lawrence Cottage. He consulted
with a few associates as to what had transpired and returned
back to his hotel room in Edgartown and slept.

Major questions arose as to his intentions towards Kopechne
at that late hour and whether or not he was inebriated.

Kennedy would not report the accident to police until 9:50

a.m. the following morning. A diver had already recovered her body from the vehicle an hour earlier. Kennedy dictated a statement recounting the events. He agreed with the text, but did not sign the typed version.

Without any direct eyewitnesses, the facts behind the tragedy became difficult to sort out. Kennedy's handlers leaped into full damage control and he cooperated minimally with investigators.

Kennedy would be put on trial and cited for negligence and leaving the scene of an accident. The Kennedy name likely prevented him from being indicted for manslaughter and/or driving under the influence. He would be given a two month suspended sentence and one year probation. His driver's license would also be suspended for 16 months. Shortly following Kopechne's funeral, his wife would suffer her third miscarriage since their marriage.

The international scandal and resulting negative publicity prevented Kennedy from entering the presidential races in 1972 and 1976. Prior to the accident, he was the overwhelming Democratic Party favorite. He would enter the 1980 Democratic primary, but lost handily to incumbent President Jimmy Carter. His reputation could never successfully evade the *Chappaquiddick incident* and its consequences.

The magnitude of this profound calamity would have sobered up most men permanently. For Kennedy, his subsequent litany of unseemly behavior and debauchery was only beginning. His East Coast *frat boy* style of recklessness, overindulgence and arrogance became well documented. The majority of these incidents were alcohol fueled.

Two of his Washington D.C. embarrassments occurred at the *La Brasserie* restaurant. Both summarized his disregard for conventional and restrained behavior when it concerned himself. In December 1985, he introduced the *Waitress Sandwich* to colleague and drinking companion Senator Christopher Dodd. Reportedly, the pair was dining with young dates in a private room on the restaurant's first floor annex. All four became excessively drunk.

While their dates left the dining room to use the bathroom, the two men requested the co-owner of the restaurant to have a specific female server join them. Kennedy reportedly manhandled the waitress upon her entrance and playfully tossed the much lighter woman atop a table. He then positioned her upon the lap of Dodd who was sprawled in a chair. Kennedy leaned himself on top of her and grinded his genital area against hers.

The waitress would escape bruised, shaken and angry over the assault. She ran out of the room. Kennedy playfully laughed off the incident. His foursome left shortly afterwards once they'd settled the bill. During that era, the repulsive act was dismissed as another Kennedy escapade. The offended victim had no reason share any amusement. Dodd has predictably denied the event ever occurred.

Two years later at *La Brasserie*, Kennedy would attempt a pants lowered frontal assault with an obliging young congressional lobbyist. They selected their bedding space next to the restrooms, secured only by a partially closed flimsy accordion door. Their sexual encounter on the carpet followed a wine dominated lunch in a private upstairs room. A waitress accidentally interrupted their frolic. *La Brasserie* would shutter permanently in August 2005.

Despite his dizzying embarrassments, Kennedy remained oblivious to scrutiny and self-control. Age and illness eventually slowed his pace. The man who never would be president was credited professionally with an impressive legislative career. He served as a U. S. Senator representing Massachusetts for nearly 47 years. He was the second most senior member of the Senate when he died still in office at the age of 77 from brain cancer on August 25. 2009.

His hedonistic exploits would be eclipsed by his lengthy career in public service as evidenced by numerous awards and honors. His legacy of political accomplishment would elevate him into a role model. Acknowledging his example would require rose tinted glasses to view his accompanying lifestyle choices.

Oliver North Establishes His Own Rules
National Security Council Headquarters
17th Street and Pennsylvania Avenue NW, Washington D.C.

In late 1985, Lieutenant Colonel Oliver North of the National Security Council decided to unilaterally initiate an American foreign policy decision. He wished to shift funds towards a paramilitary group of anti-Sandinista rebels called the *Contras*. The Sandinistas were the reigning socialist government of Nicaragua.

The major obstacle with his objective was that Congress had prohibited any funding to the Contras. This legal blockage proved incidental to North. He would find a way.

Beginning in early 1981, Reagan administration officials had secretly been facilitating the sale of weapons to the Islamic Republic of Iran. The Ayatollah Khomeini led government was officially sanctioned by the United States with an arms embargo at this time. The arms deal was originally initiated to influence Iran to release 52 American diplomats and citizens taken as hostage on November 4, 1979 at the Tehran based American embassy.

The early sales proceeded without affecting the hostage crisis. On January 20, 1981, the hostages were released following 444 days of captivity.

Despite the strained relations with the United States government, Iran had an insatiable need for weaponry as a result of their war with neighboring Iraq. This conflict began on September 22, 1980 with a full-scale invasion into Iran by Iraqi military forces. The war would continue nearly eight years before ending in stalemate on August 20, 1988. The United States shamelessly sold arms to both warring sides until 1986. In November 1986, the weapons transactions were publicly revealed. Included in the list of munitions sold were TOW and HAWK missiles.

North seized the opportunity to divert camouflaged revenues from the Iranian arms sales to fund Contra insurgency activities. He also raised private donations for their cause. President Reagan was a strong proponent of the Contra cause. There was no linkable evidence that Reagan had authorized or was even aware of North's actions. Following a congressional investigation, North was dismissed from his position.

In 1988, North was indicted for conspiracy to defraud the government. His televised testimony during his trial the following year elevated him into a celebrity. His forceful, direct and confident demeanor impressed viewers. He insisted that Reagan approved and supported his activities. Whether his testimony was truthful is subject to speculation. He was found guilty of obstructing the U.S. Congress, destroying documents, and accepting an illegal gratuity.

He was sentenced to two years probation. In 1991, a prosecution witness claimed that his testimony had been tainted. All charges against North were dropped. Post-trial, North attempted to parlay his brief renown into political office. He ran and lost for a U.S, Senate seat in Virginia during 1994. He shifted projects into hosting a conservative radio talk show during the 1990s. He wrote and co-wrote several books. His name recognition steadily ebbed.

In 2018, he was named president of the lobbying group the National Rifle Association. Within a year, he clashed and became involved in a power struggle with their chief executive. The issue involved the organization's tax-exempt status and charges of financial improprieties. North exited his NRA position in 2019.

TWISTED TOUR GUIDES.com

A Family's Tortured Legacy Mirroring American Involvement In Vietnam
Chuong Family Residence:
5609 Western Avenue NW, Washington D.C.

Tran Van Chuong and his wife Than Thj Nam Tran led an adventurous existence of intrigue, manipulation and diplomacy before their eventual killing in 1986. Their emergence into public prominence began during the Japanese occupation of Vietnam in World War II.

Tran was a lawyer in the town of Bay Lieu during his early professional years. He married advantageously to a member of the extended Vietnamese royal family. Her father was Than Trong Hue, the country's National Education Minister. Her mother was a daughter of Emperor Dong Khanh. The couple lived in affluence attended by a staff of two dozen servants.

Japanese military forces entered Vietnam in September 1940 and stayed until August 1945. French colonial administrators under the Vichy government remained in charge for the majority of that period. Than Tran-Chuong was distinguished for her beauty and cunning. She would be accused by the French secret police of judiciously sleeping with Japanese officials to further her husband's advancement within the occupation government. The French labeled her the *Pearl of the Orient* for her sensuality, stealth and raw ambition.

Tran Van Chuong became the first Foreign Secretary under the temporal Empire of Vietnam regime. During the final two years of World War II, the Japanese ruthlessly administered the country. Their indifference towards the people resulted in a massive squandering of resources and severe famine reportedly killing over 2 million.

During this bleak period, communist rebels led by Ho Chi Minh mobilized and maneuvered to build support for their cause of an independent nation. They assisted starving individuals with food, gave farmers seeds for replanting while soliciting recruits. Upon the Japanese surrender in 1945, the original French occupiers presumed that they would simply re-govern their former colony. They were mistaken.

Vietnam became unified in their goal of establishing national independence and expelling the French presence. The struggle for later political control ultimately evolved into a confrontation of political philosophy. To clearly understand the independence movement involves wading through a succession of failed treaties, divided loyalties and commitment miscalculations on warring sides.

Simplified, Hanoi would become the communist center with allegiance to the People's Republic of China in the north. Saigon remained the more westernized society in the south supported by the United States via millions of dollars in assistance. The clouded reality became far from simplified.

During the French Indochina War between 1946-1954, the Chuongs took flight from the communist guerrilla fighters. The family was smuggled safely into Saigon by a Catholic organization. The couple was disguised as a monk and peasant woman.

Tran Van Chuong would eventually resurface through family connections as South Vietnam's ambassador to the United States and an observer at the United Nations during the early 1960s. He would resign his position in protest during 1963, denouncing his government's anti-Buddhist policies and ensuing massacres between May and November.

The Chuong's had a son and three daughters. Their second daughter, Le Xuan, became the wife of Ngo Dinh Nhu, the brother of South Vietnam's first President Ngo Dinh Diem. His reign would endure eight years but was perceived as corrupt. President John Kennedy had lost confidence in Diem's capacity to lead the country and conduct the war effort against his communist adversaries in the north. The United States military was already deeply invested in the conflict. President Eisenhower had initially allocated millions of dollars in aid and Kennedy had begun sending military advisors.

On November 1, 1963, South Vietnamese military generals launched a takeover of the country with purported assistance from the CIA. Diem and his brother Nhu initially escaped, but were apprehended the next day and executed on orders by Duong Van Minh. Their bodies were discovered mangled in the back of an armored car. Nhu's wife Le Xuan was traveling through Beverly Hills at the time of the coup d'etat purportedly peddling her memoirs.

Le Xuan would cultivate her own legacy as a calculating and ruthless enchantress like her mother. John and Jackie Kennedy despised her. She was profiled in numerous major media outlets as the infamous *Madame Nhu*, employing her beauty and adroitness for her own raw ambitious advancement. Observers considered her the *most detested* woman in Saigon for her arrogance and illicit intrigues.

Upon the death of her husband and brother-in-law, she would abruptly recede from prominence. She skipped out of the Beverly Wilshire Hotel leaving her bill partially unpaid. She hid out briefly in Paris. When the new South Vietnamese government requested her extradition back to Saigon to face justice, she fled to Rome. She was reunited with her four children, but tragedy would ultimately accompany. In 1967, her oldest daughter died in a car crash in Longjumeau, France. Her youngest daughter, an IT sector lawyer would be killed on April 16, 2012 in a traffic accident on her way to work in Rome.

The coup against Diem would alter the level of American participation in the war. The instigator of the change, Duong Van Minh would become South Vietnam's next president. John Kennedy would be assassinated 20 days later. Historical observers are divided on what would have been Kennedy's subsequent strategy in Vietnam.

Under his successor President Lyndon Johnson, American military presence escalated substantially. That decision would trigger catastrophic consequences.

Tran Van Chuong's resignation as ambassador and allegiances to Diem darkened his future in Vietnam. The couple remained in their Washington D.C. duplex. The relationship with their daughter became estranged.

Their only son, Tran Van Khiem was formerly a press officer for Diem. He was stranded and imprisoned in Saigon following the presidential coup. He endured years of imprisonment emerging with a damaged body and mind. The Chuong's would pay dearly for their abandonment of him.

On July 24, 1986, he would exact revenge upon his elderly parents by strangling both to death at their home. He was declared unfit for trial and sent to the St. Elizabeth Hospital. Seven years later, he would be released and deported to France where he had a child named Pierre living in Paris. His sister, Le Xuan would die in exile in Rome at the age of 86 on April 24, 2011. She was working on her long delayed memoirs that would finally be published by L'Harmattan in October 2013.

Denial And Unaccountability Thwart A Presidential Front Runner
Gary Hart's Former Residence:
517 6th Street SE, Washington D.C.

Gary Hart had been tagged as a womanizer and serial philanderer since managing Senator George McGovern's 1972 presidential campaign. He had been married to Lee Ludwig since 1958, but reportedly never allowed an obstacle such as a marriage vow to impede temporal hedonism.

Following McGovern's defeat against incumbent Richard Nixon, Hart planned his own political trajectory. He defeated incumbent Republican Senator Peter Dominick in Colorado's 1974 U. S. Senate election. During his first term, he served on the committee investigating the Three Mile Island accident. He was narrowly re-elected in 1980 and distinguished himself by sponsoring the Semiconductor Chip Protection Act of 1984.

That same year, he narrowly lost the Democratic presidential nomination to former Vice President Walter Mondale. Incumbent President Ronald Reagan easily defeated Mondale. Hart decided not to seek re-election to the Senate in 1986. He spent the next year planning his presidential run.

His timing seemed perfect and he had the backing of the party's leadership. He had positioned himself to represent a fresh vision for the Democratic Party in the upcoming 1988 election. Articulate, aligned with tech interests and in his early-fifties, Hart represented a potential agent of progressive change. He was widely considered the frontrunner for the democratic nomination once New York Governor Mario Cuomo indicated that he would not enter the race in February 1987.

Hart's rumored past indiscretions were in close pursuit to destroy his reputation. He officially announced his candidacy on April 13, 1987. He couldn't restrain himself from quickly sabotaging his campaign.

Upon his declaration, the media covering his campaign honed in quickly towards their familiar issue. Interrogations regarding prior claims of womanizing overshadowed questions regarding policy positions, campaign strategy or prominent issue topics. Hart was became fatigued by the incessant inquiries and made an unwise and fatal challenge.

He encouraged the media pack to follow him. He stressed that they would observe only his uneventful social existence. One newspaper, the *Miami Herald* would cash in on his offer.

During the last week of April, the executive editor of the *Herald* was contacted by phone from an anonymous caller. She claimed that she had proof that Hart was having an affair with her Miami based roommate. The caller claimed to have this proof via photographs and phone records substantiating their intimate time together. Her friend was an attractive blond named Donna Rice.

The caller stressed that Rice was flying up to Washington D.C. that Friday evening to spend the weekend together with Hart in his townhouse. Generally amidst a presidential campaign, the likelihood of a candidate's available free weekend would be improbable. His planned campaign stop to Kentucky that weekend had been cancelled. There was no published replacement venue. The editor instinctively sensed that the information was genuine. He assigned an investigative reporter to cover the lead.

On Friday, May 1st, the reporter caught a 5:30 p.m. flight to Washington D.C. Ironically Rice was also aboard. Upon arrival, he drove to Hart's known address and staked out the property. Hart's front door opened at 9:30 p.m. with he and Rice emerging outside together. She would spend the evening overnight inside.

The *Herald* editor and a staff photographer flew to D.C. early the next morning to confirm the sighting. That evening the threesome viewed Hart and Rice exit via the townhouse back entrance. The couple strolled to over Hart's car parked nearby. Soon after, they returned through the front entrance. The editor sensed that Hart appeared agitated, potentially aware that he was being followed. When he returned outside via the back entrance, the *Herald* trio approached and confronted him about his relationship with Rice.

Hart knew instinctively that he'd been caught overstepping an indulgence. He denied being involved in any relationship and alleged that he'd been set up. He claimed that Rice was simply working as a campaign aide. His practiced excuse had evaded disclosure previously. The stakes were far greater. He was now a serious presidential candidate and internationally known personality.

Donna Rice would soon be outed as his mistress. She'd met him at a New Years Eve party in Colorado. She'd later accompanied him on an overnight sailing aboard an 83-foot luxury yacht called the *Monkey Business*. A damning photograph of her sitting on Hart's lap soon appeared first in the *National Enquirer* tabloid and then hundreds of newspapers. She was grinning broadly and he was wearing a white T-shirt with the forever damning imprinted *Monkey Business Crew*.

The story appeared in the Sunday, May 3rd *Herald* edition. The accompanying media tsunami overwhelmed any potential evasive or damage control. Other unflattering reports surfaced regarding his 1984 unpaid presidential campaign debts and suspected past dalliances.

Both Hart and Rice continued to deny vehemently any impropriety. Their denials were unconvincing. Polls were taken nationally regarding Hart's truthfulness and to determine if Americans were legitimately concerned regarding a candidate's sex life.

Hart determined to take a self-orchestrated high road and avert disclosure. Unfortunately that pathway was crumbling into oblivion beneath his feet. He endured the media barrage and dissection of his character for a single week.

He claimed to be *bent but not broken* from the invasive media coverage. He blamed the controversy on numerous sources except his own actions, stupidity and arrogance. He suspended his presidential campaign.

Immediately after, he rented a cottage in Oughterard, Ireland to reportedly spend time with his son. He maintained contact with key members of his presidential campaign team. His campaign manager, Congresswoman Patricia Schroeder, took the opportunity upon his withdrawal to enter the presidential race. Indifference towards her entrance and insufficient fundraising prompted her own withdrawal four months later.

Hart's isolation in Ireland convinced him that suspending his campaign was premature. Perhaps he'd reasoned that American voters really didn't care about a candidate's sexual history. President John Kennedy's numerous affairs by then had been widely exposed and his legacy remained intact and generally positive.

In December 1987, Hart returned to the presidential race with modest fanfare. He declared on the steps of the New Hampshire Statehouse: *Let's let the people decide!*

They did. Unfortunately, he polled poorly in the New Hampshire primary earning only 4% of the vote. He withdrew his candidacy for a second and final time. Massachusetts Governor Michael Dukakis swept the Democratic nomination. Vice-President George H. W. Bush then annihilated Dukakis in the 1988 general election. Dukakis won only ten states.

Hart had completed misread the public reaction towards his infidelity. Most American's *did* care about a candidate's marital fidelity as future President Bill Clinton would experience, Clinton eventually acknowledged his deception and asked public forgiveness.

Hart's deception worsened more profoundly and evolved into a perception regarding his character. He could not bring himself to acknowledge or show minimal remorse towards his act of adultery or any of the women he had maligned previously.

His continued denials despite overwhelming evidence made any future pronouncement suspect. Could this individual be trusted to lead the nation? This question would be repeated frequently with subsequent administrations.

Following his second withdrawal, Hart resumed his law practice. His continuing ambition remained to rehabilitate his reputation and become relevant once again in political affairs. He gave numerous speeches, became involved with various commissions and wrote several published texts regarding upgrading national security.

He mused publicly over the idea of resurrecting another presidential run during late 2002. He had still not entirely comprehended the basis for his previous rejection. His political train had already passed the station. There remained only a nonexistent level of support for a President Gary Hart.

In October 2014, President Barrack Obama and longtime friend Secretary of State John Kerry tossed him a ceremonial bone. He was named the United States Special Envoy for Northern Ireland. The position has become extinct. It has remained vacant following the resignation of Mick Mulvaney in January 2021.

Donna Rice took a voluntary professional leave of absence following the avalanche of publicity accompanying the scandal. She resigned from her marketing position with a pharmaceutical company. There would exist no *normal* to return to.

She modeled in commercials and advertisements for *No Excuses* jeans, turning down more lucrative exploitive offers. She reportedly *reconnected* with her Christian faith and disappeared from public exposure for several years. She married in 1994 and became affiliated with an organization called *Enough is Enough* advocating Internet safety. There was no public indication whether Gary Hart ever apologized to her for his weekend invitation in 1987 or her resulting compromised privacy and notoriety.

TWISTED TOUR GUIDES.COM

The Largest Drug Cartel and Subsequent Bust
Reputed Drug Operation Headquarters:
407 M Street NE, Washington D.C.

Partners Rayful Edmonds III, 24, and Tony Lewis, 26, orchestrated an extensive and sophisticated drug cartel during the 1980s. Their criminal operation thrived amidst D.C.'s flagrant drug epidemic. They controlled reportedly half of the cocaine, heroin and PCP trade both as retailers and suppliers. They purchased their primary inventory from rival Los Angeles based Crips and Bloods gangs who had direct supply lines based in Colombia. Their cashflow became staggering, their network sprawled throughout the region and their territorial competition rivalries were lethal.

Mayor Marion Barry vehemently denied that major gangs operated within the boundaries of D.C. Given his own dependence and addiction, Barry was far too compromised to offer moral leadership. He senselessly denounced a *Washington Post* article tracking more than 30 homicides attributed to turf war rivalries between Edmonds' gang and competitors. The value of human life had plummeted to a fresh depth.

By 1985, Edmonds' well-insulated family base and operation had attracted the intense scrutiny of the Drug Enforcement Administration, FBI and D. C. Metropolitan Police. The three entities cooperated on a joint two-year investigation designed to permanently eliminate the cartel.

Sunday, April 16, 1989 was the projected date for the principal drug bust designed to culminate the investigation. The preparatory work involved intimate wiretapping, cultivating informers and isolating the cartel's primary operators. The clandestine opportunity nearly evaporated due to internal information leaks.

Their element of surprise appeared lost, so law enforcement authorities forwarded their apprehension efforts to Saturday, April 15 in the early evening. They arrested Tony Lewis at his home in Arlington, Virginia and captured Edmonds III at his girlfriend's house inside the 900 block of Jefferson Street NW.

Arresting officers spread out to an additional dozen addresses within D.C., Maryland and Virginia. A prime location included Edmonds' grandmother's house in the NOMA district, considered to be the operational headquarters.

Amidst the chaotic arrests, many suspects had vanished. Television crews followed several of the apprehension teams. Some of the suspects were caught attempting to transfer assets to other locations and modify their names to other associates on their bank accounts, assets and vehicle registrations. Nine of Edmond's relatives were taken into custody.

Edmonds' trial that included ten associates would be held at the Quantico Marine Corps base and last 56 days. Unprecedented security was employed for jurors for fear of retaliation by Edmonds' remaining network. Both Edmonds and Lewis were sentenced to life imprisonment without the opportunity for parole. Upon the decision being announced, Edmonds maintained his innocence publicly claiming authorities were looking for someone to blame for the drug problems on the D. C. Streets.

Edmonds played the race card following his trial in an unconventional manner. All twelve of his jurors were black. He claimed that if the jury had been racially integrated, he would have received a fairer verdict. He was quoted: *I'm not racist, but white people would have taken their time. They would have gone by the law.*

By 2022, Edmonds and Lewis had remained incarcerated for 33 years. Both men would exhibit multiple proclamations of their remorse towards the damages they were responsible for. The magnitude had finally occurred to them. Would acknowledgement be acceptable enough?

Life in prison without the possibility of parole as a jail sentence has come under renewed scrutiny nationally. In February 2021, U.S. District Judge Emmet G. Sullivan reduced Edmonds' sentence to 20 years, citing Edmonds' nearly two decades of cooperation with prosecutors in other drug and homicide cases in D.C. and other parts of the country. His additional pending 30-year prison sentence in Pennsylvania has clouded any early release scenarios.

Lewis remains incarcerated in a federal prison in Cumberland, Maryland. His son, Tony Lewis Jr. has coordinated rallies and protest initiatives targeted towards President Joe Biden to release his father.

For their victims and their peers and relations, the release of either Edmonds or Lewis would be incomprehensible. Their eventual liberation would be interpreted as an affront to justice. The mechanisms of the judicial appeal system continue to debate the pair's ultimate merit for release. Their cumulative victims live daily with the consequences and carnage from an earlier era that the pair contributed towards significantly.

Washington D.C.'s Reputed Mayor For Many Lifetimes
Crack Cocaine Arrest Site:
Westin Hotel: 1400 M Street NW, Room #727
(Formerly Vista International Hotel)

Marion Barry lived through several lifetimes of political change during the final quarter of the 20th century. He is most remembered for being filmed in January 1990 lighting a crack cocaine pipe inside a Vista International Hotel room. This instance of indiscretion and humiliation obscured a lifetime of legitimate achievement in politics and civil rights activism.

Barry was born in Mississippi in 1936 and reportedly picked cotton as a child during his harsh formative years. During the 1960s, he earned a master's degree in chemistry at Fisk University. While pursuing his studies, his involvement with social reform commenced. He reportedly was a participant with the Freedom Riders, a neighborhood organizer and chairman of the Student Non-Violent Coordinating Committee. He was arrested on several occasions for participating in protest sit-ins.

He would never employ his university degree. Instead, he relocated to Washington D.C. in 1965 to start a Non-Violent Coordinating Committee chapter. He gravitated towards local politics, ultimately his consuming passion. He ran for a school board position and then the D.C. city council. In 1977, a Hanafi Muslim group member shot him just above his heart during a two-day siege of a District office building.

He survived the superficial wound. He considered himself ready to attain his higher ambition. The following year, he ran for mayor.

Barry's support then was multi-racial. Supporters viewed him as a progressive and positive force. He won the mayoral election and two subsequent terms. Observers credited him with installing programs providing summer youth jobs, home-buying assistance and placing thousands of black employees in upper level city jobs, once exclusively for white applicants.

Barry cultivated an image of charisma and outspokenness. Behind his charm were widening schisms. By his third term, his life was in chaos and spiraling out of control. His marriage was failing, his late night partying proliferating and his drug and alcohol abuse worsening.

In the fall of 1989, Barry was arrested on a misdemeanor drug charge after being accused of using cocaine while staying at the Mayflower Hotel. The most volatile charge was soon to follow.

On January 18, 1990, he strolled willingly into an FBI drug sting. Barry and supporters have suggested that he was being targeted for his high-profile status and progressive racial agenda. Others observed that his fall was merely inevitable.

An FBI informant, Rasheeda Moore had a previous relationship with Barry and according to his memoirs hounded him to meet her at the Vista Hotel lobby. Moore was a teacher and former model in her 30s. According to Barry, she was a heavy cocaine addict and he simply a casual user. Their initial break-up occurred when he caught her smoking crack cocaine in their room at the Grand Hyatt Hotel during an AIDS fundraiser. He smashed her pipe and attempted to flush five crack rocks down the toilet. Following this confrontation, he avoided her for months afterwards.

Barry claimed that the FBI staged hotel room #727 with hidden cameras and supplied drugs. They used a threat of imprisonment for a prior bench warrant as the means for securing her involvement. According to Barry, the FBI scripted her conversation and even babysat her children during their reunion.

Barry obediently followed her upstairs anticipating sex. When she encouraged him to share a crack pipe, he complied. He was immediately detained and arrested once he lit and began inhaling the contents. Video footage of his participation was leaked and distributed globally. He was charged with 11 counts of cocaine possession and three counts of perjury.

His subsequent trial before a multi-racial jury became hung on the majority of charges. Several of the jurors concluded that he'd been unethically set-up. He was convicted of only a misdemeanor count of drug possession. He would not be retried on the charges.

Barry would serve only six months in prison casting himself as a *political prisoner*. The irony behind the timing of his arrest was that Washington D.C. was suffering in the midst of a destructive crack cocaine epidemic.

Upon his release, many residents considered him a hero and martyr. In 1992, he won election as a Ward 8 councilman. Two years later, he was re-elected mayor. His shocking comeback became a national comic punchline and not universally applauded. Congress stripped Barry of much of his mayoral control. He declined to seek a fifth term that he certainly would have won. Anthony Williams became his successor.

His redemptive road would continue with several bumps en route. Barry would be arrested in 2002 when traces of marijuana and cocaine were found in his car when he was stopped in the Buzzard Point neighborhood in Southwest D.C. No charges were filed and Barry maintained the drugs had been planted.

In 2005, he was put on probation for not filing or paying income tax for several years. The following year he would be detained by police for driving too slowly. On the evening of July 4, 2009, U.S. Park Police at Anacostia Park arrested him and charged him with stalking a woman.

Barry missed the attention and adulation he received from politics. In November 2004, he ran for the Ward 8 city council seat and won with 96% of the vote. He continued in that position until his death at 78 on November 22, 2014. Leading up to his final collapse, he had struggled with diabetes, a blood infection, prostrate cancer and had a liver transplant in 2009.

Marion Barry's life mirrored the comedy and pathos of a contemporary tragedy. Many of his accomplishments have been diminished. Yet his legacy will permanently be the first name associated with the office of Mayor of Washington D.C.

Marion Barry, Jr.
(1936 - 2014)
"Mayor for Life"

BARRY
MARION
MARION
CHRISTOPHER
MARION BARRY CHANGED AMERICA
WITH HIS UNMITIGATED GALL TO STAND
UP IN THE ASHES OF WHERE HE HAD FALLEN
AND CAME BACK TO WIN.
- MAYA ANGELOU - 1995

**Scientist, President, Obscene Phone Caller
American University:
4400 Massachusetts Avenue, Washington D.C.**

In 1990, Robert E. Berendzen was a respected astronomer, professor and President for ten years at American University. During the first quarter of that year, he felt a compulsion to make indecent phone calls to households within the Fairfax area.

One of his calls was directed to the home of a Fairfax police officer on March 28. His wife answered. Berendzen discussed engaging in group sex and various other personal sexual fantasies. That same evening, he made three calls to her and the following day ten. She operated a day care center during the daytime hours. Each nuisance call varied in length from twenty minutes to an hour.

Several of his calls had no reference to sex. He identified himself as a real estate agent and that his wife as a psychologist. Despite the upsetting nature of the contact, he could usually converse rationally. He would then abruptly veer into vulgar language and begin boasting about having sex with his young son and daughter. Berendzen was indeed married, but his two grown daughters had already left the household.

The length and frequency of the calls made tracing relatively easy. Each call originated from Berendzen's office at American University. He was promptly arrested and a trial date was scheduled for June 28th.

The trial was moved up an entire month at the request of Berendzen's attorney. On May 23, Berendzen waded through a curious courthouse audience eager to witness firsthand this odd perpetrator sit in the defendant's chair.

While under the effects of an earlier induced truth serum, Berendzen described how he had suffered emotional, physical and sexual abuse as a child living in Dallas, Texas. Reportedly, he suppressed the effects of an abusing adult woman close to him until 1988. That year he visited his childhood home to attend his father's funeral.

The trial lasted ten minutes. Berendzen pled guilty to misdemeanor counts of making indecent calls. His jail time was waved on the condition that he continued to receive psychiatric treatment.

The sheriff deputy assigned to escort Berendzen out of the chambers described the courtroom atmosphere as *chaos*. Spectators and the press were unruly. According to the deputy: *We had the press out front, a bag lady in the cafeteria eating everybody's lunch and breakfast, and the whole criminal docket in one courtroom. The best thing to do was get him out of here.*

Following the courtroom bedlam. Berendzen resigned as president of American University. The victimized police officer and his wife filed an $11 million lawsuit against Berendzen and the university. The case was resolved with a financial settlement. Once the settlement was publicly announced, more than two dozen daycare providers in the region reported to police that they had also received similar obscene phone calls.

Two years later, Berendzen would return to American University as a full-time professor. He remained there until his retirement in August 2006. He continued work with numerous astronomical organizations, consulted with NASA and coordinated several major international conferences based on his expertise.

A Story That Sprouted No Legs
Chevy Chase Elementary School:
4015 Rosemary Street, Chevy Chase, MD

Massachusetts Congressman Barney Frank became one of the first openly gay elected officials when he publicly acknowledged his sexual orientation in 1987. His admission was not voluntary. His name had surfaced in a scandal involving a male prostitute, Steve Gobie whom he had housed and hired with personal funds as an aide, housekeeper and driver. Frank had originally met Gobie two years previously on April Fools Day to procure sexual services.

Gobie parlayed the use of Frank's Capitol Hill apartment to operate an escort service. He also maintained a relationship with Gabriel Massaro, the principal of Chevy Chase Elementary School. He used a guidance counselor's office after hours to ply his trade.

The consequences of Gobie's disclosed indiscretions far underachieved his expectations. Gobie indicated that Frank was aware of his operation. Massaro claimed that he resigned from his position before being fired. The anticipated bidding war Gobie anticipated for *his* story never materialized. He ended up providing his version free to the *Washington Times* in the hopes of securing a book contract and earning massive royalties. The envisioned book project never happened. Gobie abruptly disappeared from public view offering nothing substantial to extend his narrative.

The House of Representatives formally reprimanded Barney Frank on July 26, 1990 *for improperly using his office to help a male prostitute*. He had little difficulty winning re-election to a sixth term that November. He remained in office until January 2013 choosing not to seek re-election the year before. Democrat Joe Kennedy III succeeded him. Frank published his own autobiography in 2015.

A Serial Killer With A Varied Murder Base, Washington D.C.
Second Shooting Victim: 1400 Block Oak Street NW, Washington D.C.
Jack Bryant Murder: Safeway Barbershop, 3400 Block of 11th Street NW, Washington D.C.

Elizabeth Hutson Murder: 19th Street and Park Road NW, , Washington D.C.
James Swann's Apprehension: 939 Florida Avenue NW, Washington D.C.

James Swann, Jr. became known as *The Shotgun Stalker* trawling the streets of Washington D.C. during 1993. His random drive-by shootings terrorized residents and walkers within the Mount Pleasant and Columbia Height neighborhoods.

Most of his attacks followed an identical pattern. Swann would slow his car down next to an isolated victim and fire a 20-gauge shotgun at them before driving away. The shootings were generally conducted during the evening hours. He would kill four and wound five before his apprehension.

Swann was born in 1964, but exhibited signs of mental illness during his early years. He later refused professional help and lived with his sister in New Jersey, working periodically as a security guard. His sister evicted him and he lost his job at a drugstore when he continuously walked backwards during his shift.

He began splitting his time between New Jersey, New York and Philadelphia. His schizophrenia worsened. He claimed to hear voices within his head prompting him to kill. The most prominent voice he claimed was Malcolm X, who urged him to concentrate his targets within northwest D. C.

For eight weeks beginning on February 23' 1993, Swann terrorized the city. Police initially had difficulty tracking his patterns or motivation. His first target was in high-crime district Columbia Heights. His shot missed. Fifteen minutes later, Swann wounded a man severely in the face partially blinding him within the same neighborhood,

Three days later, he walked inside the Safeway barbershop on 11th Street wearing a concealing mask. He blasted Jack Bryant to death as he sat in a barber chair. He then wounded another 68-year-old man with a second shot. Police originally arrested a 31-year-old man for the shooting after two witnesses identified him. The unreliability of the witnesses and ballistics tests cleared the suspect.

Throughout the first series of shootings, investigators classified each as drug or gang related. On March 4th, the distinctive 6' 4" Swann continued his spree by wounding a 43-year-old man.

He then abruptly shifted his firing location. His next target would be Hope Hallock, 23, who he wounded on March 17th in the Mount Pleasant district. This neighborhood was wealthier and had a significantly lower crime rate than Columbia Heights. Five days later, he murdered Elizabeth *Bessie* Hutson walking her dogs between 19th Street and Park Road.

Police finally realized that they were dealing with a serial killer targeting random victims. On April 4th, Swann returned to Columbia Heights shooting at and missing a woman walking alone. Less than a week later he wounded two individuals and killed a 35-year-old man.

On April 19th, Swann made his final killing and a critical slip-up. He first missed several targets while cruising inside his small blue Toyota. He then shot and killed Nello Hughes, 61. Swann was fleeing the crime scene when he sped through a red light. He was sighted by off-duty police officer Kenneth Stewart.

Stewart tailed Swann to Florida Avenue where he caught up with him in a parking lot. Swann attempted to elude Stewart on foot. He was caught and arrested. His shotgun was recovered in the back seat of his vehicle.

Investigators and forensic psychologist attempted to comprehend Swann's behavior. Following most of his shootings, he commuted to Harlem, stopping for food and then hiring a prostitute.

At his hearing, Swann would be tried on four counts of murder and ten counts of attempted murder. On September 27, 1994, he would be found *not guilty by reason of mental defect*. He would be confined at St. Elizabeth Hospital.

Swann's hospital internment has raised the question regarding his actual state of mental instability. He reportedly has boasted about his killing spree to fellow inmates. One of the strangest observations about him was a t-shirt that he enjoyed wearing imprinted with *THRILL TO KILL*. His father gifted the disturbing garment to him.

Swann has been denied numerous furlough requests. His visits were intended to be under his father's supervision. He reportedly still suffers from hallucinations. He is housed where he should remain permanently.

**The Final Breaking Point Of An Arkansas Lawyer
Vincent Foster Suicide Location:
Fort Marcy Park, 700 George Washington Memorial
Parkway, McLean VA**

Vincent Foster had constructed a credible professional reputation within the Arkansas legal establishment. When his boyhood friend Bill Clinton was elected President in the 1992 election, he welcomed the opportunity to assist him during his transition period before assuming office.

Foster learned abruptly and painfully that the rigors and pressures of Washington D.C. were far more invasive and destructive than Little Rock, Arkansas. During the transition period when Foster was vetting a number of top appointees, he began complaining to his personal physician over feelings of depression and anxiety. He experienced panic attacks that had the effect of gutting his soul.

There was no one able or capable of consoling or shielding him once the intense media and political attacks began. The Clinton administration transition faced early snafus including an Attorney General nominee that had failed to pay taxes for nanny services. Shortly following, a financial impropriety scandal tainted the White House travel office. *Travelgate* resulted in seven firings, negative press and the threat of a Congressional investigation.

Foster shouldered the blame, but likely prematurely. The *Travelgate* storm had been blown enormously out of proportion. It withered into insignificance. The escalating fears that Foster internalized convinced him that his own professional reputation was near ruin. Returning back to a legal practice in Arkansas had ceased to become a legitimate alternative.

Foster, like many who have suffered the debilitating effects of depression, could not envision simply waiting out the imminent crisis. His concerned sister arranged for him to speak with a psychiatrist and also suggested two additional confidential practitioners. His fear towards compromising his security clearance tempered his follow-up. He telephoned one contact, but hung up when he only got an answering machine.

Politics is a dangerous arena for the emotionally vulnerable. Character assassination is bloodsport. Media commentators and rival political partisans sniff weakness and often attack without discretion. Foster couldn't shake his obsession over the damage of a potential Congressional inquiry. He spent the weekend of July 17-18, 1993 accompanying his sister to the Maryland shore for rest and recuperation.

On Monday, July 19th, no one realized that he was formulating a personal exit strategy. He spent the day reportedly in his office with the door closed wrapping up legal and family matters, his father's estate details and sending out thank-you notes.

The next morning should have brightened his perspective. Supreme Court nominee Ruth Bader Ginsburg and FBI head Louis J. Freeh were breezing through their confirmation hearings, certain to be appointed. He no longer cared judging by his response of the news to a colleague.

He ate his lunch alone on the couch of his office. Around 1:00 p.m., he picked up his suit coat and strolled to his car. He informed his office staff that he'd be returning, but didn't carry his briefcase with him. He folded his suit jacket neatly on the front passenger seat and drove out to Fort Marcy Park. There were no eyewitnesses to his activities. Did he hesitate over this next act?

Fort Marcy Park was a Civil War fortress constructed to protect the Chain Bridge approach to Washington D.C. Foster mounted a diminutive trail to arrive at a cannon near a grouping of park benches. He likely reflected before lifting an old revolver into his mouth. He fired once. His body would be discovered at approximately 5:30 p.m. resting on a hillside slope near the canon.

His personality collapse was rumored, but his abrupt, isolated and unforeseen death suggested the possibility of murder. An exhaustive inquiry involving 125 witnesses, DNA tests, physicians, lawyers and FBI agents followed. Their findings confirmed that his actions constituted a legitimate suicide.

His death would become another scandal attached to the Clinton administration only six months old.

Suicide proved insufficient and counterproductive for conspiracy theorists and presidential critics. With his death, Foster became fingered as *the man who knew too much*. He was maliciously linked with a succession of accusations including the Whitewater scandal, a romance with Hillary Clinton and a litany of constructed insider abuses. None would later be substantiated nor proven.

Vincent Foster opted by his self-destruction to cease the personal attacks and character assassination levied against him. The depth of his desperation would be acknowledged posthumously, but not to the satisfaction of Clinton detractors. He would not become the last tragic casualty on the grounds of Fort Marcy.

On January 25, 2022, Kevin Ward, the mayor of Hyattsville, Maryland killed himself with a self-inflicted gunshot wound. Political life on any level is capable of darkening the perspective of the soul.

Fort
Marcy
1861-1865

The Spy Trapped By The End of the Soviet Union
Ames Couple Residence:
2512 North Randolph Street, Arlington, VA
CIA Headquarters:
1000 Colonial Farm Road, Langley, VA

The 1989 fall of the Berlin Wall and subsequent dissolution of the Soviet Union was the worst thing that had ever happened to Aldrich Ames. He was a 31-year veteran of the Central Intelligence Agency (CIA), but infamously became known as spying for the Russians since 1985.

Ames was a CIA case officer whose initial assignment had been in Ankara, Turkey. He also had worked in New York City and Mexico City. In April 1985, he was assigned to the CIA's Soviet and Eastern Union Division at CIA Headquarters in Langley, Virginia. He spoke Russian and specialized in Russian intelligence services. That same year he married his deputy, Maria del Rosario Casas. Two years earlier he had divorced his first wife.

The new position became a lucrative opportunity for Ames that he promptly exploited. He voluntary sought out KGB officers at the Soviet Union Embassy in Washington D.C. His *ideal* job placement earned him a comfortable salary of $50,000. He yearned for more.

During the summer of 1985, Ames met frequently with a Soviet diplomat passing on confidential information about CIA and FBO contacts. Amongst his most valued information was identifying technical operations targeting the Soviet Union. Several of the Russian operatives that Ames had identified were subsequently arrested and reportedly executed.

Ames' motivation for betraying secrets was not ideology. He was compensated handsomely and continued his activities even following the collapse of the Soviet Union. He was reportedly paid $1.88 million during the first four years of his spying activities.

Ames' newfound wealth raised attention within the CIA. A ten-month investigation was begun in May 1993. The monitoring included intensive physical and electronic surveillance of his activities. Ames was unaware that he was under microscopic observation. He had planned to meet with his Russian handler in Bogotá, Columbia followed by a planned visit to Moscow.

Fearing Ames might abruptly disappear within Russia, Ames was arrested along with his wife on February 21, 1994. He protested his innocence, but at his trial he pled guilty to spying for the Soviet Union and subsequently the Russian Federation. Ames admitted that his information had compromised virtually every Soviet agent within the CIA. Officials indicated that over 100 intelligence operators had been identified and at least ten executed.

The remorseless Ames confessed that he never feared being caught by the FBI or CIA. Instead, he feared Soviet defectors who might finger him. His plea bargain deal spared him the death penalty. He was sentenced to life imprisonment without the possibility of parole. He was ordered to forfeit his entire assets. His wife received a modest five-year prison sentence for tax evasion and conspiracy to commit espionage.

The CIA was roundly criticized for not monitoring Ames' activities sooner. CIA Director James Woolsey refused to dismiss or demote any of Ames' peers or supervisors. Woolsey irrationally bargained on the furor subsiding. His gamble failed and he later resigned under pressure.

Ames remains incarcerated, rotting away and forgotten within the Federal Correctional Institution in Terre Haute.

TWISTED TOUR GUIDES.com

**Dick Morris: The Fall Of A Man Of Former Importance
Extramarital Affair Location:
Jefferson Hotel**

1200 16th Street NW, Suite 205, Washington D.C.

In August 1996, Dick Morris was on the cusp of reaping personal glory by being the subject of an impending *Time* magazine article. The feature story credited Morris' advice and strategy for the resurgence of President Bill Clinton's reputation.

Morris' elevated status followed a 1994 mid-term election debacle where the Democratic Party had lost majority control of both the Senate and House of Representatives. Morris had engineered an image resurrection and was considered Clinton's closest advisor.

Morris and his wife Eileen had arrived into Chicago to bask in the accolades promised by the Democratic National convention. The United Center basketball stadium would host the event. The Morris couple would be prominently seated and feted amidst the VIP section.

Clinton appeared certain to defeat two weak opponents in the upcoming November election. They included former Senate Majority Leader Republican Bob Dole and Reform Party nominee Ross Perot.

Dick Morris was credited with successfully arranging Clinton's reputation back in order. His own universe would soon dissipate into disgrace. He and his wife were staying in a luxury suite at the Sheraton Hotel. Their stay would become aborted when news circulated rampantly regarding two stories appearing in the *New York Post* and *Star Magazine*.

The reports indicated that Morris had been engaged in a yearlong extramarital affair with a 37-year-old call girl from Virginia named Sherry Rowlands. The two met habitually inside suite 205 at Washington's Jefferson Hotel. To impress Rowlands with his prominence, he'd allowed her to read sensitive political correspondence and listen in on phone conversations with Clinton.

The article in the *Star* revealed explicit details, displayed compromising photos and cited texts from tape recordings in their possession. Rowland had decided to cash in lucratively on her relationship with Morris. The *New York Post* became aware of the forthcoming story and published their own scoop before the *Star*.

The *Star* was no ally of Bill Clinton. During his initial run for the presidency, the publication had unveiled the story of his previous 12-year affair with Gennifer Flowers. Their extended coverage of the scandal nearly sabotaged the Clinton campaign before it developed any traction. There was no doubt the supermarket tabloid would muddy Morris' reputation and attempt to drag Clinton into the slop.

The impending revelations cast Morris as a pariah. He vehemently argued with other top Clinton advisers that he could fight off the scandal and survive. They had no intention of allowing his distraction to eclipse Clinton's rise to the summit. Morris had to go. He went.

Morris, 48, had no bargaining leverage. He had overestimated his importance, bragging incessantly about his power to his peers. When he resigned, he couldn't and didn't deny the allegations. He claimed that he didn't wish to subject his wife and family to the sadism of *yellow journalism* that he was well acquainted with.

Morris would earn a unique distinction with *Time* magazine based on his steady rise and sudden fall. He was featured on two consecutive covers. The September 2, 1996 issue lavished him with a flattering profile entitled *The Man Who Has Clinton's Ear*. The following week after his scandal broke, Morris and his wife were profiled with a headline: *The Morris Mess: After The Fall*.

Morris had wormed his way in steadily to become a Clinton confidant. His rise did not endear him with many existing insiders. He was politically savvy enough following multi-decades of experience to understand his vulnerability. He was easily expendable. Clinton would offer no condemnation for Morris' actions, not being in a morally credible position to do so. He simply thanked him for his services and wished him well in the future.

The subject of prostitution would taint Morris' reputation once again during the early 2000's. Not astonishingly, he described himself as a *sex addict*. His name was outed as a client with a D. C. escort agency called Pamela Martin and operated by Deborah Palfrey. The *D. C. Madam* as she would become labeled committed suicide in May 2008 after her conviction and shortly before her sentencing.

The road towards redemption for Morris has maintained a stony surface.

While his name still elicited recognition and comic punchlines, he released a 1997 book entitled *Behind The Oval Office*. The edition tossed minor gravel towards Bill and Hilary Clinton. Their relationship with Morris soured. He became their frequent critic, particularly during Hilary's Senate and Presidential runs.

In his ongoing efforts to sustain relevancy, Morris frequently appeared on *Fox News* telecasts and on various local and nationally syndicated radio talk shows. He continued his political consulting practice domestically and even in international election campaigns. Critics lambasted his reputation for consistently predicting incorrect election result outcomes.

Morris appears frozen on the fringe of national politics with neither political party enthusiastic towards inviting him back into the mainstream. He remains married to his wife Eileen.

**An Extended History of Presidential Impropriety and Infidelity
The White House:
1600 Pennsylvania Avenue NW, Washington D.C.**

The Bill Clinton-Monica Lewinsky scandal became the costliest extra-marital affair for an American President. It historically wasn't the first.

Lewinsky became an unpaid White House intern in July 1995. By the end of the year, she was hired for a paid posting in the Office of Legislative Affairs.

During this period, she became acquainted and intimate with President Bill Clinton. The pair reportedly shared nine sexual encounters within his Oval Office extending into March 1997. She was not naive with her pursuit and Clinton had an extended history of marital infidelity. The relationship was doomed from the outset. He had no plans to leave his wife Hilary for her.

In April 1996, her employment superiors transferred her to the Pentagon where she became an assistant to chief Pentagon spokesman Kenneth Bacon. Their move was motivated by a suspicion that Lewinski was spending excessive time with Clinton. She unwisely confided to a co-worker Linda Tripp about her relationship with Clinton. Tripp rewarded her disclosure by secretly recording their conversations beginning in September 1997. Lewinski left her position that December.

Tripp would turn the tapes over to Independent Counsel Kenneth Starr who was conducting a separate investigation into another potential scandal called *Whitewater*.

In January 1998, news of the affair became public. The Clinton administration responded with full damage control protocol. Clinton tiptoed around the issue by denying that he had engaged in an *improper* sexual relationship or affair.

His tactic backfired. By then, too many legitimate sources knew the truth. Lewinsky had stored a damning and unconventional piece of evidence. She kept a blue dress that she'd once worn stained with Clinton's semen.

As the scandal raged wildly throughout the world media, Clinton finally apologized and acknowledged his duplicity. A Republican Party majority Congress impeached him. A U.S. Senate that lacked sufficient votes to cast him out of office spared him the indignity of conviction.

Both Clinton and Lewinsky's characters were ravaged by the infidelity. Both would survive the assault. He completed his presidential term to become a respected statesman with less scrutiny on his personal life. She endured the ridicule and defamation and reinvented herself on multiple occasions. She is currently identified a social activist, film producer, television personality and fashion designer.

Her legacy ironically rebounded better than that of her predecessors.

Sexual impropriety and marital infidelity has a deep-rooted history within the Chief Executive position. Power and privilege have always allured interest as an aphrodisiac. Bill Clinton was not the first to recognize this reality.

In many respects, his behavior was tame. Siring children out of wedlock has not been an unusual pastime for several prior Presidents. Proving the allegations has been difficult.

George Washington was reputed to be the father of his country, but also the father for several of his slaves. He made the decision to free all of the enslaved individuals that he owned in his will. This action would not take effect until after his death in 1799.

Thomas Jefferson inherited Sally Hemings as a slave from his father-in-law, John Wayles. Upon her arrival to Paris in 1787 to work and live with Jefferson, her status changed. She became a *free* woman and paid servant, since France did not recognize the legality of slavery.

The widowed Jefferson began sexual relations with her during their two years there. Throughout his presidency between 1801-1809, she remained his mistress. They had six children together. Jefferson neither confirmed nor denied the children's heritage. Their relationship remained publicly undocumented. A book published in 1997 resurrected the story. DNA analysis commissioned the following year confirmed a direct linkage between Jefferson and one of the Hemings descendants tested.

John Tyler served one term as President between 1841-1845 following the death of William Henry Harrison after only 31 days in office. He never successfully won the office and following a rupture with his own Whig Party, he formed a new party called the Democratic-Republican Party. He was unsuccessful during the 1845 campaign losing decisively to James K. Polk.

Tyler was a prodigious breeder during his lifetime fathering eight children with his first wife Letitia and seven additional with his second wife Julia. He was accused of the sexual exploitation of his slaves by fathering additional children to increase his household. Worse, he reportedly sold some of his sons to increase his finances. Hard evidence substantiating this popular allegation then is scarce.

Perhaps the worst sex scandal involved President Grover Cleveland prior to his winning elective office. Cleveland is the sole President (so far) to serve two non-consecutive terms in office. Cleveland's reputation was tainted by his evasive confirmation that he had fathered an illegitimate child while still unmarried. This act was used as a major character attack employed by his political rivals.

What was less known regarding his indiscretion was the factual truth proved far worse.

On the evening of December 15, 1873, Cleveland invited Maria Halpin, 38, to dinner at Buffalo's Ocean Dining Hall and Oyster House. She was an attractive woman a year older than Cleveland employed at a local department store. Cleveland was a portly six-foot tall bachelor who had been persistently pursing Halpin for several months previously.

Halpin finally relented and agreed to the dinner. The meal passed amicably and Cleveland escorted her home to a downtown boarding house. He overstayed his welcome and proceeded to sexually assault her. Six weeks later, Halpin realized that she was pregnant. Cleveland threatened her regarding any form of disclosure. He made it abundantly clear that he had no intention of claiming or financially supporting the child. Marriage wasn't an option for the ambitious Cleveland.

His subsequent follow-up was vile. Oscar Folsom Cleveland was born on September 14, 1874 in a hospital for unwed mothers. Folsom was the name of Cleveland's best friend. Cleveland arranged to have the child immediately taken from his mother and placed in the Buffalo Orphan Asylum. Maria Halpin was interned briefly in the Providence Lunatic Asylum, but released following an evaluation by the facility's medical director.

The medical director would adopt her son.

Grover Cleveland's political rise and eventual national exposure accelerated with his election as mayor of Buffalo in 1881. He became the governor of New York the following year and the Democratic Party nominated presidential candidate in 1884.

Facing a public relations crisis over his known illegitimate son, his campaign team conducted a smear campaign against helpless Maria Halpin. She was labeled an adventurous alcoholic that preyed upon married men. Cleveland claimed that he assumed responsibility for the boy solely because he was the only unmarried man that had she slept with. He cast major doubts regarding his fatherhood.

The exaggeration and malignment of Halpin subsided any collateral furor. His campaign was successful and he became the 22nd President.

The libel forever shamed and destroyed Maria Halpin. She would later marry and live the rest of her life in poverty and obscurity until her death in 1902. Her son was never allowed to live with her. He reportedly changed his name to James E. King, Jr. and became a Buffalo gynecologist. He died childless in 1947.

Grover Cleveland ultimately chose a child bride named Frances Folsom groomed for him. She was ironically the daughter of his longtime best friend. He'd known Frances from infancy and was affectionately known by her as *Uncle*. The couple married in the White House when she was only 21 becoming the county's then and still youngest first lady. She was then 27 years younger than Cleveland.

Warren Harding was the first President to be elected on his birthday, broadcast a speech via radio and earn office with women's votes.

Harding reportedly was the first President to conduct an extramarital affair while serving in office. The Harding legacy has been forever blackened by scandals conducted by his professional associates and peers. There were two highly profiled rumored liaisons between Harding and mistresses.

Carrie Phillips was the wife of Harding's longtime friend James Phillips. She was tall, attractive and ten years younger. Their affair began reportedly in 1905 and lasted fifteen years. While he was a U.S. Senator from Ohio, she had attempted to blackmail him into voting against a declaration of war against Germany during World War I.

She was a strong German sympathizer and an unwelcome still smoking gun leading up to the 1920 presidential election. The Republican National Committee reportedly gave her and her husband a generous stipend to leave the country. They accepted the offer.

Harding won a landslide victory over Ohio Governor James Cox dominating the popular vote and earning every state majority outside of the South. Over 200 letters written between them substantiated the Harding and Phillips relationship. The correspondence was revealed in July 2014 following the expiration of various court restrictions preventing their public exposure.

Nan Britton was a pretty blond, thirty years younger than Harding who he'd originally found employment for in 1917. They continued their affair sporadically until his abrupt death in San Francisco on August 2, 1923. She gave birth to their daughter Elizabeth Ann Christian on October 22, 1919.

Harding was never able to view the girl, but provided child support payments that were hand delivered by the Secret Service. His unforeseen death terminated these payments.

Nan Britton unsuccessfully sued Harding's estate attempted to establish a trust fund for their daughter.

She wrote a best selling book entitled *The President's Daughter* in 1927 detailing the specifics behind their affair in explicit detail. She speculated that Elizabeth was likely conceived on Harding's Senate office couch. One of his favorite intercourse spots was inside an Oval Office coat closet.

Throughout the remainder of her life, Nan Britton was branded a *degenerate*, *pervert* and *extortionist* attempting to falsely taint the already darkened Harding legacy.

Warren Harding's wife Florence had no interest in acknowledging publicly her husband's infidelity. She was considered vengeful and maintained a black book vilifying real or imagined slights by others. Rumors suggested that she hastened her husband's death by heart attack inside their San Francisco Palace Hotel suite when they were alone without medical supervision. She refused to permit an autopsy. Her wish was granted.

Harding's paternity remained clouded until 2015. His legacy protectors insisted that he was sterile. Results from a DNA genetic test that year confirmed otherwise. DNA profiling established Elizabeth Ann Christian as his daughter.

Subsequent Presidents including Franklin Roosevelt, Lyndon Johnson, and George H. W. Bush have each been linked with extramarital affairs. John Kennedy's dalliances were numerous and have been frequently acknowledged.

Privacy and discretion have become nearly impossible for national leaders. The press and social media currently devour any crumb of potential scandal. There are no longer any *off the record,* consensual or leniency agreements between the media and elected officials. Every slight, discrepancy and nuance is now blasted, often unsubstantiated, to a readership of millions. Credibility and accountability have suffered from this haste to be the initial reporting source.

Can and will there be a future Presidential sex scandal? As long as human occupy the position, there are certainly no guarantees against one.

Leveraging Infidelity Without Acknowledging Personal Indulgence
Ex-Congressman Newt Gingrich's Former Office:
Rayburn House Office Building
45 Independence Avenue SW, Washington D.C.

During his tenure as Speaker of the House of Representatives (1995-98), Newt Gingrich parlayed sexual impropriety into political leveraging against a vulnerable President. During 1998, he shepherded the House impeachment proceedings against President Bill Clinton.

The campaign against Clinton was based on allegations of perjury involving the Paula Jones sexual harassment civil case and Clinton's affair with Monica Lewinsky. These allegations would be proven factual with regard to Lewinsky. Clinton's lying during a deposition constituted a felony and became grounds for impeachment.

Gingrich received his desired political outcome when the House voted to impeach Clinton by partisan vote on December 19, 1998. Ironically, Gingrich could only partially savor the victory from his orchestrated attack. A month earlier, he had resigned his position of Speaker pressured by his Republican colleagues. In their eyes, he had failed them during that month's mid-term congressional election. More pronounced, the entire House had voted overwhelmingly to reprimand Gingrich for earlier ethical wrongdoings.

The vote of 395 to 28 effectively ended not only Gingrich's influence, but also his career in Congress. He resigned permanently two months later on January 3, 1999.

His nearly four-year Speaker legacy altered the tenor of the House significantly. Political observers have credited (or blamed) Gingrich's leadership stint as furthering the polarized gap between politics and partisanship. Any future semblance of political party cooperation has never materialized.

Gingrich's role in the Clinton scandal eventually illuminated his own sexual indiscretions and history of marital infidelity. Throughout the entire media circus, fact accumulating process and public pronouncements against Clinton, Gingrich harbored a secret. He was immersed in his own extramarital affair. His mistress was a much younger Callista Bisek, a staff aide in the office of Wisconsin Congressman Steve Gunderson. Their liaison reportedly had begun during Gingrich's early ascent towards the speakership.

Throughout his period of congressional power, Gingrich had trumpeted the imperative importance of preserving *traditional family values*. His own later acknowledged past appeared to question whether he even comprehended the definition of the term.

Gingrich's first marriage was to his former high school geometry teacher. Following 18 years of marriage and multiple alleged affairs, he divorced and married one of his mistresses. According to his first wife, he discussed divorce terms with her while she was in the hospital recovering from cancer surgery.

In 1981, she would take him to court for failing to provide proper financial support for her and their daughters. A judge ordered him to increase his financial support. His ex-wife claimed that he didn't obey the order. She died in 2013 at the age of 77.

During his second marriage shortly following his divorce in 1981, his new wife reportedly controlled their finances eventually lifting them out of debt. She opted not to share the public life of a politician's wife. Her preference seemed odd considering he'd already been serving in Congress for two years.

Their turbulent marriage would endure nearly two decades. Gingrich filed for divorce in 1999, a few months after she had been diagnosed with multiple sclerosis. One of her amusing post-marriage anecdotes was that she had declined to accept his suggestion of an *open marriage* sexually. Her approval became unnecessary by then. Gingrich disputed her version of events.

He ultimately solved his mistress dilemma by marrying Bisek in 2000, four months following his second divorce.

Gingrich flirted twice with running for president during 2000 and 2012. On both occasions, he harshly discovered that he was not sufficiently popular within his own party. The second aborted attempt confirmed that he was far past any electable potential nationally. His upward trajectory in politics had flatlined.

During his second attempt in December 2011, an Iowa based Christian group asked him to sign their organization's *Marriage Vow*. They were knowledgeable about his history regarding the sanctity of marriage vows. Rarely concise when addressing issues, he sent a lengthy response that included a pledge to *uphold personal fidelity to my spouse*.

Leaving political office became Gingrich's most lucrative reward. His private life was no longer subject to the intense scrutiny as when he was an elected offical. He became wealthy through the establishment of various organizations and causes. He also became enriched as a well-compensated speaker enabling extensive travel. Gingrich delivered then as now predictable conservative commentary through various media channels and outlets.

He announced publicly his conversion to Catholicism in 2009

stressing a visit by Pope Benedict XVI within the United States cemented his decision. The Catholic Church later conveniently recognized his third marriage as *valid*. The decision was based on the death of his first wife and their granted annulment of his second marriage.

Gingrich has shamelessly maintained a steadfast complaint against a *cultural elite* intending to create a secularized America. His own *elite* vision includes establishing a foundation of ethics, family orientation and God into a distinctly American value system.

Given his own contradictory lifestyle, he might wish to be extremely cautious towards gaining what he ultimately longs for.

**A Disappearance Vanishing Into The Waters Of The Potomac
Joyce Chiang's Last Sighting, Former Starbucks:
Connecticut Ave NW & R Street NW, Washington D.C.**

On the evening of January 9, 1999, twenty-eight-year old Joyce Chiang met with several friends for dinner and a movie. Afterwards, one of her friends offered her a ride home. En route, Chiang asked the driver if she could make a quick stop at a Starbuck's near her apartment. The friend obliged and Chiang indicated that she would walk the remaining four blocks home. Her brother, who was also her roommate, awaited her return. She never arrived.

Her disappearance immediately involved FBI investigators because she was a federal employee. Chiang was an attorney working in the General Counsel's office of the Immigration and Naturalization Service.

The next day, her billfold would be discovered at Anacostia Park and turned in. Four days later the couple who'd found it recognized Chiang's photo in local media coverage. They notified the FBI who immediately conducted a search of the park. Their efforts would recover her apartment keys, video and grocery cards, a pair of gloves and the jacket that she was last seen wearing. Her body remained missing.

For three futile months, family, friends and concerned parties staged a candlelight vigil every Saturday evening in Dupont Circle. Accompanying television and print appeals failed to stimulate eyewitnesses or individuals with assisting information.

Three months later and eight miles from where her items had been discovered, a canoeist sighted her badly decomposed body on the Potomac River. The case would subsequently remain cold with few clues for twelve years. During the

Chandra Levy botched investigation, local police speculated that Chiang had potentially committed suicide without any context as to why. Levy and Chiang had lived only four blocks apart, but investigators were reluctant to attribute their cases to a lone serial killer. Their rationalization was based on the murders being committed over two years apart.

In May 2011, D.C. police set up a press conference to announce that their conjecture of suicide was incorrect. They announced that two suspects were probably responsible for Chiang's murder. One was currently imprisoned in Maryland for a different crime and the other was living in Guyana that did not have an extradition treaty with the United States. The pair was identified as a team who abducted individuals off the street with the intention of robbery. They speculated that the two men had either tossed Chiang into the river or that she drowned attempting to escape.

Beyond that announcement, the hypothesized case has stalled without charges being filed. Evidence tying the two men directly to Joyce Chiang was never been publicly substantiated. Her friends and colleagues have eulogized her through an award established by the Georgetown University Law Center. She had graduated from their evening division in 1995 while working for Congressman Howard Berman as an immigration advisor.

A Critical Moment of Truth That Elapsed
Chandra Levy Apartment: Newport Condominium 1260 21st Street NW #315, Washington D.C.
Gary Condit Apartment: 2611 Adams Mill Road NW, Washington D.C.
Body Discovered: Rock Creek Park: Western Ridge Trail near Glover Road, Washington D.C.

Gary Condit experienced a punitive lesson regarding timing and disclosure that would haunt him professionally and personally.

During the 1998 impeachment proceedings against President Bill Clinton, Central Valley congressman Condit demanded that Clinton should *come clean* regarding his alleged sexual relationship with intern Monica Lewinski. Condit's later failure to follow his own advice effectively terminated his credibility and political legacy. His downfall unexpectedly accelerated during the summer of 2001 with the disappearance of Modesto native and Washington D.C. intern Chandra Levy.

Far from her formative Central Valley hometown, Levy, 24 was completing her final semester of study at the University of Southern California. She moved to Washington D.C. to complete a paid internship with the Federal Bureau of Prisons in the Public Affairs division. Her future appeared promising and her next stage career choice became whether to return to D.C. or pursue employment elsewhere. Her apartment lease expired at the same time her internship ended. She planned a return home in May 2001 to sort out her future plans and objectives.

On May 1, 2001 she mysteriously disappeared from her southwestern Dupont Circle apartment. Video footage from her building was unable to track her departure. Most investigative speculation targeted Rock Creek Park as her intended destination. Reconstructed data on her laptop computer search engine indicated that she'd clicked a link to a map of the location. The site is a popular jogging trial within the city that stretches north into Maryland.

Her apartment unit was located a modest distance away from entering the trail. She reportedly left her personal belongings inside her residence while she began jogging along the well-exposed public trails.

On May 6th, Chandra's anxious parents telephoned police to indicate that they had not heard from her in five days. The following day, her father followed-up the call indicating that his daughter was having an affair with a U.S. congressman. Both her father and aunt based on Chandra's confidences with the latter forwarded Gary Condit's name to police. Following the filing of a missing persons report, police entered her apartment with a search warrant.

They discovered her credit cards, identification and a cell phone left behind in her purse, an indication that her departure ensured a return. Her suitcases were partially packed for her impending flight and her answering machine was completely full of messages. Two were from U.S. Congressman Gary Condit inquiring if she was okay.

Condit initially denied knowing Levy intimately. He also expressed surprise in the discovery that her apartment lease had expired. On July 7th, an unidentified police source confirmed that Condit admitted to them about their affair. Condit became a suspect of interest also because his own apartment was a short distance away from the Rock Creek Park trail and Levy's projected entry point to the trail.

During the course of more exhaustive background checks, it

was revealed publicly that Condit had been involved years earlier in another affair with a flight attendant. The alleged mistress refused to cooperate with investigators.

The escalating investigation involving Condit stimulated speculation into his potential involvement via media leaks. Condit had a sound alibi for the day of Levy's disappearance as he was meeting with Vice President Dick Cheney as a senior member of the House Permanent Select Committee on Intelligence. As media attention intensified towards his potential involvement with her disappearance, scrutiny regarding his personal life and sexual trysts rocketed. During the height of the media frenzy, he refused to take an administered lie detector test by police.

Chandra Levy had been missing for two weeks. During this interval, valuable investigative time was squandered. As the focus shifted from examining the evident facts and potential clues, the media circus swung full pendulum.

Condit's aversion to disclosure was understandable, but ill timed. Adultery has never resonated well with constituents, particularly within the religiously influenced Central Valley. A relationship with a woman younger than his daughter and thirty years his junior was considered *unacceptable*. His own religious upbringing acclimated him to understand the harsh consequences of marital infidelity. A public admission of guilt would irrevocably doom his future. In the end, it didn't matter.

The political environment of power and federal governmental authority is rife with socially ambitious individuals clamoring for advancement. The faces and political parties shift, but the ecosystem has varied little over the decades. Power and position attract sexual encounters and there are numerous volunteers waiting for their opportunity.

Condit was married with two children. He was born and raised in Oklahoma and when his father became a pastor at a Baptist church in Ceres, California, the family relocated. He attended Modesto Community College and graduated with a Bachelor of Science degree in 1972 from California State University, Stanislaus. He set his personal sights on politics and never varied course. Immediately following graduation, he began an accelerated trajectory of success.

He started with his election to the Ceres City Council and became mayor between 1974-76. He advanced to the County Board of Supervisors, California State Assembly and finally the U. S. Congress via a special election following the resignation of House Democratic Whip Tony Coelho. Condit would win re-election for five consecutive terms earning the reputation as a conservative maverick within the Democratic Party. He periodically voted against party sponsored legislation without consequence due to his avid support base.

His own future appeared secure as he sometimes ran unopposed. Higher aspirations such as the California governorship or a U.S. Senate seat were likely beyond his reach since historically the California electorate in recent decades has not voted in any elected Central Valley legislator to the highest offices.

His presumed job security would shift irrevocably when his affair with Levy was blasted throughout the international news media. The investigative disappearance case plodded forward with few promising leads. Levy's parents were understandably desperate to keep the case in the forefront of the news.

In July, Condit agreed to allow investigators to search his apartment. He'd had two months to sanitize any potential damaging evidence. He denied directly to Levy's mother that he had anything to do with her daughter's disappearance. Still the doubts and doubters persisted in their suspicions. The case consumed the headlines during the summer of 2001.

In August, Condit accepted an interview request by ABC News anchor Connie Chung. Illogically presuming he could control and orchestrate the interview before 24 million viewers, his strategy failed. Once again, Condit denied vehemently that he had harmed or killed Chandra Levy and had absolutely nothing to do with her disappearance.

Condit poorly miscalculated the intended purpose of the interview. The only *real* question the public wanted confirmed was the degree of their relationship and sexual intimacy. He refused to address the question out of his claimed professed *respect* for his own family's wishes. He babbled on about personal integrity and even escorted Chung through an almond orchard stressing his deep attachment to agricultural roots. The interview altered few opinions and only strengthened the suspicion that he had withheld information during the criminal inquiry.

The public's obsession with the case was instantly diverted by the catastrophic magnitude of events in New York City on September 11th. The destruction of the World Trade Center Towers relegated Chandra Levy and Congressman Gary Condit into secondary coverage. Interest had decidedly waned while the world was in turmoil. Chandra Levy remained missing.

Celebrity author, Dominick Dunne, penned an audacious article for *Vanity Fair* magazine later in 2001. Dunne's piece was based on a sequence of narratives spun from a *supposed* inside source close to the Washington DC's sexual underbelly.

His story involved Gary Condit, Chandra Levy and a Middle Eastern sex procurer who was responsible for her disappearance. Dunne had been duped by his source that immediately disappeared after the article was published. Dunne spoke on a syndicated conservative talk show, prompting Condit to sue the magazine for damages. *Vanity Fair* eventually settled financially with Condit while Dunne plummeted from grace. The absurdity of the tale confirmed that no account of events was too bizarre or outrageous to be considered probable.

A milestone in the case confirmed the public and family's worst and imagined fears.

On May 22, 2002, Chandra Levy's remains were discovered in a remote stretch of Rock Creek Park after a man called 911 indicating that he'd found a skull. Detectives found bones and personal items scattered, but not buried, in a forested area along a steep incline. There was deep suspicion that her remains had been moved from a previous location owing to the distance from her projected starting point.

This sector of the park had been overlooked during earlier coordinated searches. The jogging pants she'd been wearing on May 1st were knotted at the bottom suggesting her killer might have removed them. Investigators indicted that surrounding evidence suggested murder, but no one could be certain.

Over the course of a year's exposure to inclement weather, DNA evidence was essentially absent. Investigators determined that they might also have a credible suspect based on the timing of her disappearance. Ingmar Guandique was an undocumented immigrant from El Salvador charged with assaulting two separate women at knifepoint within Rock Creek Park. Guandique proved easy for investigators to locate as he was then incarcerated serving a ten-year sentence for the non-lethal assaults.

Gary Condit meanwhile hoped that he'd weathered the worst of the scandal and confidently announced that he would run for re-election. He lost in the Democratic Party primary in March 2002. This loss was to a former aide. Condit's diminishing number of supporters felt that his opponent's actions were traitorous and opportunistic to Condit. The victor, then California State Assemblyman Dennis Cardoza won the seat in the general election and served until August 14, 2012. He resigned to become a public affairs representative and lobbyist with a law firm.

Condit quietly served out his legislative term, absent of intense scrutiny and retired from politics after astutely surveying the carnage to his reputation.

He eventually relocated to the Phoenix metropolitan area where in near anonymity, he operated two Baskin-Robbins ice cream stores. His franchises failed and he was ordered to pay restitution to the parent company for breach of contract. Fifteen years after Chandra Levy's death, he published a full disclosure book entitled *Actual Malice*. Following critical reviews and media exposure upon its initial release, the book slid immediately into obscurity. The text continued to deny his culpability and any sexual history with Levy. The time for complete and truthful disclosure had elapsed fifteen years before. Interest towards Gary Condit remained firmly indifferent.

In 2009, eight years following Chandra Levy's murder, Ingmar Guandique was officially arraigned for her killing. The prosecution's case was constructed predominantly on boastings Guandique had uttered to his prison cellmate. Gary Condit proponents argued that the former congressman had been vindicated by this arrest.

The legal action against Ingmar Guandique would follow an

erratic curve. In 2010, he was convicted of Levy's murder and sentenced to 60 years in prison. Five years later, following appeal, Guandique would be granted a retrial. His counsel successfully argued that the prosecution's prime witness had a documented history of fabricating testimony and soliciting law enforcement officials with supposed confessions to improve his own internment status.

The fresh trial immediately raised serious questions regarding the informant's credibility. The judge dismissed the charges against Guandique at the prosecutor's request. In May 2017 he was deported to his native El Salvador seemingly closing his involvement in the case.

As for Condit, he has continued to protest that the alleged sex scandal claims resulted in his losing his fortune, job, closest friends and D.C. colleagues. He cast himself as a tragic victim of circumstantial media frenzy. Chandra Levy was unavailable for her reaction to his complaints.

Could Condit's full cooperation have sped up the investigation and possibly resulted in more credible suspects? His reticence to *come clean* and even submit to a lie detector test reflects a morality tale regarding the double-edged blade of expedient truthfulness. Whether he had been completely forthright from the inception of questioning or not, the consequences of a confirmed dalliance would likely have doomed his career anyway. Evasiveness proved more expedient, self-serving and ultimately shortsighted. When truth mattered most, he remained ambivalent.

We'll probably never know how Chandra Levy's life may have blossomed and flourished. We have direct evidence regarding the fate of Gary Condit. Power and moral ambivalence rarely conclude well.

CHANDRA LEVI'S APARTMENT BUILDING

GARY CONDIT'S APARTMENT BUILDING

ROCK CREEK PARK TRAIL

SECTION WHERE BODY WAS FOUND

One of America's Darkest Days: 9/11
The 9/11 Pentagon Memorial:
1 N Rotary Road, Arlington VA

American Airline flight #77 departed from Dulles International Airport on the morning of September 11, 2001 bound for Los Angeles. Less than 35 minutes into the flight, five Saudi passengers affiliated with the al-Qaeda movement stormed the cockpit. They forced the 58 passengers, pilots and crew members to the rear of the aircraft. One of the hijackers, trained as a pilot, took over control of the plane.

His intended destination was nearby. The hijackers were counting on the element of abrupt surprise, as their intended target was the Pentagon building. Contrary to their expectations and demands, passengers aboard the plane relayed the news of their hijacking to their friends and family via their cell phones. The doomed victims could do nothing to prevent the inevitable.

The Saudi pilot steered the plane towards the western side of the facility. At 9:37 a.m., the fully fueled Boeing 757 slammed into the Pentagon building igniting an explosion and fire that would require several days to fully extinguish. A section of the building collapsed into rubble. All aboard the plane were killed. One hundred and twenty-five additional victims including emergency workers on the ground would be added to the fatality count.

The horror of that collision would only be numerically exceeded by the damage and carnage inflicted upon the World Trade Center Buildings in New York City. The grim sequence of events became a dark day in American history.

The damaged sections of the Pentagon would be rebuilt in 2002 with employees returning to those sectors in August.

During the immediate aftermath following the attack, a temporary memorial was established on a hill at the Navy Annex overlooking the Pentagon. People would solemnly visit and pay tribute to the 184 who died and others who were injured on the ground. One year later, the *Victims of Terrorist Attack on the Pentagon Memorial* was dedicated at Arlington National Cemetery.

Architects Julie Beckman and Keith Kaseman submitted the winning design for the 9/11 Pentagon Memorial. The effect is a brilliant example of conceptual design. The layout consists of 184 illuminated benches, arranged according to the victim's ages over a 2-acre plot. Each bench is engraved with the name of a victim. The benches representing the interior Pentagon fatalities are arranged facing the building's south façade. A shallow lighted pool of flowing water is positioned under each memorial bench. A wall along the edge of the Memorial begins at a height of 3 inches rising to 71 inches. This height represents the age range of the victims starting at 3 years old to 71 years old.

The Memorial was officially opened on September 11, 2008, exactly seven years following the tragedy. Each year an American flag is hung on the section of the Pentagon struck by American Airlines Flight #77. This section of the building is lit up in blue lights.

It is often thought and hoped for that such Memorials reminding visitors of tragic events, may one day end their reoccurrence. Sadly, successive generations add their own defining stories. Washington D.C. is a town littered with monuments, history and memories.

The December 7, 1941 attack on Pearl Harbor was once coined *a day that will live in infamy*. As veterans of World War II increasingly expire and relations with Japan have long ago stabilized, the day has lessened in significance for many younger citizens. September 11th, 2001 currently remains a reminder of national vulnerability and tragedy. The harsh lesson learned should never be downplayed or worse, someday forgotten.

366

The Profound Darkness of John Muhammad's Soul
Beltway Sniper Victim's Sites:

James Martin: Shoppers Food Warehouse (Now Giant), 2201 Randolph Road, Wheaton, MD

James Buchanan: Fitzgerald Auto Malls, 11411 Rockville Pike, Rockville, MD

Prem Kumar Walekar: Mobil Station (Now Sunoco), Aspen Hill Road and Connecticut Avenue, Aspen Hill, MD

Sarah Ramos: Leisure World Shopping Center, 3701 Rossmoor Blvd., Norbeck, MD

Lori Ann Lewis-Rivera: Shell Station, Connecticut and Knowles Avenues, Kensington, MD

Pascal Charlot: Georgia Avenue at Kalmai Road, Washington D.C.

Dean Harold Meyers: Sunoco Station, 7203 Sudley Road, Manassas, VA

Kenneth Bridges: Exxon Station, Interstate 95 Exit, Fredericksburg, VA

Linda Franklin: Home Depot, Intersection Arlington Blvd. And Leesburg Pike, Seven Corners, VA

Jeffrey Hopper: Ponderosa Steakhouse, State Route 54, Ashland VA

Conrad Johnson: 14100 Block of Grand Pre Road, Aspen Hill, MD

Brookside Gardens:
1800 Glenallan Avenue, Wheaton, MD

The demons that prompted John Allen Williams to murder strangers by sniper fire were complex and incomprehensible to understand. His hatred seemed personified by a sense of empowerment over determining life and death.

What influences created these demons?

Williams, better known as *John Allen Muhammad* changed his surname in October 2001 shortly following the 9/11 attack on New York City's World Trade Center complex and the

Pentagon.

The unraveling of his personality began more than a decade earlier. He was born in Baton Rouge, Louisiana on New Years Eve, 1960. The family moved to New Orleans when his mother was diagnosed with breast cancer. She died when he was three. His father abandoned him and his maternal grandfather and an aunt raised him.

He enlisted during August 1978 in the Louisiana Army National Guard at Baton Rouge as a combat engineer. He transferred to the conventional army in 1985 and trained as a mechanic, truck driver and specialist metalworker. He qualified as an expert marksman.

His tours of duty included Fort Lewis, Fort Ord and in 1991 he served in the Gulf War in Kuwait. He earned numerous honors for his service and was honorably discharged as a sergeant in April 1994.

While on active duty in 1987, he joined the Nation of Islam. He helped provide security after his discharge in 1995 for the *Million Man March* on the Capitol.

His personal life deteriorated. He had married twice and fathered three children. His second wife sought and was granted a restraining order for alleged abuse. In 1999, the troubled Muhammad kidnapped his children and transported them to Antigua. He was reportedly engaging in credit car and immigration document fraud. It was during this abduction that he would encounter Lee Boyd Malvo, who later partnered up with him on his infamous string of murders.

Malvo would testify that Muhammad had indoctrinated him into believing that his ultimate goal was to establish a camp in Canada where homeless children would be trained as terrorists. In Muhammad's deluded logic, he initiated his goal with a nationwide scourge of terror. He envisioned a ransom to stop the killings as the source of funding for his terrorist camp. At his later murder trial, his defense attorney stated his *true* ultimate goal was to kill his ex-wife Mildred in order to regain custody of his three children. Like most of his sparsely publicized rhetoric, little of it made sense.

John Muhammad and Lee Boyd Malvo's legacy of violence would begin on February 16, 2002 at a hillside residence in East Tacoma, Washington. The first killing was a bungled revenge murder. It became the sole homicide that seemed accompanied by a plausible motive.

John Muhammad had instructed Malvo to kill the best friend of his ex-wife. She had assisted his former spouse's escape from their abusive relationship. The murder was intended as repayment for her aid.

Malvo's relationship with Muhammad has been scrutinized extensively. Malvo claimed that his older accomplice exerted a Machiavellian influence over him that was punctuated by a pattern of sexual abuse. He followed instructions without questioning or conscience.

Malvo botched the instruction by shooting the first person that answered his knock. Keenya Cook, 21, was the niece of the intended victim, living at the residence in the midst of sorting out her own life. She was in the process of undressing her baby daughter for a bath while preparing food on the kitchen stove. She had just broken up with her child's father and had moved in with her aunt and cousin. She managed a woman's clothing store.

The hurried gunshot to her head was fatal and Malvo fled the scene. Investigators and family were baffled by a seemingly absence of motive. It wasn't until Muhammad and Malvo's later East Coast murders that the killing was linked directly to the pair. Malvo confessed, while Muhammad remained defiantly silent.

From February until October 2002, the pair traveled cross-country between Washington State to their end destination in Washington D.C. via southern states. They engaged in a robbery and shooting rage killing six more individuals and wounding seven. Their victims were identified in Los Angeles, Tucson, Denton, Atlanta, Montgomery and Baton Rouge. Neither perpetrator would ultimately stand trial for these murders.

Muhammad and Malvo arrived into the D.C. metropolitan area at the beginning of October. Muhammad was driving a blue 1990 Chevrolet Caprice. A firing port was created above their New Jersey license plate enabling them to shoot and remain concealed. The contraption enabled easy escape following their attacks.

On October 2nd, Muhammad fired a shot through a Michael's craft store in Aspen Hill, Maryland. The bullet narrowly missed a cashier and was presumed by police to be random. James Martin was shot to death one hour later in the parking lot of a Shoppers Food Warehouse store. The following morning, four people would be killed within a two-hour span in the Aspen Hill district and nearby Montgomery County, Maryland. A fifth was added that evening in the Takoma neighborhood of D.C.

On October 4th, a woman was wounded in the chest in the parking lot of the Spotsylvania Mall in Spotsylvania, VA. By now, the shootings were being linked and journalists were converging to cover the events. School officials reassured the public they were exerting every cautionary measure possible. Security was tightened and all outdoor activities were canceled. The D.C. metropolitan region was paralyzed in terror.

Muhammad began spacing out his shootings two to three days apart. He was monitoring news coverage of his killing spree and attempting to exhort authorities to provide him with funds to cease the murders.

Conscious of the public announcement regarding school safety, Muhammad shot 13-year-old Iran Brown critically as his aunt was dropping him off at the Benjamin Tasker Middle School in Bowie, MD. He survived despite serious internal injuries. At the crime scene, investigators discovered a shell casing and the Tarot Death Card with written inscriptions.

On October 9, the spree continued further south into Virginia with the shooting death of Dean Meyers at a Sunoco gas station. Two days later, Kenneth Bridges was killed at an Exxon Station near Fredericksburg, On October 14, Linda Franklin was killed inside a covered Home Depot parking lot at the Seven Corner Shopping Center.

The desired panic sought by the perpetrators had enflamed into its desired effect. Service stations had begun to install tarps to conceal their clientele. Numerous media dispatches identified the sniper's vehicle as a white van, slowing the accuracy of the investigation.

On October 17, either Muhammad or Malvo became overly cocky. One of them telephoned the Montgomery County Police Department to indicate that he was responsible for the murder of two women during a liquor store robbery a month earlier in Montgomery, Alabama.

What the caller didn't realize was that only one woman had died and that fingerprint and ballistic evidence were available from the case. Over 400 FBI agents from around the country were working the capturing the newly monikered *Beltway Sniper*. A fingerprint from the gun in Montgomery was traced to Lee Boyd Malvo from an earlier warrant in Washington State. He was immediately paired with John Muhammad and the Bushmaster .223 rifle registered to him. The trail quickly led on October 22nd to the license plate tracking of their blue Chevy Caprice.

The information would be distributed to the news media for global circulation. The net was closing rapidly on Muhammad and Malvo. They hadn't completed their rampage nor were aware that their freedom was nearly over. How long they had chosen to continue was never revealed.

On October 19, Jeffrey Hopper was shot fatally in a parking lot near the Ponderosa Steakhouse in Ashland, Virginia. Three days later, bus driver Conrad Johnson was gunned down while standing on steps at a bus stop in Aspen Hill, Maryland. He would become their final victim.

The closure of the carnage came discreetly on the morning of October 24. The blue Chevy Caprice was spotted at a rest stop parking lot off of I-70 in Maryland. Within an hour, law enforcement had set up a perimeter blockage to prevent any escape. During the morning, a team of Maryland State Police, Montgomery County SWAT officers and Hostage Team special agents arrested the sleeping pair without a struggle.

The first trial of Muhammad was conducted in Virginia during October 2003. He was charged with murder, terrorism and the illegal use of a firearm. His extortion attempt was also revealed. On November 17th, he was convicted and sentenced to death. He would be returned to Maryland to face charges. He would be convicted on six counts of murder and given six life sentences.

As Virginia still conducted capitol punishment, his death sentence precluded any punishment that his other murder convictions might result in. Muhammad sullenly protested his innocence throughout the proceedings. He requested prosecutors to terminate any appeals to spare him his death sentence.

On November 10, 2009, John Muhammad would be executed at the age of 48 at the Greensville Correctional Center in Jarrat, Virginia. His calloused premeditation and complete disregard for human life forged him into an unsympathetic figure. He declined to make a final statement prior to his death by lethal injection. His body was cremated and the ashes given to his son in Louisiana.

Malvo's defense team attempted to parlay his juvenile status as an argument against conviction. During Muhammad's Virginia trial, Malvo stated that he had been the triggerman for every shooting. His tactic was employed to spare the death penalty for Muhammad. The precision aim of the shootings and his own lack of arms experience made his confession implausible. During the Maryland trial, he admitted that he had lied. His detailed testimony filled in numerous gaps of the pair's activities and travels. He freely confirmed the murders that they were suspected of.

Malvo would be sentenced to life imprisonment without the possibility of parole. He is currently interned at the Red Onion State Prison in Pound, Virginia. The facility is designated as a Supermax security prison housing 848 inmates and considered one of the toughest national institutions with stringent controls.

Films and media portrayals have documented the D.C. Sniper's exploits. These exposés have attempted to piece coherence into the pair's monstrous actions. Malvo has periodically attempted to shed light into the unimaginable darkness behind their thinking. He has since married, but there remains only a slight probability that he will ever experience freedom again.

An engraved memorial stone with each of the Maryland, D.C. and Virginia victims is located as an oasis setting inside the Brookside Gardens facility in Wheaton, Maryland. The 50-acre property is landscaped with terraced tropical gardens, winding streams, walking trails and shady gazebos. It is a serene alternative to the horror that once characterized the petrified region. It symbolizes the antithesis of a shrouded soul that John Allen Williams could never evade.

James Buchanan

Prem Kumar Walekar

SARAH RAMOS

LORI ANN LEWIS-RIVERA

CONRAD JOHNSON

BROOKSIDE GARDENS

BROOKSIDE GARDENS
WE REMEMBER
JAMES D. MARTIN
SILVER SPRING MD
JAMES L. SONNY BUCHANAN
ROCKVILLE MD
PREM KUMAR WALEKAR
OLNEY MD
SARAH RAMOS
SILVER SPRING MD
LORI A. LEWIS RIVERA
SILVER SPRING MD
PASCAL E. CHARLOT
WASHINGTON DC
DEAN H. MEYERS
GAITHERSBURG MD
KENNETH H. BRIDGES
PHILADELPHIA PA
LINDA FRANKLIN
ARLINGTON VA
CONRAD E. JOHNSON
OXON HILL MD

**Tossing Retirement Funds Into A Failing Career Vortex
Congressman Don Sherwood Residence:
110 D Street SE, Washington D.C.**

The downward trajectory of Congressman Don Sherwood began with a 911 call on September 15, 2004. Police responded to a woman who had locked herself in his apartment bathroom.

Cynthia Ore claimed that Sherwood was choking her. He responded that he'd only been giving her a backrub. No charges would be filed as both decided that the circumstances had already progressed too far. The police report was simply filed and nearly forgotten.

Only it wasn't.

A former campaign rival who'd lost to Sherwood that same year dredged up the report. She distributed the document to several newspapers and television stations. The situation soon became awkward for the married Sherwood. He initially described Ore as merely a *casual acquaintance*. His brushing off tactic didn't succeed.

His next move resulted in his admission that they'd conducted a five-year affair together, but there had been no abuse. His tracks became muddier when Ore filed a $5.5 million lawsuit accusing him of repeatedly assaulting her during their relationship. His upcoming re-election was only a year away.

He decided to toss good money after a bad cause. He settled the lawsuit with an alleged payout of $500,000. Half was paid up front and the other half payable upon the conclusion of the election. His attempt at damage control was intended to silence more injurious disclosure.

Sherwood wagered that the support from his strong Republican ties including Pennsylvania Senator Rick Santorum and President George W. Bush would suffice within his 10th district. He hoped that by expressing genuine contrition regarding the affair and repeating that he'd never physically abused his mistress. In televised ads, he reminded voters that he would *keep on fighting hard for you and your family*.

His Democratic opponent Chris Carney didn't bother with subtleties in his advertising. Carney was a former Defense Department consultant and navy lieutenant commander. He was unapologetically poised for battle and was a certified expert shot. His ads were targeted directly towards Sherwood's jugular vein and most exposed vulnerability. The background in all of his advertising displayed the text *repeatedly choking* and *attempting to strangle plaintiff*.

Sherwood was flailing with a defensive stance and no credible return ammunition. He lost decisively in the election 53% to 47%. Carney would win one additional term following his victory. Republican Tom Marino, a former U.S. Attorney, would defeat him in 2010.

There exists a fraudulent sentiment that American voters are becoming less judgmental towards the sexual indiscretions of their elected leaders. Adultery while serving in office remains almost universally frowned upon. Don Sherwood became yet another example. He doubtlessly regrets the financial settlement he negotiated with Cynthia Ore prior to the total collapse of his political career.

**The Unexplainable Murder of An Activist
Wanda Alston Murder Site:
3808 East Capitol Street, Washington D.C.**

The unexplainable knocked on the front door of civil rights activist Wanda Alston and departed with only a drug clouded motive and stolen life. On March 16, 2005, William Martin Parrott, Jr. desperately pounded on his *friend* Wanda Alston's door requesting money. He had been bingeing on crack cocaine and needed cash to continue his accelerated spree.

She refused. He began stabbing her.

They continued to struggle but the confrontation was one-sided. He was armed, hefty and reckless. She was physically small and unprepared for the onslaught. He continued to slash her until she collapsed and died from her injuries. Parrott stole her credit cards and drove off with her car. He was apprehended the following day confessing his actions. He could not explain why he had killed Alston and would later plead guilty to second-degree murder.

Alston held an elevated political position as D.C. Mayor Anthony Williams's liaison to gays and lesbians. She was very popular and approximately 1,000 people would attend her memorial service.

Parrot would offer his own apologies in the courtroom and through his legal representation. He would not placate those closest to Alston. He could only offer his own narrative of disintegration.

Depression, loss and drug addiction became his rationale. His diabetic father had recently died after his legs had been amputated. He had lost his job and source of income as a medical technician at a morgue. His second marriage had dissolved. His own diabetic condition began resembling the early stages of his father's.

His coping mechanism evolved into substance abuse. It worsened from introductory alcohol and marijuana into crack cocaine. It is a familiar descent. He dabbled in outpatient treatment, but relapsed. He attempted to conceal his addiction from his mother, children and the woman who would become his third wife. All of his efforts ultimately proved futile leading up to his knifing confrontation with Alston.

Addiction is a powerful beast defying rationality. The addict usually recognizes the accompanying destruction and havoc spread to themselves and others. Some individuals proved capable to overcome addiction. Many simply deteriorate beyond recovery.

For Parrott, his sole remaining outcome could only be punishment. He was sentenced to 24 years of incarceration by a D.C. Superior Court Judge.

A Modest Transitory Accommodation For A Future President
Senator Barrack Obama's Apartment:
227 6th Street NE, Washington D.C.

Newly elected Illinois Senator Barack Obama arrived into Washington D.C. during 2005. He settled upon a one-bedroom Stanton Park apartment building with modest furnishings. For three years, the unpretentious dwelling served his essential needs offering an old bathroom, miniscule kitchen and diminutive stove.

The meager space offered a convenient location to Capitol Hill and simplicity, ideal for Obama's then preferences. His wife Michelle would later confide in an interview that she would have never lived there.

Obama was in a position to afford better. He was a rising star within Republican political circles. His book royalties for two published works had amounted to significant revenue. He was a sought after public speaker. He kept the apartment for a portion of his 2008 presidential campaign until his lease expired. Once he earned the Democratic nomination and the race tightened, he required Secret Service protection. A change of residence became essential. He relocated his family's living quarters and protection entourage to an entire wing of the Hays-Adams Hotel.

Upon his election, the family moved across the road to the White House.

TWISTED TOUR GUIDES.com

**The Hot Cash Sting That Froze A Congressman's Legacy
Money Transfer: Ritz Carleton Hotel Parking Lot
1250 South Hayes Street, Arlington VA**

Democratic Congressman William Jefferson updated an old
tactic of concealing *hot* money inside a domestic residence.
Instead of hiding the cash under a mattress, he chose his
freezer. In August 2005, the FBI raided Jefferson's home and
freezer discovering $90,000 in tracked currency. The
currency was divided into nine bundles and wrapped in
aluminum foil inside pie crust containers.

The stash was part of a staged $100,000 bribe destined for
Atiku Abubaker, then the vice president of Nigeria. This first
installment was designed to enlist Abubaker's help in gaining
approval from the country's telecommunications authority.
Jefferson's influence and position was a key role to a deal that
Virginia businesswoman Lori Mody was financing. Mody and
Jefferson had formed a temporary alliance over this project.
Jefferson was due to earn a significant cut.

In 2005, Jefferson was a sitting member of the House Ways
and Means Committee. He was an ideal conduit for
facilitating grayscale commerce. Jefferson was parlaying his
committee position and clout to arrange African business
deals. Mody's project was simply one additional deal that he
was navigating through the perilous waters of rogue
transactions.

Mody and Jefferson met in the parking lot of the Arlington
Ritz Carlton Hotel on July 30. She transferred a briefcase to
him stocked with traceable bills. The transaction was
completed seamlessly. Jefferson was very guarded in his
remarks towards her. He neither examined the contents of the
briefcase nor acknowledged its purpose.

Unknown to Jefferson was that Mody had been a cooperating

witness for the FBI since March. The transfer was being filmed on five different cameras as evidence. The FBI provided the money and car that Mody was driving.

The confirmation video footage and Mody's sworn statements enabled the FBI to raid Jefferson's Congressional offices in May 2006. Undaunted by the mounting pressure, he narrowly won re-election despite being named as the subject in a corruption probe. Voter turnout for the election was barely over 16%. He would be relieved of his House Ways and Means committee post afterwards.

Thirteen months later, he was indicted on sixteen felony charges related to corruption, racketeering, conspiracy, money laundering, obstruction of justice and other offenses. In 2008, he once again sought re-election despite the indictments. He lost narrowly to Republican candidate Anh *Joseph* Cao.

At the conclusion of his late 2009 trial, he was found guilty on eleven of the sixteen corruption charges. He was sentenced to thirteen years in prison, the longest ever for a member of Congress.

On May 2012 he began serving his sentence at the federal prison facility in Beaumont, Texas. He appealed his case following a U.S. Supreme Court ruling on similar issues. On October 5, 2017, he was ordered released after a U.S. District Judge dismissed seven of ten charges against him. He would ultimately only serve five and a half years in prison.

Jefferson's riches to rags fall marred an impressive career trajectory. He spent his formative years working alongside his father on their family farm. He earned his law degree from the Harvard Law School before entering politics as a legislative assistant.

He unsuccessfully lost twice in elections for Mayor of New Orleans and once for governor of Louisiana. His election to Congress came in 1990 following the retirement of 10-term incumbent Lindy Boggs.

Jefferson would serve nine-terms and become the state's first black congressman since the end of Civil War Reconstruction. Little of that distinction will be remembered once his legacy was permanently iced during 2005 inside his freezer.

A Street Mugging Worsened By Incompetent Emergency Non-Treatment
David Rosenbaum Mugging Site:

Gramercy Street at 38th Street NW, Washington D.C.

At the end of 2005, David Rosenbaum had decided to retire from the *New York Times* following a distinguished 35-year journalistic career. He had worked as the editor and/or chief correspondent for numerous departments and crafted his reputation on his analysis of national politics. Although retired, he kept his desk at the *Times* Washington Bureau with the intention of continuing as a contributing writer.

On January 6, 2006, cousins Michael Hamlin and Percy Jordan, Jr. were trawling the Northwestern sector streets of D.C. in a vehicle seeking out vulnerable victims for expedient robberies. They sighted Rosenbaum walking alone in a neighborhood near his residence. They parked and returned to confront him. They stole his wallet and then Jordan slammed him in the head repeatedly with a heavy plastic pipe. Rosenbaum collapsed on the pavement. The young men drove off.

Store surveillance cameras later recorded the pair using Rosenbaum's credit cards. They would be subsequently arrested. Hamlin was quick to blame his cousin for the physical assault. Both would be convicted and given prison sentences.

The story evolved into a second tragedy upon Rosenbaum's collapse. He would be transported by ambulance to the Howard University Hospital emergency room. Due to his incoherence triggered by the blows, hospital staff presumed that he was intoxicated. They based their conclusion on his inability to speak and numerous vomiting stretches. One emergency medical technician did note the evidence of trauma.

Dropping his case to low priority, the emergency staff ignored him for hours. This miscalculation resulted in delayed treatment ultimately causing his death due to complications two days later.

Three days following his death, the chief of the D.C. Fire and Emergency Medical Services attempted to defend his staff's actions and delayed follow-up. He claimed that four medical assessments were properly taken and all standards of care and measures were performed.

Had David Rosenbaum not been a prominent member of the press corps, the story may have expired with that response. The *New York Times* had no intention of permitting a cover-up.

The travesty of misdiagnosing his condition and ignoring his treatment would provoke a scathing public report by D.C.'s inspector general. Public apologies would follow and along with reciprocal threats of expensive litigation. Immediate reforms were mandated for emergency services. The scandal extended nationally and would affect numerous other hospitals.

Rosenbaum's wife would die from cancer six months later. The family agreed to forgo a lawsuit in exchange for the creation of a task force to investigate and improve D.C.'s emergency services. The commission was established in March 2007 and named the Rosenbaum EMS task force.

Presumably protocol changes were addressed and enacted at Howard University Hospital. Unfortunately it required the cruel death of a well-connected journalist to prompt an efficiency review. For the unknown number of previous voiceless victims, this change would result posthumously.

**The Cowardly Knifing Of An Aspiring British Politician
Alan Senitt Murder Site:
3124 Q Street NW, Washington D.C.**

Alan Senitt was a 27-year-old North London political activist volunteering in D.C. for Virginia Senator Mark Warner's political action committee *Forward Together*. He'd arrived in the United States on June 9, 2006.

Senitt had aspirations of a dedicated career in politics. He had graduated with an MA in International Studies and Diplomacy from the School of Oriental and African Studies at the University of London. He further laid his professional groundwork working for House of Lords member Greville Janner, the World Jewish Congress and serving as director for the Coexistence Trust charity. He ran as the Labour Party candidate in North London during the May 2006 local election.

On July 9, 2006, only one month after arriving, he was escorting a female friend home. Three men, one armed with a gun and the other a knife, accosted them. Two of the men grabbed Senitt as the third attempted to sexually assault Senitt's companion. In the ensuing struggle, Senitt was stabbed and his throat slashed.

The three men fled in a car driven by an adult woman. They would all be apprehended and arrested the same day. The foursome was charged with murder. One perpetrator was a 15-year old male preventing his name from being publicly revealed. Each participant would plead guilty and receive extended prison sentences.

An Overnight Stayover Goes Astray
Robert Wone Murder Site:
1509 Swann Street NW, Washington D.C.

Robert Wone, 32, was a practicing attorney living with his wife in suburban Oakton, Virginia. He worked as general counsel with *Radio Free Asia* in downtown D.C. He took the position two months after leaving a commercial real estate law firm. The position required a substantial pay cut, but provided Wone with a sense of purpose following the professional burnout he'd experienced.

On August 2, 2006, Wone completed his workday and headed to a continuing education legal seminar ending at 9:30 p.m. He spoke with his wife afterwards while heading to his *Radio Free Asia* offices to speak with the night staff. His intention afterwards was to spend the evening with a college friend Joe Price to avoid an extended commute back to Oakton. His anticipated arrival time to Price's rowhouse was 10:30 p.m.

Joe Price had met Wone in college at William and Mary University. He'd graduated in 2003 to earn a law degree from the University of Virginia. He was very active in the gay community and had an existing relationship with Victor Zaborsky, a local marketing manager. In 2004, they added an additional partner into their relationship, Dylan Ward, a Georgetown graduate. They considered themselves a family unit maintaining a polyamorous relationship with each other.

At 11:00 p.m., neighbors heard a scream during a newscast. Zaborsky made a 911 call at 11:49 with paramedics arriving minutes later followed by the police. Joe Price telephoned Wone's wife shortly after midnight to inform her that her husband had been stabbed in the back and was at George Washington Hospital. When she arrived with members of her family, they discovered that Robert Wone had expired from being stabbed in the chest and stomach.

The case and investigation went from strange to bizarre. All three men would deny involvement in Wone's death or claim any sexual relationship with him. They attended his funeral where Price served as a pallbearer. They speculated collectively that an unknown intruder had killed him. No motive or signs of burglary accompanied their claim.

Police investigators doubted their conjecture from the outset. They alleged that the crime scene had been tampered with and the area around Wone's body had been cleaned. Investigators meticulously examined the crime site and residence in detail.

Wone's autopsy revealed evidence of some degree of suffocation, potentially a pillow, and puncture marks on his neck, chest, foot, and hand. Cadaver dogs found a blood residue in a dryer lint trap and the patio drain suggesting that someone washed themselves in the back patio area and then dried the wet clothes in a dryer.

The investigation dragged on. In 2007, the Metropolitan Police revealed that they were close to making an arrest in the murder case.

The long-awaited arrest never resulted. In October 2008, an obstruction of justice charge would be filed against Dylan Ward and one month later against Price and Zaborsky. In December, additional charges of conspiracy were filed against all three men.

The conspiracy trial began on June 17, 2010 and concluded without any of the defendants' testifying. Twelve days later, the presiding judge found each man not guilty of all charges. Ironically, that same judge indicated that she personally believed that the men knew who killed Wone. She was not convinced beyond a reasonable doubt that they were guilty of their charged offenses.

So who killed Robert Wone and why? His widow filed a wrongful death lawsuit against Price, Zaborsky and Ward that was settled in August 2011 for an undisclosed sum and agreement.

Robert Wone has subsequently become lionized by several organizations through memorials and scholarships. His murder case remains open. The infamous rowhouse on Logan Circle sold in 2019 for $2.1 million despite its notoriety. The buyer was the son of the owner of the McLean Development and Apartment Management Company.

The Wolf Legislating The Chicken Coop
Congressman Mark Foley Residence:
137 D Street SE, Washington D.C.

Congressman Mark Foley clarified the profile of an *Internet predator* by example with his peers. Republican Party leadership requested his abrupt resignation on September 29, 2006. This extreme action followed accusations that he had sent suggestive emails and sexually explicit text messages. His recipients were teenaged boys who were serving and had previously served as congressional pages.

Pages have used by the Senate and Congress since the early 19th century. Appointed and sponsored by an elected official, they must be sixteen years old and attend school. Their duties consist primarily of delivering correspondence and legislative material within the Congressional complex. Other duties include preparing the chamber for legislative sessions and carrying bills and amendments to respective desks. Pages attend class in the early morning and live together in dormitories.

Foley had developed a congenial reputation amongst House pages during his eleven years in Congress. He represented the 16th District in Florida that then included Port Charlotte, Port St. Lucie, and Palm Beach.

The scandal began on September 28, 2006 when ABC News reported that during the previous year, Foley had initiated an inappropriate request via his personal AOL email account. He had asked a former page to send a photo of himself directly to Foley. The issue might have concluded there when Foley confirmed that he had sent the email. His office indicated that it was a common practice for pages to submit photographs for reference material for future recommendations.

That explanation unraveled into unforeseen chaos when

another page who'd viewed the report came forward the following day with far more damaging material. ABC News reported viewing excerpts of sexually explicit instant messages sent by Foley to that page. These messages made overt references to sexual organs and actions. ABC News tipped off Foley's office earlier that day of the impending telecast.

In prior generations, a politically connected individual might have dismissed the charges as hearsay or slander. Foley conceivably could have bullied and destroyed the reputation of a vulnerable informer. With printed out email and instant messenger texts, the proof remained visual unless a recipient opted to delete it. The whistle blowing page had kept the texts. They traced directly to Foley. Mark Foley had only a single option. He resigned that evening preventing the House of Representatives from expelling him. His long-term future in Congress was already unsteady despite a secure Republican district. The revelation of the emails ended any hopes of his November re-election against Democrat Tim Mahoney.

Additional pages would come forward with charges against him and texts establishing a pattern of inappropriate behavior dating back to his entry into Congress. Another House Republican and the House Clerk had already warned Foley in 2005. Clueless and arrogant, he simply ignored their advice.

More accusations against Foley would follow during his year of disgrace. His advisors attempted to thwart even more serious actions against him. Foley publicly insisted that he wasn't a pedophile and that he had not had followed up by contact with a minor. He simply identified himself as a gay male. He further claimed that he had a drinking problem and made his inappropriate communications while intoxicated. Foley's solution to the scandal was to check himself into a rehab clinic on October 2nd.

The disclosure into Foley's history and pattern of messaging triggered an investigation by both the FBI and Florida Department of Law Enforcement. Just how deeply they investigated Mark Foley's activities was subject to extreme criticism by many observers. Both law enforcement agencies inquiries resulted in no criminal findings. Congress and Foley denied investigators access to *critical* data.

There was little interest by the Republican Party to pursue or dredge up additional damaging material. The November 2006 mid-term election proved ill timing. The party would lose control of both Foley's seat and their House majority. Foley appeared superficially an odd candidate to indulge in the misconduct that derailed his career. He was the Chairman of the House Caucus on Missing and Exploited Children. His committee had introduced legislation targeting sexual predators and created stricter guidelines for tracking them.

Following his inglorious exit from Congress, Foley returned to Palm Beach and entered a real estate enterprise. To salvage his tattered reputation, he announced publicly his new relationship with a Palm Beach dermatologist. He later initiated a local political radio show. He resurfaced briefly politically during the Donald Trump presidential campaign as a staunch supporter.

Constitution Incongruity Over The Separation Between Church and State
Fellowship Foundation Headquarters:
133 C Street SE, Washington D.C.

The Fellowship Foundation is considered one of the more influential religious lobbies operating within Washington D.C. The organization that is called *The Family* by members is an all-male, tight-lipped institution offering fundamentalist interpreted bible teaching, counseling and living accommodations. Elected political representatives from both parties have historically attended sponsored activities and even resided on-site.

The Fellowship was for decades registered as a church enabling tax-exempt status. The 12-bedroom, 8,000 square-foot house is situated in one of D.C.'s most expensive neighborhoods. Outsiders consider the organization a private club advocating Christian doctrine. Insiders were a prestigious collection of political power brokers.

Knowledge regarding the group and their three–story red brick edifice evaded close scrutiny until 2009. Three of its former high-profile residents confessed to adulterous affairs. The three included Nevada Senator John Ensign, South Carolina Governor Mark Sanford and Mississippi congressman Chip Pickering.

The infidelity scandal elevated the organization's profile to the attention of the Office of Congressional Ethics. Their tax-exempt status was revoked soon afterwards. The Fellowship Foundation has consistently publicly downplayed their collective influence. The most consistently shared rule that members adhere to is silence regarding the group's specific activities.

One consistent admission is that they maintain the traditions and follow the teachings of Jesus Christ. The Faith Foundation was established during the 1930s as a coalition of businessmen. Their reported dogma stressed that the Great Depression was divine punishment from God. President Franklin Roosevelt's New Deal policy and organized labor groups were identified as evil influences orchestrated by Satan.

The group's fundamental philosophy has remained the *consecration* of America to God first with an aggressive expansion of nationalism globally. Sound familiar?

The current membership reputedly is predominately Republican, but Democrats are welcome, provided that they concur with the group's fundamental aims. The Christianity that the group espouses may have scant resemblance in the eyes of many to the actual teachings of Jesus from Nazareth. This criticism is common towards fundamentalist right-wing political organizations with religious heritages.

These organizations presume no conflict between the Constitution's stated separation between church and **state**. Their priority remains an interpretation of God's will provided it promotes their political agenda.

The Final Degradation Of A Lifelong Bigot and Anti-Semitic
US Holocaust Memorial Museum:
100 Raoul Wallenberg Place SW, Washington D.C.

A lifetime of hatred, ignorance and prejudice prompted 88-year-old gunman James Wenneker von Brunn to enter the United States Holocaust Memorial Museum. Nearing 1:00 p.m. on June 10, 2009, von Brunn drove his car to the 14th Street entrance of the museum. He entered the building and immediately confronted Museum Special Police Officer Stephen Tyrone Johns.

The two men were unfamiliar. Von Brunn raised a Winchester Model 1906 .22 caliber rifle and without provocation shot Johns once in the upper torso. He would later expire from his injury at the George Washington University Hospital. Von Brunn would fire twice more in the direction of two officers. They returned a volley of eight rounds wounding him in the face.

Von Brunn's attack was the second recorded intended assault upon the museum. In 2002, two white supremacists plotted to destroy the building using a fertilizer bomb. They were arrested before their plan materialized.

James Wenneker von Brunn seemingly came from a stable parental background in Houston, Texas. His father was the superintendent at a steel mill and his mother a piano teacher and homemaker. He received a Bachelor of Science degree in journalism in 1943 at St. Louis' Washington University. He then served in the Navy between 1943 until 1957. He was the commanding officer of PT boat 159 during World War II receiving a commendation and three battle stars.

Upon his military retirement, he worked as an advertising executive and producer in New York City for twenty years. Behind his sturdy veneer was a seething bigot, anti-Semitic and Neo-Nazi.

His anti-social behavior first emerged in 1968 with a six-month jail sentence in Maryland for fighting with a sheriff over a DUI charge. He was later linked to an attempted kidnapping upon approaching the Federal Reserve's Eccles Building armed with multiple weapons. During the 1980s, he was convicted for additional burglary, assault and weapons charges resulting in his serving six and a half years in prison.

He joined various militant ultra-right wing organizations touting extremist views, denial of the Holocaust and Aryan supremacy. As his health declined due to congestive heart disease, his outbursts and behavior became erratic. His political philosophy darkened towards violent confrontation targeted Jewish interests, blacks and President Barack Obama.

Von Brunn armed entry into the museum was a solitary act of defiance. He victimized Stephen Tyrone Johns who had politely opened the entrance door for him. Johns was a member of the privately contracted Wackenhut security team protecting the building. He was married with a son and two stepsons. His funeral would be held on June 19, 2009 at Ebenezer AME Church in Fort Washington, Maryland. Over 2,000 people attended the service.

President Obama and numerous international humanitarian organizations would condemn the murder. Following the shooting, federal authorities raided Von Brunn's apartment in Annapolis, Maryland. They reportedly seized a rifle, ammunition, computers uploaded with child pornography and a peculiar painting of Jesus standing adjacent to Adolf Hitler.

On June 11, 2009, von Brunn was charged with first-degree murder and firearms violations. He pleaded not guilty to all charges. In September, the judge ordered him to undergo a competency evaluation to determine if he could stand trial. The testing would never be administrated. While incarcerated at the Federal Correctional Complex in Butner, North Carolina, he died on January 6, 2010 of natural causes in a hospital located near the prison.

A Sexting Weiner Prolongs A Series Of Poor Decision Making
Rayburn Office Basement Wellness Center
45 Independence Avenue SW, Washington D.C.

For reasons incomprehensible during 2011, Congressman Anthony Weiner determined that he needed and could arouse desire in younger women. He sent an email to a 21-year-old woman with an accompanying link to a sexual suggestive image of himself. He was posing with an erection barely concealed by his boxer briefs. The married Weiner's innovative approach to seduction not only captured his recipient's attention, but a global audience's when his actions and revealing image were disclosed publicly.

Many of the photos were reportedly taken inside the basement Wellness Center in the House of Representative's Rayburn Building. Weiner was a popular representative from New York's 9th congressional district wining seven successive terms.

This action was apparently not singular. It was also reported that he had sent sexually explicit photos and messages to other women before and during his marriage. He rationalized the harmlessness behind his actions by confessing that he had never met any of the women nor engaged in a physical relationship with them.

The accompanying public furor was swift. On June 16, 2011, he announced his intention to resign his congressional post. One week later, he was unemployed.

The damage to his political career appeared permanent then. Strangely in April 2013, Weiner presumed that the abbreviated memory public had forgotten his past indiscretion. He brazenly entered the New York City mayoral race. His renewed public attention prompted further ridicule. Additional photos of Weiner were released along with his admission that he'd sexted three women since his congressional resignation. The masochistic Weiner remained in the race until the gruesome end, finishing a distant fifth in the Democratic primary.

Weiner had learned nothing from his political banishment and exile. Following an article in the *Daily Mail* in September 2016, the FBI began an investigation into a report that the clueless Weiner was still targeting younger forbidden fruit. His laptop was seized revealing a sexting relationship with a 15-year-old girl. That seizure also caused controversy later in the Clinton-Trump presidential campaign.

On May 19, 2017, Weiner pled guilty to one count of transferring obscene material to a minor. His wife, fatigued by his antics and likewise the poseur, filed for divorce just prior to the guilty plea. Weiner would spend 21 months in federal prison at the Federal Medical Center in Ayer Massachusetts.

There was no indication as to whether he cultivated a fresh audience for his explicit physique during his internment. Upon his release in 2019, he was required to permanently register as a sex offender.

**A Pretender Marries and Ultimately Murders His
Patroness to Society
Viola Herms Drath Residence:
3206 Q Street NW, Washington D.C.**

Albrecht Gero Muth found his ideal entree into an illusionary life of glamour, prestige and security. Working as an unpaid German intern for the National Committee on American Foreign Policy (NCAFP), Muth met the widowed 70-year-old Viola Herms Drath. She was an established German-American socialite who'd been a fixture within D.C. society for over thirty years.

Drath had established credibility whereas the 26-year-old Muth could only offer youth and a vivid imagination. During her lifetime, she had served as a diplomat and authored eight textbooks utilized in over 150 colleges and universities. She was an accomplished editor, commentator and correspondent for numerous media outlets. During President George H. W. Bush's administration, she was a foreign policy advisor and member of numerous prestigious political and social organizations.

She had married Francis Drath in 1947 after meeting him in Munich while he was the deputy military governor of Bavaria. Their marriage of 33 years produced a son and daughter before his death in January 1986. Muth wormed his way into her life subsequently and the oddest of pairings married in 1990.

Muth was a dreamer and illusionist. He portrayed himself as a secret agent, diplomat and militia leader. He fabricated a preposterous story regarding an elderly German Count that had fallen off an elephant in India and needed to appoint a successor to his rank before his death. Muth was selected. He adopted the title of Count Albrecht to the certainty of no one. His credibility strayed further in 2003 when he claimed the rank and began wearing the uniform of a brigadier general in the Iraqi Army. His charade extended into organizing a memorial ceremony at Arlington National Cemetery to honor fallen American soldiers.

For twenty-one years, the couple remained together although indications of domestic violence by Muth had been reported prompting repeated police visits. His drinking reportedly aggravated his aggression. The level of abuse culminated on August 11, 2011 when Drath was found dead in the bathroom of her residence. She had been beaten and strangled to death. Muth was arrested, convicted of first-degree murder and sentenced to 50 years in prison. He is currently incarcerated at the Federal Correctional Institution in Butner, North Carolina.

Occupy D.C. and Identifying the One Percent
McPherson Square:
1500 I Street NW, Washington D.C.
Freedom Plaza:

Pennsylvania Avenue at 14th Street NW, Washington D.C.

During the autumn of 2011, a protest movement began in New York City's Zuccotti Park located in the Wall Street financial district. The aim of the movement was to identify economic inequality and challenge the influence of money in politics.

The *Occupy* organization identified their membership as 99% of the American population. They stigmatized the 1% of the population that represented the largest concentration of wealth. Their unfocused manifestations concluded that occupying banks, corporate headquarters, board meetings, social media and university campuses would further their aims. Their hopes revolved around paralyzing traditional business and governmental operations.

The movement expanded to Washington D.C. and within scattered urban cities. On October 16, 2011, Dr. Cornel West, an activist and Princeton University professor was arrested along with 18 others. They had launched a protest condemning economic inequality on the Supreme Court steps. Over the next three months, increased national media exposure and scattered confrontations dominated the local movement's activities.

McPherson Square and Freedom Plaza became two prominent protest locations beginning in October 2001. Several of the participants decided to camp out on both properties. Sanitary conditions worsened with each passing week resulting in a streaming infestation of rats.

The squatters were ordered to vacate their encampments by January 31, 2012. By February 4th, police began disbursing the majority of tents, arresting those who resisted and allowing sanitation workers to remove hazardous materials.

Approximately fifteen tents remained throughout the remainder of the winter and spring. On June 10th, *Occupy DC* protesters removed the remaining tents from McPherson Square. They vowed to supporters that the protests would continue. They didn't.

The long-term impact of identifying the 1% did nothing to alter their fortunes and influence. The subsequent decade entered an unprecedented period of sustained financial growth in both real estate and equities. The gap between wealth and impoverished simply widened further.

FREEDOM PLAZA

The Man Without A Country and His Questionable Protest
Booz Allen Hamilton Building:
1500 I Street NW, Washington D.C.

The debate over the proper labeling of Edward Joseph Snowden will likely shadow his life until its conclusion. He has viciously been called a *traitor*, *dissident* and *coward*. Equally passionate are his defender's claims that elevate him to *hero*, *whistleblower* and *patriot*.

In 2013, Snowden was hired by National Security Agency (NSA) contractor Booz Allen Hamilton following previous employment with Dell Computers and the CIA. His role as a computer intelligence consultant accessed him to highly classified information. He had developed a prior reputation as a *computer wizard* and distinguished himself professionally.

Snowden claimed that his intimate access disillusioned him towards the ethics behind the programs he participated in. He further claimed that he raised his objections through internal channels but was routinely ignored.

On May 20, 2013, Snowden flew to Hong Kong after leaving his job with Booz Allen Hamilton regional Kunia Camp, Hawaii facility. He made a fateful decision that promised no aborting or redemption from. In early June, he revealed thousands of classified NSA documents to at least four journalists. The data resulted in unflattering stories internationally regarding his allegations of intimate acts of American surveillance and espionage. Booz Allen Hamilton terminated his contract on June 10th, the day after he disclosed releasing the files.

On June 21st, the U.S. Department of Justice announced two charges against Snowden for violating the Espionage Act of

1917 and the theft of government property. The Department of State immediately revoked his passport.

Two days later he hastily flew into Moscow's International Airport. He was now a man without a nationality and valid passport. Russian authorities restricted his movements to the airport terminal for over one month. He was then granted the right of asylum for one year, which would require repeated extensions. In October 2020, he was granted permanent Russian residency.

His landing destination immediately raised questions regarding his true motives. Snowden claimed his that leaks were designed to warn and inform the public what is conducted in their name and can be done against them. U.S. officials condemned his actions noting the potential grave damage done to American intelligence capabilities. Neither party was translucent over the extent of this damage.

Snowden's public observations and arguments certainly appeared plausible. Individual privacy and security remains a vanishing and nearly extinct right with online access. However, Snowden's own legacy became tarnished and compromised.

As history has demonstrated, Russian President Vladimir Putin is not a leader that has historically granted indulgences without a certainty of return favors. Snowden is currently working with a Russian IT company during his exile. There is no evidence that he has channeled his idealism towards reforming Russia's internal citizenry surveillance system.

Three years later, another contract employee of Booz Allen Hamilton would breach security protocol.

On October 5, 2016, Harold Thomas Martin III was arrested over allegations he'd used his access as government contractor to remove confidential classified data and potentially exploit important NSA documents.

It was never determined what motivated Martin's theft. There was no specific indication that he intended to engage in conventional espionage. He did initiate contact via Twitter with Kaspersky Lab, a Russian cyber-security firm. A raid by the FBI and Maryland State Police on his modest residence unearthed over 50 terabytes of classified data inside his house, a locked shed and his vehicle.

Martin's case resulted differently than Snowden's. He reportedly never accessed any of the files that he'd removed from government facilities. He was dismissed as a data hoarder with only grandiose delusions. At his March 2019 trial he pled guilty to the charge of *Willful Retention of National Defense Information*. He was sentenced to nine years incarceration. He is currently interned at the Federal Medical Center in Devens, Massachusetts.

The examples of Snowden and Martin raised serious ethical questions regarding the access outside contractors have to sensitive data. At the same time, Snowden's revelations disturbingly confirm that Americans are vulnerable to covert surveillance by their own government. These inquiries are absent of search warrants, permission or probable cause.

Edward Snowden has made the most upon his outing as informer. He married Lindsay Mills in 2017 and they have one child. His future relationship with the United States government is clouded. He will likely never be welcomed back without a public trial and incarceration. He will remain a permanent outsider within Russia regardless of the length of his residence.

The Man Without a Country may continue to preach his ethical motivations and concerns for our privacy and security.

His voice remains muted to most American listeners by choice. His covert action of betrayal reeks. The consequences that he recklessly imposed on data exposed individuals are unforgivable. He lost the majority of his credibility the instant he entered and then remained within Russian territory.

**A Carjacking Shocking By The Result and Perpetrators
Anwar Vehicle Crash Site:
75 N Street SE, Washington D.C.**

The carjacking death of Mohammad Anwar proved as shocking in consequence as the ages of the perpetrators. On March 23, 2021 at approximately 4:00 p.m., two young girls, 13 and 15, asked Anwar for a ride near the Navy Yard Metro station. He drove a gray late model Honda Accord sedan as an Uber Eats driver.

After driving a few blocks he halted the vehicle near the 1200 block of Van Street SE. One girl tasered Anwar, partially disabling him. The other presumably attempted to commandeer his vehicle. Amidst their struggle, the driver's door remained open. Anwar was still partially wedged in the driver's seat and partially hanging out of the vehicle. As he tried to regain control of his car, it accelerated. The vehicle slammed into railings as it turned east onto N Street SE in front of the Washington Nationals Park Parking Garage C.

The car hit a tree and smashed several parked cars before flipping over. Anwar was ejected onto the sidewalk where police found him limp and motionless. Medics would transport him to a nearby hospital where he later expired.

Two uniformed National Guard troops nearby pulled the girls out of the wreckage as the car wheels continued to spin. The girls immediately lied to bystanders indicating that the car belonged to them. They were detained at the scene and later arrested.

Anwar, 66, had immigrated to Springfield, Virginia in 2014. He was a father and grandfather, survived by a wife and two adult children in the United States. He had four grandchildren living in Pakistan.

The two female perpetrators had a prior history of carjacking. Due to their ages, they were neither identified publicly nor tried as adults. Each accepted plea-bargains allowing them to plead guilty to felony murder in exchange for dismissing other charges. Both were sentenced to the care of a youth agency until considered rehabilitated or reaching the age of 21.

Author, photographer and visual artist Marques Vickers was born in 1957 in Vallejo, California. He graduated from Azusa Pacific University in Los Angeles and became the Public Relations and Executive Director for the Burbank, California Chamber of Commerce between 1979-84.

Professionally, he has operated travel, apparel, wine, rare book and publishing businesses. His paintings and sculptures have been exhibited in art galleries, private collections and museums in the United States and Europe. He has previously lived in the Burgundy and Languedoc regions of France and currently lives in the South Puget Sound region of Western Washington.

He has written and published over one hundred books spanning a diverse variety of subjects including true crime, international travel, social satire, wine production, architecture, history, fiction, auctions, fine art, poetry and photojournalism.

He has two daughters, Charline and Caroline who reside in Europe.